ca

THE
PARANORMAL

THE
PARANORMAL
A GUIDE TO THE UNEXPLAINED

ANTHONY NORTH

BLANDFORD

First published in the UK 1996
by Blandford, A Cassell Imprint

CASSELL PLC
Wellington House
125 Strand
London WC2R 0BB

Distributed in the United States by Sterling Publishing Co., Inc.
387 Park Avenue South, New York, NY 10016-8810

Distributed in Australia by Capricorn Link (Australia) Pty Ltd
2/13 Carrington Road, Castle Hill, NSW 2154

**A Cataloguing-in-Publication Data entry for this title is
available from the British Library**

ISBN 0-7137-2615-6

Typeset by Keystroke, Jacaranda Lodge, Wolverhampton
Printed and bound in Great Britain by Hartnolls Ltd, Bodmin, Cornwall

Contents

Information Talents

Time Anomaly

Introduction

IT WAS a pleasant night in the summer of 1983. The day had been a normal one for my wife and me – there had been nothing to prepare us for the events of that night. We had been asleep for a couple of hours when we were awakened by someone rattling the letterbox on the front door. Rubbing sleep from my eyes, I cursed – guessing who it was. It would be the Duty Airman.

At the time I was in the Royal Air Force, serving on a British missile base. Quite often my job involved being called out in the middle of the night to investigate security problems on the base; so immediately I braced myself for several hours of work.

Our bedroom window was just above the front door. I got out of bed and opened the window to tell the Duty Airman that I'd be down presently. But, looking down at the door, I was surprised to see that there was no one there.

I put the incident down to imagination, or maybe a freak gust of wind. I never believed for one second that the Duty Airman had rattled the letterbox and left, for the house was situated in a square of houses with a large expanse of grass between us and the main road. It would have taken a good minute for the Duty Airman to have walked out of the square, and throughout this period he would have been in my view from the window – the square was very well lit. And I had heard no vehicle come or go from the square.

I went back to bed, told my wife that there was no one there and snuggled back down to sleep.

A moment or two later the letterbox rattled again. This time, though, it was followed by the sound of footsteps walking away from the door.

I jumped out of bed once more and hurried to the window to look out, knowing that footsteps could not be caused by a gust of wind and knowing equally that I could not have imagined them – my wife had heard them too.

But for the second time there was no one at the door and the square was completely deserted. Baffled, I returned to bed.

My wife then said that our invisible visitor was her dead grandfather, coming to tell her that her grandmother had died.

I was sceptical, to put it mildly. My wife's grandmother was ill, but she had been ill for over ten years, having severe heart trouble, and there was no reason to expect her death at this particular time. Only a couple of days before my wife had talked to her on the phone and she had seemed perfectly normal. At the time, I might add, we lived some two hundred miles away from her.

Next morning a telemessage dropped through the letterbox with the news that my wife's grandmother had died the previous day.

My wife had had a similar, though less startling, experience when her grandfather died. In this case we knew he was dying, but on the day of his death, while we were travelling on a bus, my wife turned to me and said, out of the blue, that we must send a wreath. She *knew* that he had died.

Between these two deaths my wife had experienced a whole host of paranormal events. They began when we were staying with her same grandmother, who one day said that her husband still rattled on the letterbox from time to time, just as he did in life when coming home. And from then on, whenever we visited her grandmother, my wife used to feel her grandfather's presence about the house. One day she was in the bathroom when the room suddenly went very cold and she felt her grandfather's presence. She said, 'Hello, Grandad. What do you want?' At that, the room warmed up and the presence receded.

To add a final note of weirdness to these events, when I decided to write about this case many years later, my wife and I sat for nearly an hour one morning discussing it, and immediately after we stopped, as if on cue, a hearse passed by.

These are just a few of many such happenings experienced by my wife and me – several of which will be featured in the coming pages. Much of the above can be explained rationally. The hearse could have been mere coincidence. The feeling of the presence in the house could be simple suggestion after my wife had been told by her grandmother of her own experiences – which in turn could have been the product of hysteria following a bereavement. But when two people hear the same rattling letterbox and the same footsteps so close to a further bereavement, of which neither could possibly have had any knowledge, then alarm bells must surely go off, suggesting the interaction of things beyond the scope of accepted material science. And it must be a sobering thought to think that, at the very moment you are reading this, hundreds of similar events are happening the world over.

This book is my attempt to explain such happenings. But where, among the claims and counter-claims within the subject, does one begin to make sense of it all?

What questions are asked?

Do you believe in ghosts? Do you believe in telepathy? Or do you believe that anyone who claims to believe in such phenomena is a crackpot?

Well, perhaps we should forget all these questions. For instance, what are you saying when you say you believe in ghosts? Rationalize your statement and you will quickly discover that it has no foundation in logic. You are simply upholding a belief system.

Similarly, what are you saying when you say the believer is a crackpot? Can you prove that he or she is insane? Can you totally disprove the claims once and for all? Many have tried, but the sceptic has failed to discredit the paranormal, clinging to a few cases that are obviously fraudulent, and falling back on statements such as 'this is coincidence'.

This is equally the upholding of a belief system, for dismissing paranormal phenomena as coincidence – a thing no one yet understands the mechanics of – is simply answering a mystery with the unexplained. The sceptic is falling back on safety – to accept the phenomena would be an affront to his intellect, an intellect that discounts the paranormal's existence.

My approach is substantially different. I'm neither a believer nor a sceptic. However, I've looked at enough authenticated cases to know that *something* is going on that is as yet unexplained. So perhaps the question that should really be asked is: do you believe that something is going on that gives the *impression* of the existence of ghosts, telepathy, *et al*?

By looking at the subject in this way we remove it from preconceived notions and can attempt to lay solid foundations upon which to build a theory.

In the late-nineteenth century science attempted to come to terms with the paranormal. But after a brief courtship the two parted company, only coming together occasionally in these days of modern, and spectacular, scientific success in other areas. But why has science become so reluctant to study this field?

Science is the observation and understanding of phenomena within nature. By this definition, science should be pumping resource after resource into the paranormal. However, there is a reason why scientists ignore the paranormal – and, in one way, a valid reason.

Science has a structure. To the people who create this structure it is virtually the last word upon how the universe functions. This is principally due to man's need for safety. Ever since thinking man looked up to the heavens and realized his insignificance within the vastness of the universe he has had to build systems of thought that keep him safe. In earlier, more superstitious times, philosophers built theologies around a benevolent God who created us special within the universe. But as the popular God waned and scientific materialism grew, then logical understanding took over from beliefs in God, making the universe chaotic and the product of blind chance without God. Only thinking man can rise above this chaos by exhibiting intellectual superiority over the universe by virtue of scientific theory. And, armed with his scientific theory, man can delude himself that he knows what is going on – and will ignore any attempt to make chinks in his academic armour.

Indeed, throughout the history of scientific advancement, any bright spark who comes along to upset the academic apple cart usually spends most of his life the victim of ridicule.

But the present structure of a chaotic universe exists for another, admittedly related, reason. It is also there to remove science from the metaphysics of religion and beliefs in an overall guiding intelligence. And the paranormal stinks of other-worldly interference.

Another problem of acceptance is the lack of repeatable experimentation and theory. Things are just not scientific if they cannot be replicated in experiment after experiment. Elusive qualities such as the paranormal are too shy to satisfy this requirement. But nothing to do with the mind is repeatable in all experimentation. Yet psychology is accepted as a science.

As for theory, the 'facts' of the paranormal seem to clash so consistently that theorizing finds its roots in quicksand.

And, finally, scientists are frightened of the fraud. And here I don't blame them. There are far too many weirdos cashing in on the paranormal. Whenever they are identified the whole field suffers. And this distorts the picture. No scientist will take the risk of being conned if it means financial backers becoming reluctant to put money into his future research.

A great deal of evidence for the paranormal is anecdotal. Much of it is suspect. Attitudes to anecdotal evidence should be cautious. But the vital question to be asked is, out of all the anecdotal material available, could *some* of it be factual?

Considering that cases of the paranormal have existed in all cultures, through all known times, and are just as prolific today as in the past, I fail to see how there can be smoke without fire. But this does not necessarily mean that the paranormal is caused by things beyond the grave. Perhaps the paranormal needs to be redefined.

In the old days manifestations of the paranormal were classed as supernatural: they came from a world of spirits. In 1882 the Society for Psychical Research was set up to investigate paranormal phenomena in a more scientific way. By the 1930s the American psychologist J.B. Rhine had founded the science of parapsychology, inventing such terms as 'extra-sensory perception'.

Treating the paranormal as 'beyond normal' rather than 'supernatural' brought it a little more respectability. But I would go further. The paranormal is an integral part of life. We cannot exist without it. It is not paranormal but normal. Ghost sightings and telepathic abilities are simply phenomena at the extremes of normality. Therefore, what I offer in this book is a survey of the 'extrenormal' – though, for convenience, I shall continue to use the term 'paranormal'.

But why do we need to understand the paranormal? Isn't life that bit more interesting if there are mysteries to jolt the imagination? Yes. And the story of scientific advance over the centuries demonstrates that the understanding of one mystery usually gives birth to another. However, to use this argument is to deny the paranormal importance. The main reason for embarking upon this study is to show that the paranormal, and the understanding of it, could provide the next level of understanding of existence.

The average scientist will scoff at this. But that is only his safety mechanism working overtime as he gains comfort from the scientific structure he understands. He feels that if I am right his structure will fall. But is this the case?

Aristotle said that the earth was the stationary centre of the universe. Nearly two thousand years later Copernicus said that the earth revolved around the sun. Religious academe was in uproar. Galileo confirmed that Copernicus was right. He barely survived with his life after standing before the Inquisition. Newton decided the issue, and the walls of Jericho came tumbling down.

Genesis tells us that God created the earth, and all life upon it, in six days. Man was born in God's image. Then along came Darwin and showed that man was descended from a primate. And the walls of Jericho came tumbling down.

Gregor Mendel was a scholar who crossed two pea plants to produce a hybrid. Academe said: 'So what?' Genetics didn't fit the then-accepted structure. For fifty years it was ignored. Then it was accepted. And the walls of Jericho . . .

. . . *didn't* come tumbling down.

Why not?

Because the structure of knowledge could be adapted to absorb genetics without seriously undermining any of its proven truths. In fact, whenever the walls of Jericho came tumbling down, it was at the cost of either the Bible or unproven truths. I believe this is true of a proper understanding of the paranormal.

Many researchers have spent many years trying to unravel the secrets of the paranormal. How have they fared?

Dismally, I'm afraid. Not one incidence of the paranormal has been proved to have taken place. There are two possible reasons for this failure. First, the paranormal doesn't exist. The investigators have all been deluding themselves, following an impossible dream. Or, second, they have been barking up the wrong tree – devising their theories and conducting their research in the wrong way. But which of these explanations is correct? Perhaps both.

Let me explain.

Most psychical researchers have one thing in common. They have assumed that the phenomena they are investigating are occurrences not related to normal life – they say such things as 'that person is psychic', as if the normal person is not. This attitude pushes the paranormal out of the mainstream; relegates it to a backwater. Then the researchers moan that the media treats their subject as a great joke. Well, maybe they have only got themselves to blame. It is they who removed it from normality in the first place. And can they really expect science to pump in millions of pounds of academic research on something of no apparent use?

If they want to stop the media making fools of them, if they want science to take the paranormal seriously, if they want to find out what is really going on, then it is time that they sat back and looked very closely at just what it is they are doing.

Let's think about that emotive subject, life after death. What element of life could possibly survive death? Is it the physical body? Clearly not – we can see that rot. Then it must be the soul. But what *is* the soul? Well, you can take your pick which explanation you prefer – all are mystical, tenuous and unprovable. Let us look, then, at what we *know* survives death.

There are, essentially, two parts of us that survive death. If we have produced an offspring then our genetic make-up survives in the genes of that child. And collected memories of our life survive in the minds of those who knew us.

Which leads us to ask, what *is* life? What do we know about it for certain? We know that life consists of a body (the cellular construction) and that part of us which interacts with, and reflects upon, society, in a non-physical way (the mind). And both these elements survive death through inherited genetic (or cellular) characteristics and memories in other people's minds.

These points are important, because they show that life is more than the sum total of the individual. Life becomes, essentially, communal. And, if we see life in this way, we can understand the communality of a species. Evolution grasps this concept in a physical, genetic sense, but it can be applied to the mind, too.

Contemporary man is shaped by physical genetic characteristics inherited from his forebears. But he is also shaped by the thoughts of his ancestors. When we read an old book, such as the Bible, and live according to its principles, we are being influenced by our forebears. But could our ancestors' thoughts influence us through another, less obvious, mechanism? Could thoughts not written down on paper affect us too?

We may not have found a mechanism for such a mind intrusion yet – as has been found with DNA – but it is tempting to accept its existence. Ancient thoughts may come to us every day through instinct, impulse and *déjà vu*.

The scientist, engineer and science-fiction writer Arthur C. Clarke once wrote: 'Today we not only lack a Newton or Einstein of the paranormal, we still await its Aristotle. . . .'

I believe these words to be untrue. We have had our Aristotle. He was the eminent psychologist Carl Jung, with his theory of a collective racial unconscious lying below our personal mind – a communal mind-store. For he encapsulated the idea of the communality of the mind of men. He gave credence to the concept of inherited, innate memories being passed on through the generations.

However, instead of accepting the implications of the collective racial unconscious, most psychical researchers misunderstood what Jung was saying. They ridiculously over-simplified the concept into the 'group mind', as if, somewhere, there was this huge brain into which we all input as if it were a computer data bank.

That is like saying that there is a massive gene shop which hands out genes. The concept is ridiculous. There is no gene megastore, but we all have our own corner shop. A collective unconscious would work in a similar way. Basically, we all have within us, and individual to us, a little memory shop that is overstocked and brimming with thoughts and images of our species past.

I suppose the best way of looking at it is to think of mind as energy. And, as any scientist will tell you, energy cannot be destroyed. It can simply be transformed. And this could well be life after death.

But, of course, it could be much more. For it could also be a data bank of information. In it could be the lives of our ancestors, which could, conceivably, be reincarnated in our present life, manifested as spirits, or even hallucinated as a ghost. And it could also contain contemporary information, such as the fact that a friend or relative has just died, giving the impression of telepathy.

The message here is that reincarnation, ghosts, spirit manifestation and telepathy do not exist. They are merely various explanations to account for a single phenomenon – inherited memory. There are not lots of different phenomena. There are simply lots of different tags to confuse us.

At least, that is the crux of my argument here.

* * *

The paranormal can be conveniently split into four main groupings. These are the manifestation of supposed life-after-death experiences; mind-over-matter abilities; information talents; and time anomaly. I shall survey each grouping in turn, before going on to attempt an explanation of the paranormal in terms of understanding the human condition and its relationship to the universe and reality itself.

Each grouping can be sub-divided into specific phenomena. Life after death takes in reincarnation, Spiritualism and ghosts. Mind over matter includes magic, the poltergeist and psychokinesis. Information talents include telepathy, clairvoyance, dowsing and astral travel. And, finally, time anomaly includes time slip, precognition and prophecy.

In my view, the use of such terms is academic, and I use their 'official' tags purely for ease of explanation. Indeed, some researchers would argue over my categorizations. For instance, the poltergeist is thought, by many, to be a ghost, and should therefore be included in the life-after-death grouping. I leave it up to the reader to decide who is right.

LIFE AFTER DEATH

Reincarnation

THE THIRTEENTH Dalai Lama of Tibet died in 1933. Three days after his death, still sitting on his throne, he turned his head to the east. This was taken as a sign that the search for his successor should begin in that direction. Two years later the regent conducting the search arrived, alone, at the sacred lake of Lhamoi Latso and there he received, in a vision, the guidance he had been hoping for. He would find his new leader – still a child – living in a house with turquoise tiles near a monastery with roofs of jade green and gold.

By 1936 the monastery had been identified as the Kumbum monastery and the house located, in the nearby village of Takster. Inside, the searchers found a two-year-old boy. In 1939, after vigorous research and testing, the boy was placed upon the Lion Throne. The fourteenth Dalai Lama of Tibet had been found and inaugurated, continuing an unbroken line from the first Dalai Lama of 1391.

What was placed upon the throne, of course, was not simply a small boy but the incarnation – the thirteenth – of the first Dalai Lama. The Tibetans were giving expression to the belief that upon death the soul can be reincarnated to inhabit a new physical form.

Belief in reincarnation is thousands of years old. Even in modern times, it has been estimated, two thirds of the world's population hold reincarnation as a fundamental belief. A recent Gallup poll showed that 25 per cent of the population of Britain believed in reincarnation.

In 1956 an amateur hypnotist called Moray Bernstein caused a sensation by describing, in his book, *The Search for Bridey Murphy*, a number of hypnotic regressions he had induced in a Colorado housewife, Virginia Tighe. During the sessions, Mrs Tighe described her life in a previous incarnation as Bridey Murphy, an Irishwoman from Cork, who had died, at the age of 65, in 1864. What made the case so impressive was the fact that many of the details of her life in Ireland were able to be authenticated, although Mrs Tighe had never visited Ireland and had no Irish connections.

It is not known where belief in reincarnation began. Ancient Egyptians accepted that royalty and aristocracy might be reincarnated and that through these 'great' souls leaders were invested with age-old wisdom. In ancient Greece, Plato believed that without successive lives there could be no life in the universe. Such a belief became firmly entrenched in Western philosophy with Plato's theory of Ideal Forms. Here, every object we can make, every thought we can have, is an echo of its ideal form created for eternity in some spaceless, timeless void.

Reincarnation, or rebirth, is alluded to in the world's oldest known sacred books, the Hindu Vedas, dating from about 1000 BC. The Upanishads, which go on to explain the main tenets of the Vedas, also refer to it. In the *Mahabharata*, an epic poem composed between about 400 BC and AD 200, the god Krishna says to Prince Arjuna, 'Both I and thou have passed through many births.'

Fundamental to Hinduism is the *samsara*, or 'wheel of rebirth'. Reincarnation is caused by the imperfections of a soul when it first manifests in the world. Such imperfections cause ignorance and desire, forcing the soul to cling to the world through materialism or earthly desire. It then becomes the task of the soul to realize and purify itself. When this is achieved, it leaves the samsara and is reunited with brahman, the world spirit or absolute.

Samsara is influenced by karma, the principle that the mental and physical deeds of a lifetime decide the soul's rebirth. Karma allows good, which is rewarded, and bad, which is punished. Such reward and punishment is manifested through incarnation into successively lower or higher life forms. Between such incarnations there is a period of rest in order for the soul to contemplate its progress. To assist the soul to purify itself, birth is seen as a process of misery. It is in the best interest of the soul to seek brahman, because the number of incarnations it can go through are limitless. Only with purity can the wheel of rebirth be escaped.

Buddha taught that the individual has two selves. The lesser self dies with the body, but the greater self survives. Personality, or ego, dies with the lesser self, breaking up into small pieces. In the period prior to rebirth some of these pieces intermingle with pieces of other lives to form a new personality. This personality enters the life force, or greater self, and achieves rebirth.

Buddhism, like Hinduism, teaches that the soul's task is to overcome earthly failings and attain spiritual perfection. To achieve this, desire, hatred and delusion must be overcome. The consummation of this process is nirvana, the negation of existence, usually understood, positively, as a form of ineffable peace.

Such highly developed philosophies built around reincarnation may make us forget that there can be practical, earthly reasons to instil a belief in it. In Hinduism, we can see it as part of the socio-political control mechanism. Hindu society is based upon the caste system, where a person must remain in the social caste to which he was born. Such castes range from that of the aristocratic and powerful brahmins to those of the much-abused underclass known as the untouchables. The notion of reincarnation reinforces the system by, on the one hand, giving hope and, on the other, imposing fear. Do good in life and you may go up a caste in your next life. Do ill and you may go down. Be an untouchable and do ill, then in your next incarnation you may well be spinning a web.

That a belief in reincarnation can be seen as part of a socio-political fear mechanism does not, of course, invalidate the existence of reincarnation, any more than the manipulations of the early Christian Church towards, for example, depressing the status of women, invalidate the existence of God. Nor can the socio-political thesis wholly explain why belief in reincarnation is prevalent – in a form that places less emphasis than Hinduism upon the survival of individual personality – in Buddhist society, where the strict caste system of Hinduism does not exist.

Today reincarnation is widely accepted by a variety of peoples. In many African tribes it is taken so much for granted that infertility is looked upon as a curse because it blocks the rebirth of souls. Many Amerindian tribes believe that the personality is successively reborn: a child is named according to its previous life, which is revealed to the mother through dream imagery while she is still pregnant. And many people in modern Western society find reincarnation credible – influenced perhaps by cases like that of Bridey Murphy.

Hers is not an isolated case. Consider, for instance, that of Naomi Henry from Exeter in the southwest of England, who became the subject of hypnotist Henry Blythe. During a number of hypnotic regressions she spoke of her previous life as Mary Cohen, who, like Bridey Murphy, came from Cork. In 1790 she was living on Greengates Farm near the village of Grener. Bit by bit she told of life on the farm, marrying a violent husband and losing her children, astonishing researchers with her knowledge of Irish life at that time. She even relived her last minutes on her deathbed at the age of 70.

What are we to make of such cases? Do they confirm the existence of reincarnation? Or could it be that there are less other-worldly things going on within the human mind?

Cryptomnesia

IN 1956 Dr Edwin Zolik, then a psychologist at Marquette University, extracted a past life from one of his subjects under hypnosis. The life was that of Dick Wonchalk, a riverman. A solitary individual, he did 'nothing much, just lived off the land' as he spent his time piloting his flat-bottomed boat. He eventually died, in 1876, after a month's illness, with no one around to care for him (his family had been killed by Indians when he was a child). He remembered regretting not making friends and only rarely meeting or mingling with people.

Dr Zolik is one of many researchers who have analysed past-life regression through hypnosis. One of the first was the French psychic researcher Colonel Albert de Rochas. Beginning in 1904, he hypnotized 19 subjects, noting that they easily manifested past lives. However, he also realized that verification of these lives was extremely difficult; he often found inconsistencies between historical records and testimony under hypnosis.

Such caution has not always been shared. In the 1970s the Bloxham tapes astounded viewers when the British Broadcasting Corporation (BBC) broadcast a documentary about them. Compiled by Cardiff hypnotherapist Arnall Bloxham, these taped hypnotic regressions were called 'the most staggering evidence for reincarnation ever recorded.' Jeffrey Iverson, who produced the documentary, went on to write his book, *More Lives than One?*, about them.

The central subject of the tapes was a Welsh housewife, Jane Evans. She produced six past lives, which were particularly remarkable for the sheer detail packed into them. Her earliest life was in England, as Livonia in third-century York. Still in York, in the twelfth century she was Rebecca, wife of Joseph, a Jewish moneylender. Her third life took her to fifteenth-century France where she was Alison, an Egyptian servant of the merchant prince Jacques Coeur. A century later we find her in England again as a lady-in-waiting to Catherine of Aragon. Her fifth life was in London in the early eighteenth century, where she was a sewing girl called Anne Tasker. And finally she was Sister Grace, a nun living in America in the 1920s. Her accounts of each of these six lives displayed an accurate and detailed knowledge not only of historic events but also of social life styles. This apparent veracity was seen by many as convincing evidence for reincarnation.

There is evidence, too, of another sort – from psychotherapy. The sanctioning of hypnosis as valid clinical treatment by the British Medical Association in 1955, and by its American equivalent three years later, led to the development of a whole new area of therapy – past-life therapy. Since the 1960s dozens of therapists have cured a whole multitude of phobias, fears and aversions by taking their patients back to traumas experienced in previous lives.

Dr Denys Kelsey is one psychotherapist who has used hypnotic regression to treat a host of psychosomatic ailments. One patient was a young woman who had a deep-seated fear of flying. Taking her back 'beyond birth', Dr Kelsey brought out the incarnation of a British Royal Air Force officer who had been trapped in his cockpit and faced the terror of crashing. Once the woman was aware of this previous incarnation, she overcame her fear.

So successful is this form of therapy that in 1980 therapists got together to form the Association for Past Life Research and Therapy in Riverside, California. In 1982 therapist Dr Helen Wambach decided to survey past-life therapy through the association. Analysing data from twenty-six therapists, she gleaned the astounding fact that of 18,463 patients 94 per cent had regressed to one or more previous lives.

The success of past-life therapy may seem at first glance to offer iron-clad evidence for reincarnation. But there are indications that something entirely different is going on.

The clue to what that something different is could well come from arguments over plagiarism. Time after time an author has published a piece of work only to be branded a cheat because something almost identical has already been produced by an earlier writer.

The blind and deaf-mute American writer Helen Keller wrote, in 1892, a much-acclaimed short story, 'The Frost King'. Within months of publication it was discovered that it was a modified version of Margaret Canby's *The Frost Fairies*. Helen Keller had no memory of ever coming across Margaret Canby's work, and, indeed, it seemed unlikely because she could only read by touch. However, it was later revealed that a friend had read a selection of Canby's stories to her over a decade before. Helen Keller had simply forgotten.

To understand how this happened, we have to think of our mind as a vast store holding memories of every experience we have had. It is like an iceberg, with only a fraction of its bulk above water level. This fraction is the conscious mind, which holds 'everyday' memories. However, from time to time memories from the sunken unconscious mind can surface. Not recognized as memories, they seem like original ideas. This is the phenomenon known as cryptomnesia.

Dr Zolik began research to see if cryptomnesia could explain the knowledge displayed by those of his subjects who claimed to have lived previous lives. Under re-hypnosis, he asked them for the sources of their information. The sources he discovered in this way were invariably works of fiction. For instance, Zolik matched the life of Dick Wonchalk to a film seen by the subject, who was able to name the cinema he had seen it in. The film had become to him a symbol of his own solitary life and he had identified completely with it.

The earliest known connection between past-life regression and cryptomnesia dates back to 1906. A 'Miss C', when hypnotized, claimed to be Blanche Poynings from fourteenth-century England, the close friend of Maud, Countess of Salisbury. Investigation showed that the source of the past life was a novel, *Countess Maud, or the Changes of the World: a Tale of the Fourteenth Century*, published in 1892.

The Finnish psychiatrist Dr Reima Kampman also undertook research into cryptomnesia. His subjects were a group of secondary-school children, of whom some thirty produced past lives, including one who manifested no fewer than eight. Particularly interesting was the regression of one girl to the life of Dorothy, daughter of an English innkeeper in the twelfth century. Her account of English life was, according to Kampman, 'amazingly explicit'. During one regression the girl suddenly abandoned her native Finnish language and sang a song in what appeared to be a form of English. The language was identified, by Professor Ole Reuter, as Middle English, and the song as an old canon song, 'The Cuckoo Song'. Some seven years later Kampman had the opportunity to re-hypnotize the girl, whereupon he took her back to the source. She spoke of a book she had 'flicked through' in a library to kill a moment of time before her bus arrived. Investigation identified the book as *The Story of Music* by Benjamin Britten and Imogen Holst, which contained 'The Cuckoo Song' in its original Middle English.

Speech in an apparently unknown foreign language is quite common under hypnosis. Known as xenoglossy, it can be quite startling. Professor Erika Fromm of the University of Chicago once hypnotized a patient as an exercise in front of students. The 26-year-old was regressed through his life. When he returned to three years old he stopped speaking English and broke into fluent Japanese, talking continually for nearly twenty minutes. It turned out that between the ages of two and four, during World War 2, he had been interned in a camp in California where Japanese was spoken. Yet he was only aware of knowing a couple of words himself.

Such is the power of recall of the human mind during hypnosis. But what about Jane Evans, the central subject of the Bloxham tapes? In her first life she was Livonia, wife to the tutor of Constantine, later emperor of Rome, and she described how she had watched the young Constantine being trained in the use of weapons by Marcus Favonius Facilis. The names (with the exception of those of Livonia herself and Facilis), places, events and customs described by Livonia have, where they could be checked, proved to be historically correct – an apparent impossibility unless she really had lived before. But then the researcher Melvin Harris came upon a novel published in 1947 – *The Living Wood* by Louis de Wohl. Full of accurate historical detail of the period, it concentrated on Constantine, and in one passage has him being tutored in Roman weaponry by a certain Marcus Favonius Facilis. And one of its characters is named Livonia.

It is hard not to believe that Livonia was a figment of Jane Evans's imagination, conjured up as a memory of a novel read long before. This is a particularly attractive theory if we consider the fantasizing that we know goes on in the mind under hypnosis. Indeed, such fantasizing – role playing is perhaps a better description – is often used by psychiatrists to help in the cure of psychological trauma. Which may tell us why past-life therapy is so often successful. Trauma is often associated with denial of the reasons for the manifestation of the problem. Going to a therapist who practices past-life regression and connecting the trauma with a previous life makes it easier for the patient to identify the problem. So past-life therapy may be helpful in psychotherapy but it in no way confirms the reality of the past life exhibited. We are simply dealing with psychological role play.

So cryptomnesia seems to be the complete answer to reincarnation. But is it?

Memory is the fallout of knowledge based upon learning processes. We do something in life, and the event is encoded as memory, so as to improve our behaviour or regulate our activity. For instance, as a child you eat cheese and decide you don't like it. Your reaction is stored in memory. Should you come across cheese again, your memory stimulates you to reject eating it.

The predominant scientific view of memory is that such information is stored in nerve fibres within the brain. The actual process of memorizing is said to exist in two specific forms. In order to avoid unnecessary memorizing, the brain has capabilities for short-term memory and long-term memory. Consider your ability to recall a ten-digit number. If the number is of no importance to you it will exist as short-term memory for perhaps as little as a couple of seconds before being forgotten. However, should it hold importance – a new telephone number, for instance – the number will transfer from short-term memory to long-term memory, and you will remember it.

For cryptomnesia to work, in the context of past-life recall, the source for the past life must have been passed to long-term memory. But can we apply this process to cases such as the Finnish girl flicking through a book? Is it really conceivable to imagine her passing a whole song from short-term memory to long-term memory in this way?

I have no doubt that cryptomnesia is a valid ability. But it does not fit the accepted scientific memory model as presently understood – it does not fit what we know about memory recall. To 'explain' reincarnation by cryptomnesia is to answer a mystery with a mystery. Cryptomnesia is not accepted as normal. It is, in a word, paranormal. Hence, the mystery of reincarnation also remains. And we haven't even touched upon the major evidence as yet.

Possession

IN THE late 1960s Helen Wambach began a ten-year survey during which she regressed 1,088 subjects. She conducted a statistical analysis of the past lives thus revealed, collecting data concerning sex, race and class. She found that 49.4 per cent of the past lives were female and 50.6 per cent male. Splitting the lives into time periods (they ranged from 2000 BC to the 1900s), she discovered that the number of lives per period rose or fell in line with known population growth or decline – for instance, past lives from the nineteenth century were double those of the sixteenth century but only a quarter of those of the twentieth century. Class ratios also corresponded to the reality of the time – on average 70 per cent of the lives were lower class and 10 per cent upper class. There was a steady rise in the number of middle-class lives from the 1500s onwards.

This is a thoroughly scientific survey, rigorously following experimental and statistical rules. The next stage should be independent verification. In any other field such impressive results would have statisticians flocking to do the follow-up research. Yet, as far as I'm aware, no verification has been independently attempted.

Such is science's fear of understanding the paranormal. And this process of denial does not end here.

Kumari Shanti Devi was born in Delhi, India, in 1926. She was a normal little girl until the age of four, when she claimed to be the wife of Kedar Nath Chaubey from Muttra, some hundred miles from Delhi. Enquiries showed that Kedar Nath had lost his wife ten years previously and, surprisingly, all the girl's comments on this past life were confirmed as accurate.

Eventually Kedar Nath wrote to a cousin in Delhi, asking him to call on the girl. The cousin was recognized by Shanti. Later, Kedar Nath visited her and she flung her arms around him. Shanti, along with three researchers, was taken to Muttra, where she immediately recognized several other relations and even took the researchers to a place where Kedar Nath's wife had hidden some valuables. They were not there. But later an embarrassed Kedar Nath admitted that he had found the items previously and removed them.

This last point clearly hints at reincarnation, as it is unlikely that Shanti could have known of the existence of the hiding place. However, the more sceptical researchers have an easier explanation – collusion, the motive being to raise Shanti to the higher caste of her previous-life family.

Luckily, not all such cases come from caste-ridden India. In England, in 1907, three-year-old Dorothy Eady fell down stairs, knocking herself unconscious. Coming round, she began to have dreams concerning a temple and gardens. As she grew older she became convinced she had lived in ancient Egypt, becoming the lover of King Sety the First, around the thirteenth century BC. A priestess sworn to celibacy, she became pregnant, and the disgrace forced her to commit suicide. She became so convinced of this previous life that she moved to Egypt, living her entire life in a primitive village close to the ruins of Sety's temple. She died in 1981, taking her belief with her to the grave.

Japanese farmer's son Katsugoro was born in 1815. At the age of nine he began to speak of being the son of another farmer in another village who had died of smallpox in 1810 when he was six years old. Katsugoro had never visited the village of his previous life, but he described it exactly and he demonstrated intimate, verifiable knowledge of his other family.

In May 1957 the sisters Joanna and Jacqueline Pollock, aged eleven and six, were killed in a car accident in Northumberland in the north of England. In October 1958 their mother gave birth to twins Jennifer and Gillian. It was noticed that Jennifer had a scar on her forehead that was identical to one that her dead sister Jacqueline had carried. When the twins were four months old the family moved from their home in the town of Hexham to Whitley Bay, some twenty-five miles away on the Northumberland coast. Three years later the twins were taken back for the first time and they remembered Hexham with remarkable accuracy. When Mrs Pollock decided to sort out some toys that had belonged to her dead daughters, the twins recognized them and even named the dolls correctly. One day their mother overheard one of the twins speaking about the car crash, yet they had never been told how their sisters died.

Perhaps the most fascinating case on record occurred in 1877 in Watseka, Illinois. Thirteen-year-old Mary Lurancy Vennum had an epileptic fit and remained unconscious for five days. When she came round, she told her parents that she had been to heaven and talked with her dead brother and sister. From then on she began to go into trances when she would become possessed by other people. A friend of the family, Asa Roff, told her parents about his own daughter, Mary, who had had similar fits and had died about twelve years before. The family consulted Dr E. Winchester Stevens, who placed Mary Lurancy under hypnosis, when she told him that she had been taken over by evil spirits. Having an interest in psychic phenomena, Dr Stevens asked to talk to a 'spirit guide'. Mary Lurancy produced a guide whom Asa, who was present, recognized as his dead daughter. The next day Mary Lurancy 'became' Mary Roff, and she remained so for four months before reverting back to her own personality. Her life as Mary Roff was confirmed as recognizably exact by Asa. Apart from the odd trance, following this reversion she led a perfectly normal life.

What are we to make of such cases? Dr Ian Stevenson has come, since the publication in 1966 of his book, *Twenty Cases Suggestive of Reincarnation*, to be regarded as the greatest authority on reincarnation. He has examined about 1,600 cases and unearthed some fascinating facts, such as that children with remembrances of alcoholic past lives have an appetite for alcohol in their present lives. In some two hundred cases he has found birthmarks which correspond to fatal knife or bullet wounds from previous lives. Such discoveries lead him to believe that the human personality may go 'much further back in time than conception and birth'. He postulates a third factor of influence in addition to our genetic make-up and environmental experiences.

This is not to say that Stevenson accepts reincarnation as fact: 'We can never show that it does not occur; nor are we ever likely to obtain conclusive evidence that it does.'

This is the difficulty. Take the Mary Lurancy Vennum case above. If we accept that something strange went on – and the Vennum case is the gem in the believer's arsenal – does it necessarily involve reincarnation? Asa Roff was present at the original hypnotic regression of Mary Lurancy. Could some form of telepathy be at play here? Dr Stevens was interested in psychic phenomena. Could Mary have known this and simply indulged in role play? Could cryptomnesia account for her knowledge of Mary Roff's life? Did she really 'live' as Mary Roff during those four months, or was it a performance that the Roffs went along with because they so wanted their daughter to be alive?

So many unanswered questions. Yet in the mind of one researcher the mystery is not as mysterious as we are led to believe. In 1981 Ian Wilson's *Mind Out of Time?* hit the bookshelves. One of the great modern debunkers of the paranormal, Wilson replaces reincarnation with a no less intriguing but definitely more normal idiosyncrasy of the mind – multiple personality.

Multiple Personality

WE ALL exhibit various moods which can drastically alter the way we think and act. Multiple personality can be seen as the ultimate separation of these different forms of behaviour. Usually as a result of extreme psychological trauma, various elements of the sufferer's personality separate and become autonomous. The host – the original personality – is often only vaguely aware of these rogue personality fragments. Should the condition become prolonged, then each personality fragment can become a separate whole personality.

To the observer, the sufferer becomes increasingly irrational as each personality rises to take control of the host at different times. Indeed, when the sufferer is exhibiting traits of multiple personality in its extreme form, it is as though many different people are occupying the same body, sometimes unaware of each other, sometimes aware of the existence of other personalities, and often antagonistic towards them.

Treatment attempts to integrate the varied personalities back into a cohesive whole by the use of hypnosis and psychotherapy. It is not always successful.

A classic case of multiple personality was that of Christine Beauchamp, who came to the attention of Dr Morton Prince of the Tufts Medical School in Boston towards the end of the nineteenth century. Christine, a student, was close to nervous breakdown when she consulted Dr Prince. Under hypnosis she produced a much more relaxed personality whom Prince called B-2 (B-1 was the original Christine). When hypnotized, B-2 kept rubbing her closed eyes. This proved to be the first sign of another personality, B-3, trying to come out, wanting her eyes open, insisting that she had a right to see. Eventually B-3 asked to be called Sally. Though bright and mischievous, Sally was not as clever as Christine.

A hatred developed between Christine and Sally, with Sally playing vicious practical jokes on her host. On one occasion she went out into the countryside and collected a boxful of snakes and spiders, which she knew Christine hated. She addressed the box to Christine, who opened it and went into hysterics. Sally would also force Christine into embarrassing situations, leaving her personality in charge of their body to lie her way out of them.

This feud continued until the appearance of a much more mature B-4, who defended Christine. Dr Prince decided that if he could merge Christine with B-4, thereby suppressing Sally, he could make the true Christine surface. Sally fought to the end as Dr Prince carried out hypnotic sessions to this end. He finally achieved almost total success, but now and again Sally would briefly re-emerge.

The most famous case of multiple personality is perhaps that of Christine Sizemore, who was also known as Eve White. Her story is told by Thigpen and Cleckley in their book, *The Three Faces of Eve*. Christine was a rather priggish born-again Christian who consulted the doctors because she suffered from blackouts. During one consultation she said that her husband had been angry with her for going out shopping and buying sexy clothes – a shopping spree she had no recollection of. At a later consultation she suddenly changed her entire attitude and persona, becoming a smoking, drinking woman who loved virile men. This personality called herself Eve Black. Talking to her, Dr Thigpen discovered that Eve had been with Christine since she was six. Emerging from a blackout, Christine had found herself being beaten for hitting her sister – which she could not recall doing.

There are obvious similarities here with the Beauchamp case. A rather restrained person manifests an alter ego which sheds the conventions and inhibitions of the host and loves to cause trouble for her. And, like Christine Beauchamp, Christine Sizemore also eventually manifested a third personality, Jane, who became far more integrated and sensible than the others. Even the cure is similar, with Thigpen going on to integrate the personalities into a whole – although in a later book, *Eve*, Christine revealed that the disintegration of her personality returned and she manifested up to thirty separate personalities.

There are hundreds of documented cases of multiple personality on record, with the sufferers manifesting various elements of themselves either to cope with particular situations or to punish themselves.

Sometimes a rogue personality can exhibit extreme criminal tendencies. One such case is that of Billy Milligan from Ohio, who during 1979 committed a series of rapes on a local university campus. He was found to have at least nine personalities, one of which, a frustrated lesbian called Regan, committed the crimes.

It can be seen from these cases that there are many similarities between multiple personality and incidences of reincarnation. The separate personalities, once fragmented, seem to have a predilection for exhibiting personal traits. So it is logical to assume that they could attempt to 'ape' personages from the past, perhaps with the help of cryptomnesia. The alter ego may strive to strengthen itself as a distinct individual by taking on board fantasized, fictional experiences. In this way its existence is given credibility.

When the more sceptical researchers discovered the existence of multiple personality, it was hailed as the final death blow to belief in reincarnation. But is this really the case?

Multiple personality may well explain some cases of reincarnation. But it cannot explain every case. And there is a problem with multiple personality. Most mainstream psychiatrists today deny its existence. They look upon it simply as an incorrect diagnosis in the past of psychological disturbances that can be better understood as neuroses.

Looking at the history of psychiatry, we find that multiple personality became a popular diagnosis in around 1840, but had fallen out of favour by about 1910. The vast majority of cases fall into this period. It is as though the phenomenon only existed when there were specialists prepared to accept its existence. How could this be?

Multiple personality became a fashionable diagnosis at a time when demonic possession was beginning to be shunned, but before standardized theories of the unconscious mind were acceptable to the medical profession. In other words, multiple personality thrived in a time of psychological anarchy, when psychoanalysts put forward varied, and often fanciful, theories. It thrived, according to today's psychiatric establishment, because it fulfilled two essential requirements.

The first requirement can be identified within Victorian society, which insisted on the suppression of psychological idiosyncracies such as sexual perversion or hysteria. But this could be hard on the individual. By presenting multiple personality, though, patients could escape responsibility for their failings. They were the result of circumstances beyond their control, and outside their own identity.

The second requirement was a process now readily understood throughout psychiatry whereby a patient produces symptoms in line with those expected by the psychiatrist. A patient invariably tries to please the therapist by acting as the therapist wants.

We can see this process in action in the Christine Beauchamp case. The symptoms of multiple personality only manifested when Dr Prince hypnotized her. She chose to contact him, at a time when Dr Prince was well known for his theories of multiple personality. And we simply have to look at her own words: 'And I do want you, please, please, to hypnotize me again. You know it is the only thing that has ever helped me. . . .'

H.F. Ellenberger summed up the problem in his book, *The Discovery of the Unconscious* (1970): '. . . after 1910 there was a wave of reaction against the concept of multiple personality. It was alleged that the investigators, from Despine to Prince, had been duped by mythomaniac patients and that they had involuntarily shaped the manifestations they were observing.' Today what was once thought of as multiple personality is grouped together as symptoms of hysterical dissociation – namely sleep-walking, post-hypnotic suggestion and amnesia.

So it is wrong to speak of multiple personality as an accepted psychological state. It is not. And the sceptics are wrong to write off the mystery of re-incarnation by using it.

Indeed, what the sceptics miss in particular is the importance of role play. Psychiatry sees this as the primary element in the archaic phenomenon of multiple personality. I have suggested a similar thing earlier with reincarnation. In fact, role play is vital throughout human interaction. It is a practice we all wish to indulge in; a practice we all indulge in when we escape into a good novel, sit down and view a soap on television, or interact with our computer games. And yes, it is even, perhaps, a practice patients indulge in when consulting a therapist they know has an interest in past-life regression. And in understanding this point, we can see that psychiatry may well be wrong to automatically discount multiple personality in the way it does. For instance, *why* do we feel such a need to indulge in role play? Could it be that psychiatry, and academe in general, has incorrectly imprisoned us within the concept of the 'self'?

The Self

THE PROBLEM with multiple personality is that it cannot exist within the prevalent Western world view. The individual human being must be seen as an integrated whole; that is how modern life works. Our entire civilization is based upon the individual. And in this respect, multiple personality has a close affinity with reincarnation.

It is all to do with free will. As individuals we have choices. Without free will, there would be no point in making choices, for the decisions we make would have nothing to do with our individuality. Rather our choices, being already pre-determined, would have been ordained by influences outside the individual.

Buddhism does, in fact, allow for our free will. As such, the above Western view should not automatically discount our choices as irrelevant within outside influences. Except, that is, for the existence of the Ego. This is the great stumbling block. It is the Ego that raises man to such importance regarding free will. Because of the Ego, it is we, humanity, who must be in charge of our own destiny. Yet an understanding of the growth of the Ego shows us that there is not one hard, scientific fact to substantiate this view.

The history of Western thought begins with the Greek philosopher Plato in the fourth century BC. He was the first philosopher to leave a written record of his ideas. In this respect, he holds a hallowed position in the development of the Ego, and of the 'self'. For the first time a man had written about human intellect. But, as we have already seen, central to his philosophy was the idea of reincarnation. To him, everything humanity could ever do already existed in a timeless, spaceless 'form'. Man could not invent, he could only rediscover.

Plato simply intellectualized a belief, in the continuing cycle of life, that existed in all primitive cultures, although it had previously been mythologized as reincarnation. But while primitive cultures were happy being predestined to a life subservient to outside gods, in devising a man-made philosophy, Plato affronted egoistic free will.

This was reflected in Plato's pupil, Aristotle. He showed how observation, and reflection upon our observations, could increase our knowledge of the world. But, more than this, applying the science and technology derived from such knowledge allowed us to control aspects of the world and hence our increasing knowledge became associated with individual power. Aristotle taught that power could be the ultimate aim of man. His pupil, Alexander the Great, went on to become the first great empire builder.

Aristotle was not the first to recognize man's will to power. A millennium earlier the Hebrew prophet and lawgiver Moses had banished the pagan gods and cast out the idea of rebirth, putting in their place a God who saw man as the ultimate form of creation. In monotheism, man is elevated above the rest of nature. He is given a head start. He may still be subservient to an outside God, but God has allowed him his free will. He has the choice between good and evil.

This was an awesome power for man to behold. Yet, intellectually, he was still shackled by the pagan belief in reincarnation, which Plato had extended to include everything man's intellect could devise. In the fourth century AD the shackles were removed by the Christian Church Father and philosopher St Augustine of Hippo, who argued that if God created the world out of nothing, everything could not already exist in 'form'. How could God's idea of Creation have existed before it happened? Hence, St Augustine argued that only the present could exist. The past existed only as memory, and the future held nothing more than expectation. In a single philosophical stroke, he had banished Plato's forms, and the idea of reincarnation.

By the Middle Ages, Christianity was the overriding belief of the day in the Western world. Man had free will, but within the stewardship of a benevolent God. However, the argument between Christian theology and Aristotle's philosophy, which held that man didn't really need a God, remained. The first attempt to synthesize the two opposing systems came in the thirteenth century with the Italian theologian St Thomas Aquinas.

Aquinas argued that there was a distinction between 'natural' theology and 'revealed' theology. The first came from reason and experience, as in the Aristotelian model; the second involved faith and the Scriptures. Both, however, have the object of the appreciation of God.

Such a system seemed to validate both Aristotle and the Scriptures. However, Aquinas had opened a can of worms, for it was discovered that reason and experience were much mightier tools than belief. Indeed, before Aquinas's ink was dry, the Englishman Roger Bacon argued the importance of science and experimentation above the influence of custom.

For a couple of hundred years, Christianity and the growing influence of science battled it out, with science usually loosing. However, in the sixteenth century, the intellectual view approached radical change, sounding the death knell for a popular God, and raising man's Ego and the self to absolute importance. If this history has an actual turning point, then it came with another English philosopher, Francis Bacon.

Bacon wanted to free learning from the shackles of an appreciation of God. He thought learning should be geared to one overriding requirement – the advancement of man's estate. Realizing that intellect was vital to man's advancement, he sought to raise to supreme importance the pursuit of experimental science, for, as he clearly understood, 'knowledge is power'.

This announcement was timely. A contemporary of Bacon's, the Italian astronomer, physicist and mathematician Galileo Galilei, was in the process of destroying the earth-centred universe, vital to God's creation, and showing how science was our way forward. But there was still a vital stumbling block. What was it about man's intellect that made him so important? How did man's intellect work? What were the mechanics of this self that allowed us to exert such overwhelming power over the world? But the answers would not be found until the seventeenth century, the time of the French philosopher – and inventor of analytical geometry – René Descartes.

Descartes introduced the notion of 'radical doubt'. He asked, 'How do we know the world exists? How do we know God exists, or that others exist?' Most importantly, he asked, 'How do I know that *I* exist?'

These were important questions. Descartes understood that human intellect was nothing without a system whereby intellect could be understood. He argued that at the very heart of our intellect there had to be an absolute – an undeniable, self-evident truth on which to base an understanding of the world. He asked if the senses could provide such understanding? No, they cannot. Our senses can fool us. Man can dream, so does this hold power over the intellect? No, things can appear real in dreams, and while we are dreaming we cannot tell if the images are real or not. So what about mathematics, the most important tool of the intellect? Surely, whether dreaming or not, 2 + 2 = 4. No, argued Descartes. How do we know that some evil outside influence is not duping us to accept mathematics?

After pondering such obstacles, Descartes arrived at his absolute axiom. The senses, dreaming and mathematics all held uncertainty. But one thing was certain. Whether he was awake and sensing things, or asleep and dreaming, or being tricked by outside evil influences, man did think. No matter what situation man found himself in, he thought. And the fact that man was a 'thinking thing' proved both his existence and the predominance of his intellect. In Descartes' famous words, *Cogito ergo sum* – 'I think, therefore I am.'

From this fundamental certainty further self-evident truths arose. Because man, the 'thinking thing', can conceive of God, God also exists. Because God is benevolent, He wouldn't allow an evil outside being to pollute mathematics, so that, too, exists. And by using the principles of mathematics, we can understand the outside world.

Descartes validated the intellect. Yet within his philosophical system he also changed the balance of power between man and God. Previously man had existed because of God. But suddenly, because man was able to conceive of Him, God existed because of man. God still existed 'outside', but only because man's intellect allowed Him to.

The natural progression of Descartes' radical doubt led to the philosophical school known as Empiricism, of which the two leading philosophers were John Locke and David Hume.

The Englishman John Locke, who wrote in the second half of the seventeenth century, is best known for his political theory, which went on to lay the ground for developing liberal democracy. But his theory of knowledge attained great influence too. Locke had a distaste for metaphysics. Although he accepted that we should be tolerant to those who believed in God, he thought that religious belief should have no place in man's search for understanding. Similarly, Plato's theory of 'forms', validating reincarnation, which still had its proponents, was a notion that had to be banished. Locke argued that we hold no innate ideas. When we are born, we come into the world with a mentally clean slate. There is nothing in our mind to pollute us.

From this pure, unpolluted state, 'the mind is furnished with ideas by experience alone'. From seeing and hearing, and through the other senses, we gain sensations. Armed with these experienced sensations, we reflect upon them. And from such reflection, or thinking, we conceive ideas. The first ideas we have are simple ideas born from sensation, yet the mind becomes active because of them and creates complex ideas from reflection of the simple ones.

With such a view of the mind, Locke distinguished between an object in the outside world, and its appreciation within the mind. Objects, he argued, stimulated qualities. These qualities were of two types: primary and secondary. Primary qualities existed in the object itself, whereas secondary qualities produced in the mind ideas which were not in the object. In this way Locke distinguished between the appearance of the outside world and the reality of the world we conceived. In this way, man's *idea* of the world gained in importance over the world outside our mind. Suddenly, not only did God exist because of us, but so did the world.

The Scottish philosopher David Hume, towards the middle of the eighteenth century, furthered this line of thought. He argued that human knowledge came only from impressions and ideas, so the 'laws of nature' must be relegated to a position of no importance. Consider the law of cause and effect, which states that an effect, such as being shot, is the outcome of a cause, or a gun being fired. Hume asked if this is really the case. Does a cause lead to an effect, or is it just that we assume that it does because, from mental habit, we assume that because it has happened in the past it always will? Hume separated the effect from the cause, arguing that they are separate events that are related only because we decide that they are. This further derogation of the outside world went too far, as it invalidated not only all the laws of nature, but even our ability to establish them.

This intellectual cul-de-sac was, of course, unacceptable. The philosopher who showed the way out and rescued the intellect was the French writer Jean-Jacques Rousseau, almost the exact contemporary of David Hume. Rousseau, originator of the term 'noble savage', argued that man's inner nature was full of goodness and in harmony with the natural world. He rejected the view of man as a cold, clinical, thinking thing because this implied the isolation of man from his inner nature. Hence, to counter the empirical approach, he devised the concept of the self. However, Rousseau's self was more than simply the sum total of the man. Rather, it tapped a universal soul.

Such theorizing does, at first, suggest a return to Plato's forms. But even here, man had moved on. Rather, Rousseau argued that man could come to know the nature of all humanity by examining the intricacies of his own mind. As such, the importance of man was maintained, leading Rousseau to suggest that, because of his innate goodness, man had no need of kings, who ruled by the Grace of God.

While Descartes' theorizing had opened the way to Empiricism, a combination of Descartes and Rousseau led to a further school of thought, known as Rationalism. The principal philosopher here was the eighteenth-century German thinker Immanuel Kant.

Kant argued that, while the senses provide experience through which knowledge is attained, the human mind may be seen as a filter through which such experiences mingle with innate abilities to produce a peculiarly human view of the world. To Kant, every experience was a human experience. For instance, we can theorize about time and space within the universe. But this is a human explanation. Time and space do not necessarily exist as a concept in the universe at large as understood by us. Time could be of a different order.

Kant went on to argue that all people have similar filters and from this claimed that we could individually generate universal human knowledge. Applied to ethics, this meant that an individually conceived moral code was transferable to the whole of humanity. Suddenly, the individual, the self, was not only greater than God and the outside world, but an individual self could set the standards for the rest of humanity.

Many would say that this is an unfair assessment of Kant's intentions. And indeed, in one way it is. But if we follow his philosophy through to its ultimate expression, we reach the nineteenth-century German philosopher Friedrich Nietzsche.

Nietzsche thought Kant's philosophy to be too tidy. It suggested that we could eventually attain an ultimate truth. Nietzsche asked, what is truth? It was simply a concept used by individuals to convince everyone else that they should rule. 'Claims to truth,' he said, 'are really claims to power.' History was the process of individuals devising cultures, with those cultures going on to dominate others. Christianity was a prime example, with the idea of God being used to suppress the people. All laws, canons, rights and doctrines were tools of oppression.

But did Nietzsche see this as bad? Not at all. Humanity was stifled by a 'slave mentality' of obedience which kept down those who were noble. Hence, it was the duty of the noble to be strong and create their own ways of life for the lesser people to follow. Forget absolute truth. We make our own values or let others make them for us. And those who make the rules are successful, for they have attained the 'will to power'. They have become Supermen. As such, truth is what they decide to make it. Truth is a matter of interpretation. If you are powerful enough, the people will see the truth on your terms.

Man, the individual, the self, had become the ultimate, the only true source in the world, and that truth was dependent upon power.

Of course, this is just philosophy. There is not one hard, scientific fact in any of it. Yet this history of thought is fundamental to what we now see as humanity and civilization. The history of thought embodies the intellectual assumptions of our age. And it has been a slow but definite process of banishing outside influences in order to uphold the individuality of the self – the Ego. It has to. Western society is built upon it, and all the conflict, argument, cruelty, greed and power-mongering it entails.

But what does it tell us with regard to the present study? We can see that the rejection by established psychiatry of multiple personality, not to mention the banishing of reincarnation and Plato's forms, was essential to uphold the validity of the self. Any form of influence, other than a co-ordinated and wholesome self, would undermine the entire edifice of Western civilization.

And yet that edifice is seen to fall every second of every day. The edifice falls with every cry of a new-born child that takes its first breath before seeking out and sucking its mother's breast.

How does it know what to do? How has it learnt to suck? Certainly not through experience. Certainly not through intellect. Certainly not from anything approaching its individuality.

Rather, it simply knows. The information is within it, innate. It is inherited from outside its self. The knowledge exists, as if it is one of Plato's 'forms'.

Species Conditioning

MULTIPLE PERSONALITY exists. Maybe not in a form acceptable to psychiatry today. But it exists all the same. Further, although I doubt the existence of reincarnation, something exists of a mental capacity prior to birth. At this stage it is impossible to give an exact theory to explain what this mental capacity is. But there are certain patterns that can be identified from our survey of beliefs in reincarnation.

First of all, if we return to Mary Lurancy Vennum, she spoke of evil spirits and being taken over by other people. Throughout history people have been so incapacitated. In times past they were thought of as being 'possessed'. We can now see that the more likely explanation is that they were exhibiting a form of multiple personality. But what is the real difference between these two tags?

The basic phenomena produced are the same in possession and in multiple personality. So it could be argued that the only difference is our cultural interpretation of the occurrence. In our more informed, logical way we have replaced the term 'possession' with 'mind anomaly'. The phenomena are not now assumed to be produced by a 'spirit' invading the body from some supernatural other world. They are the result of the mind itself fragmenting due to psychological disorder. In other words, we have moved our cultural interpretation away from the supernatural to the 'psychological' paranormal. But have we moved this cultural interpretation too far away from possession?

I spoke earlier of multiple personality being a fragmentation of the mind of the individual, with each personality exhibiting certain characteristics of the individual. But what are these characteristics?

Some fragmented personalities are angry, others are shy; some are placid, others are vindictive. What elements of the mind are being displayed here?

It is feasible to argue that each fragmented personality is exhibiting a unique emotional element of the host. In other words, rather than multiple personality being a fragmentation of the actual mind, each personality could be a manifestation of a particular emotion within the mind.

We are all individuals. 'No two people think alike,' we say. But is this necessarily true? One thing psychology has taught us is that, although each person may be different and manifest emotion for different reasons, the emotions themselves are remarkably similar, regardless of sex, level of intelligence, age or background. It is almost as if our emotional traits are not personal to the individual, but are the product of a form of species conditioning.

In the Introduction I spoke of the 'communality' of minds and Jung's ideas of a collective racial unconscious lying under the personal mind. He believed the collective unconscious produced conditioning archetypes. I also noted above that instinct could well be a form of species conditioning. And I find it surprising that, when expressing extreme emotion, we tend to fall back on instinctual behaviour, totally suppressing the logical processes that make us what we are – or, at least, what we assume we are, because of the concept of the 'self'.

We are obviously responsible in a personal way for the behaviour that results from our emotions, but could it be that the emotions themselves are the product of species conditioning rather than personal choice? Could emotion be a subtle form of Jungian control, born from our species communality?

At present this can be no more than a philosophical speculation – although biologists seem to be heading towards the same conclusion with their discovery of genes perhaps responsible for behavioural leanings. But, in the context of reincarnation and Plato's theory of 'forms', we can see the possibility of an emotional dislocation being at the heart of the phenomenon of multiple personality.

However, if this emotional dislocation is the product of ages-old conditioning, then it is feasible that, feeding off such archaic impulses, archaic personalities could 'cling' to the emotion as a form of personal role play. If we accept this, we can see the possibility of a reincarnated personality being the mind manifestation of a previous life. But how does a person manifesting supposed previous lives decide on who to manifest from the past?

Mary Lurancy Vennum manifested the life of a family friend's deceased daughter who, like Mary, was a little girl. As to classic cases such as that of Jane Evans, isn't it probable that she would manifest personalities with whom she had had previous acquaintance, such as from a novel read and enjoyed? And isn't it true that under hypnosis we tend to mix fact with fantasy – which would explain fictitious characters? Indeed, if a person indulges in escapism and role play, as we all do when reading a novel, watching a soap or interacting with a computer game, then the role-play properties of multiple personality would echo both this process and personal bias.

If my speculations about the communality of minds are right, we can see cryptomnesia as a selection process, assisting the subject to choose which historical personalities to manifest.

But where do these personalities come from? Well, one thing cryptomnesia tells us is that the personal mind is such a vast storehouse of memory that it can hold the text of a book which the individual simply 'flicked' through. Add the communality of minds to this process and we have the memory shop I suggested in the Introduction.

One last point. The phenomenon of reincarnation is classically understood as invasion by dead souls. I discount this notion and place a psychological, rather than supernatural, tag upon the phenomenon. But perhaps this is only a different cultural interpretation.

History of Spiritualism

REINCARNATION IS a good starting point for a study of the paranormal. It has a clear 'supernatural' belief system behind it, and it allows us to clear up the matter of possession of the mind by apparently outside influences. Through redefining the cultural interpretation of such phenomena, we can see that what was once thought of as supernatural can better be thought of as psychological – albeit involving an extension of presently accepted psychological mechanisms and hinting at a new look to our understanding of the 'self'.

It is only by burying in this way the tag of supernatural activity that reasoned understanding can come regarding the paranormal. And this reasoning can also be extended to phenomena associated with that relatively recent religion, Spiritualism.

In 1847 the American clairvoyant Andrew Jackson Davis published his book, *Principles of Nature: Her Divine Revelation*, in which he wrote that upon bodily death the human spirit remains alive and moves on to one of a considerable range of worlds where it commences another stage of existence. Since the spirit has not died, but exists with full consciousness, there should be no reason why it should not communicate with those temporarily left on earth.

Davis's book was the culmination of an apparently lightning career. In 1845 he began touring America giving lectures on his 'harmonial philosophy' in which he speculated upon the origin of the universe, the survival of the soul and the requirements demanded within life for successful continued existence of the spirit life.

Two influences were uppermost in Davis's mind. The first was mesmerism, which was in the process of sweeping America. The second, and most major, was the eighteenth-century Swedish philosopher Emanuel Swedenborg.

Swedenborg was a famed scientist, scholar and engineer of his day.

However, as his career progressed he realized there were times when 'heaven opened to him', offering a number of 'visions' which we would today call clairvoyant. Typical was an experience in the Swedish seaport of Gothenburg one Saturday. He became restless and, in mid-afternoon, went for a walk. On his return he spoke of seeing a fire three doors down from his home three hundred miles away. On the following Monday the fire was confirmed, but there was no way Swedenborg could have known about it.

Convinced that such visions could only come from some supernatural source, he began collecting data and constructed a doctrine of 'correspondences' – a system that linked earthly life to the spiritual realm. His doctrine remained largely unknown in America, until Davis, a student of Swedenborgism, wrote his book.

The following year, 1848, the Fox family from Hydesville, New York State, reported hearing mysterious rapping noises about the house, apparently caused by the farmer's two young daughters. The family discovered that they could communicate with the rappings through a code they devised for 'yes' and 'no'. In this way they found out the source of the rappings was a pedlar who had been murdered in the house and buried in the cellar. The showman P.T. Barnum realized the potential in this phenomenon and took the girls to New York City. News of the happenings spread like wildfire and popular Spiritualism was born.

The first question to ask is, of course, were the Fox sisters genuine? Many years later, after a long career as a medium along with her sister and mother, one of the sisters admitted that they had faked the rappings (although she later withdrew the statement). This suggested that Spiritualism was born from a con. However, to be fair, it has to be admitted that at the time the sister in question was a destitute drunk. Such people will do almost anything for money – a factor that was instrumental in her confession. But whether the Fox sisters were fake or genuine was irrelevant. For 'mediums' had already begun to perform the most amazing feats.

One early medium was the remarkable character Daniel Dunglas Home. Born in Scotland in 1833, he was brought up in America by an aunt. Realizing his extraordinary psychic powers early in life, he had projected himself to the top of American high society by the 1850s, going on to fascinate audiences throughout America and Europe until his death in 1886.

Home was an extraordinary physical medium. Performing in well-lit rooms and in tight-fitting clothing so as not to be accused of using apparatus for his feats, he would levitate himself, furniture and other people, thrust his hands into red-hot fires and elongate his body. His performances were often accompanied by apparitions of spirits. Indeed, Home was convinced that spirits were responsible for all the phenomena he produced – he believed that when he levitated, spirits were literally lifting him up.

Home was never seriously accused of fakery. The English poet Robert Browning did attempt to blacken his reputation in the satirical poem 'Mr

Sludge the Medium', but it was thought that Browning was jealous of his wife's affection for Home.

However, not all mediums performed in such ideal conditions as Home. Most held sittings in darkened rooms. One such medium was Florence Cook, whose spirit guide, Katie King, became more famous than her.

Spirit guides were often invoked by mediums; they were representatives sent by the spirits to liaise with the medium and they would often remain faithful to their medium throughout his or her career. But Katie King seemed determined to upstage her medium and grab the limelight herself – not content with acting as an intermediary, she demonstrated her existence by materializing and walking among her audience, often sitting on a gentleman's knee.

To credulous audiences of the 1870s the existence of Katie King was a fact. However, the resemblance between Katie and Florence Cook was rather startling. Then there was the fact that the two were never seen performing at the same time. Before summoning Katie, Florence would seat herself in a curtained booth, hidden from her audience. After twenty minutes Katie would emerge from the booth, perform, and return behind the curtain. A couple of minutes later Florence would re-emerge to applause. During one performance, a Mr Volkman tried to seize Katie, to expose her as Florence dressed up, but he was prevented from doing so by the audience as Katie scurried back behind the curtain.

The British scientist Sir William Crookes went to America to investigate Spiritualism, and one of his first subjects for investigation was Florence Cook herself. Crookes claimed that Katie couldn't possibly be Florence Cook, for he had tied Florence up behind the curtains during Katie's appearances. However, evidence later accrued that suggested a romantic liaison between the scientist and the medium, although to this day it remains unproved.

Crookes was not the only academic to taken an interest in mediums. The Nobel Prize-winner Dr Charles Ricket, the French astronomer Camille Flammarion and the Italian criminologist Cesare Lombroso all became convinced of the reality of mediumistic talents. And so, too, did American psychologist William James, who went on to investigate Leonora Piper, who became, in psychic researcher Hereward Carrington's opinion, 'the greatest mental medium of all time'.

Leonora Piper never attempted physical mediumship, preferring its sister practice of mental mediumship. James began researching her after his wife had become impressed by the extraordinary knowledge she had of James's family. Indeed, James later wrote: 'Taking everything I know of Mrs P. into account, the result is to make me feel as absolutely certain as I am of any personal fact in the world that she knows things in her trances which she cannot possibly have heard in her waking state.'

James began his investigations in 1885. At this time, Piper's spirit guide was the French-speaking Phinuit. Rather than materializing, he spoke through Piper, as if possessing her. In 1887 James passed on his research to psychic researcher Dr Richard Hodgson. He made sure that all Piper's clients were unknown to her and he imposed stringent controls to prevent the leaking of information and trickery. Known to be an exacting researcher, even Hodgson was impressed.

Phinuit seemed to fade away during this period, to be replaced by a guide called George Pelham, who spoke English. In 1905 Hodgson died, but his work was continued by James Hyslop, one of America's best-known psychical researchers, who professed himself astonished by the personalities of Piper's spirit guides. As if to astound him further Piper produced yet another guide – the recently deceased Hodgson.

If Leonora Piper had proved extraordinary, so did the next medium to come to researchers' attention – the irascible Eusapia Palladino. An Italian, her already great reputation was enhanced when Professor Ercole Chiaia appealed publicly for scientists to investigate her in 1888. The then sceptic Cesare Lombroso did so, and became convinced of her powers.

Palladino was both a mental and physical medium who often levitated sitters during her seances; at times invisible hands would grasp sitters and remove them from their chairs. Eventually Hereward Carrington took her to New York, where she achieved even greater fame. But she was often caught cheating. Carrington explained: '. . . I have seen more or less the same thing happen over and over again, and know that, while she occasionally tricked, she was also capable of producing amazing genuine phenomena which have never been explained.'

It was this problem of cheating that caught the attention of escapologist Harry Houdini. A man who genuinely wanted to believe in it all, his researches convinced him that mediums simply milked a gullible public: 'We have prohibition of alcohol, we have prohibition of drugs, but we have no law to prevent these human leeches from sucking every bit of reason and common sense from their victims.'

Houdini was scathing of scientists and their involvement in Spiritualism. He, a master trickster, thought himself alone able to uncover the frauds that mediums practised. He wrote: 'The fact that they are *scientists* does not endow them with an especial gift for selecting the particular sort of fraud used by mediums, nor does it bar them from being deceived. . . .'

Soon he was on the lecture circuit himself, putting Spiritualism down at every opportunity. However, an equally well-known personality rose to do public battle with Houdini – the creator of Sherlock Holmes and arch believer, Sir Arthur Conan Doyle. Indeed, Conan Doyle went on to write his voluminous *History of Spiritualism* (1926).

An arbiter eventually appeared in the form of researcher Dr Walter Franklin Prince. In his book *The Enchanted Boundary* he wrote of Houdini and Conan Doyle: 'Both men carried on their propaganda with apostolic zeal, one to preach the gospel of Spiritualism, the other to banish the super-stition of Spiritualism.' He said Houdini '. . . stuffed so many errors into his book [*A Magician among the Spirits*]' that it held 'extraordinary bias on the whole question.' And as for Conan Doyle, bias was evident '. . . by the ingenuity of the devices through which he persuaded himself that mediums of extremely doubtful character are or were genuine.' But even the neutral Dr Prince became entangled in the furore that was Spiritualism.

Mina Crandon appeared to be a level-headed woman, with none of the eccentricities common in other mediums. Indeed, she was the wife of a respected surgeon. However, she turned her house into a form of psychic circus, displaying a remarkable array of mental and physical mediumship, including automatic writing, table turning and eventual possession by her spirit guide, her deceased brother.

Both Prince and Houdini were among researchers who investigated her, and so split were the researchers that it led to Prince resigning from his position with the American Society for Psychical Research, and Houdini being accused of deliberately planting evidence to discredit her.

Becoming known as Margery the Medium, Crandon eventually produced a fingerprint in wax of her spirit guide. Investigation identified this as the print of a previous client. The controversy surrounding her eventually became so intense that, she claimed, her talents faded away.

No less controversial was the Scottish medium Helen Duncan, who fascinated audiences from the 1930s until well after World War 2. During one sitting in Portsmouth in 1943 a sailor materialized claiming to have 'gone down' with HMS *Barham*. This ship's sinking was, at the time, classified information.

Duncan's spirit guide was perhaps the most unlikely and unbelievable guide of all. Photographs hint strongly that 'Peggy' – a young child – was nothing more than a blow-up doll-like contraption. Duncan claimed that Peggy formed out of ectoplasm from her body. In 1933 a policewoman grabbed Peggy during a seance and testified that it was nothing more than a cleverly lit undervest. Duncan was convicted of fraud and fined ten pounds (then about fifty dollars).

This was not her only brush with the law. Following more disclosures like that of the sinking of HMS *Barham*, she was arrested in 1944 on the grounds that her work posed a threat to national security. While she was under arrest, a fellow Spiritualist came forward claiming that the ectoplasm manifested from Duncan's body was nothing more than butter muslin. She was charged once more with fraud and, at her trial at the Old Bailey, was sentenced to nine months imprisonment. Because of mediums like Helen Duncan, British legal minds began to look at the old Witchcraft Act. The result was a new act – the Fraudulent Mediums Act 1951. In 1956 the authorities attempted to bring Duncan to law again under the new act. At a seance in Nottingham, the police burst into the room, seized Duncan and searched the area for props. Nothing was found. However, following the raid, she was found in shock with major burns on her stomach. Spiritualists maintained that the shock of being grabbed caused her spirit guide to re-enter her body at such speed that it had left lasting physical and mental scars. As to the validity of this, no one knows. What is known, however, is that six weeks later Helen Duncan died. Of course, her diabetes could have had something to do with it.

Amid all this controversy, a much more valuable medium came to the help of researchers in the form of Eileen Garrett, an Irish medium born in 1893. A woman with little formal education, she had a great deal of intelligence, being unique almost among mediums in that she attempted to intellectualize her powers. Her integrity endeared her to many men of intellect, including playwright George Bernard Shaw and psychologist Carl Jung. She wrote about her gift:

> To prove the existence of spirit intellectually has been left to religion and to sentiment, but neither clearly defines a way to an afterlife acceptable to the measuring rule of science. I live in a world filled with phenomena of a transcendental nature, which does not seem to allow itself to be put aside, but acts continually as a guiding force . . . I suspect that this field, discredited by those who do not experience its nature, belongs to the inner workings of what we call mind, as yet to be explored.

Her need to question her talents led to her cooperating in much study by researchers. In 1951 Garrett founded the Parapsychological Foundation in New York. Even her two spirit guides – an ancient Indian soldier, Uvani, and a physician from Saladin's court in the twelfth century called Abdul Latif – were treated with suspicion by Garrett, who never really accepted that they were spirits of the dead.

Perhaps the most famous episode connected with her followed the R101 airship disaster in 1930. Two days afterwards, Flight Lieutenant Irwin, who had died in the crash, materialized at one of Garrett's seances.

Eileen Garrett died in 1970, admired as one of the great mediums of all time, who, even in a more sceptical and scientifically rigorous world, still managed to amaze with her gift.

Garrett was a clairvoyant, who saw visions. Doris Stokes was clairaudient; she heard voices. She never went into a trance. She simply talked to her voices in the same manner as she conversed with her audience. In well-lit theatres she performed before hundreds, picking out members of the audience chosen because of the voices she heard. As well as the usual trivia she offered stark messages – once she warned a widower that his wife didn't want him to commit suicide, as he was planning to do that night. During one book launch, she reduced a journalist to tears by offering messages from her dead twin.

Stokes admitted to cheating just once, confessing that she listened to some guests before a performance and incorporated what they said into her messages. She claimed that she eventually admitted to this because her spirit guide, Ramononov, had chastised her, threatening to take away her powers if she ever did it again.

However, the researcher Ian Wilson decided to attend a performance at the London Palladium shortly before her death in 1987. Stokes relayed to members of the audience messages that seemed remarkably apt and knowledgeable. However, during the break a couple of researchers accompanying Wilson went into the audience to get the names and addresses of those who had received messages. Nearly all of them held complimentary tickets from Doris Stokes herself. As to the many parapsychologists who offered various explanations for her talent, her answer was quite bland in its simplicity: 'They just talk to me, love, and I pass the messages on.'

So what of Spiritualism today? A religion in its own right, its two periods of popular acceptance were between the 1850s and 1870s and around World War 1. In America, Spiritualism lost many followers as the New Age overtook it during the 1960s. Yet in Britain it is still popular. The Spiritualist's National Union, founded in 1901, oversees a well-organized religious structure. Indeed, most British towns have their own Spiritualist Church with healthy congregations, and several authorized Spiritualist colleges train mediums by the dozen.

Most of these mediums are poorly paid and tour the circuit from church to church, passing on their messages from the afterlife. However, sceptics point out that such a close-knit religious community gives any visiting medium access to a whole network of followers, so information about the audience is readily available.

The heyday of physical mediumship is well and truly over. Today's mediums rely on the clairvoyant or clairaudient abilities of mental mediumship. Spiritualists would explain this by saying that, in a more sceptical world, it is harder to produce physical phenomena. The sceptic would point out that in the modern world audiences have become more sophisticated, and mediums just cannot get away with their trickery these days. As an example of this, in July 1960 two researchers were allowed to film some seances at Camp Chesterfield in Indiana. Sitting through the performances in a darkened room, the researchers saw and photographed the ectoplasm and the materialization of the spirit guides. However, the developed film, which had been produced with the use of the latest image enhancers and infra-red equipment, revealed a different performance – by several of the camp members looking resplendent dressed in chiffon and gauze.

Sociological Beginnings

WHAT WAS it that caused the almost phenomenal rise of Spiritualism following the affair of the Fox sisters? The phenomena associated with Katie and Margaret Fox were nothing more than a very mild outbreak of the poltergeist activity that has happened repeatedly before and since throughout the world. How did so innocuous an event cause such a sensation?

In 1792 the English author Mary Wollstonecraft published her bestselling *A Vindication of the Rights of Women*. In her book, recognized as the cornerstone of the feminist movement, Wollstonecraft argued that women were enslaved to domestic tyranny. She denounced the denial, by men, of women's political rights, their lack of education facilities and their inequality in work. A woman's financial dependence upon men she viewed as legal prostitution.

Wollstonecraft was a contemporary of Thomas Paine, author of *The Rights of Man*, whose championing of American Independence had made him a hero in America. And with his influence, that of Mary Wollstonecraft was similarly imported. For the first time, American women dreamed of equality with their men.

With the fall of the monarchy during the French Revolution, Wollstonecraft's message further empowered women both in France and in America, where growing opposition in the North to slavery led to the formation in the South of the Underground Railroad, a network of safe houses and routes to send escaped slaves to the North. The Railroad was run almost exclusively by black women and because of this political and dangerous empowerment they were treated as heroines by the women of the Union.

Of particular fame in the years leading up to the beginnings of Spiritualism was escaped slave Ellen Craft. Setting up home in the free black quarter of Boston, she became a major political speaker for the Anti-Slavery Society. Famous at about the same time was another ex-slave, Sojourner Truth, from New York State, the very state in which Spiritualism began.

In 1843 – just five years before the Fox sisters – she began touring the Northern states. During one famous speech she was interrupted by a male heckler who told her that women were 'too frail for public life'. Truth retorted:

> That man over there say women need to be helped into carriages and lifted over pitches – *and ain't I a woman?* I could work as hard as a man and bear the lash as well – *and ain't I a woman?* I have borne five children and seen them almost all off into slavery and when I cried out with a woman's grief, none but Jesus hear – *and ain't I a woman?*

And the women's rights movement in America exploded, reaching its first crescendo in a small rural Wesleyan chapel at Seneca Falls, where America's first famous activist, Elizabeth Cady Stanton, convinced her audience that women should actively campaign for the vote. Seneca Falls was in New York State. The date of the meeting was 19 July, 1848.

In terms of geography and timing the birth of Spiritualism coincides exactly with the birth of the women's political movement. Further, from then to the present day, the vast majority of mediums have been women. Indeed, the mediums were the first women to gain influence of a real nature over Western society and so to secure release from Wollstonecraft's legal prostitution and domestic tyranny. Even the success of Spiritualism in Britain – a success greater than in any other Western industrialized nation – can be seen as a feminist rejection of a patriarchal state religion. It will be interesting to see whether the ordination of women priests into the Church of England will cause a decrease in Spiritualism.

However, feminism was not the only parent of Spiritualism. Its birth year, 1848, was the most significant year for the socio-political evolution of Western culture in the nineteenth century. Following the Congress of Vienna at the time of the defeat of Napoleon, countries throughout Europe had become increasingly disenchanted. These disenchantments finally boiled over in 1848. Italy witnessed uprisings in Venice, Rome, Messina, Palermo, Reggio and Milan. In July 1848 the Austrians crushed Italian resistance at Custoza. In May 1848 an assembly of liberals met in Frankfurt and drew up a constitution for the unification of Germany. In France, 1848 was the year of the proclamation of the Second Republic. And if this was not enough, the hatred of laissez-faire economics and of the social ineptitude of the Industrial Revolution led, in 1848, to Marx and Engels publishing the Communist Manifesto.

Simultaneously with these apocalyptic disturbances in European society, America suffered a double dose of turmoil with rumblings of social unrest that would lead, in thirteen years, to the American Civil War.

A similar state of unrest had existed in European culture in the fifth century. The Roman Empire was under severe strain as migrating barbarians hammered on the fortified walls of the empire. Society, as the people knew it, was crumbling. Augustine of Hippo then offered a theological system that allowed man to gain psychological comfort in which to hide from the nasties of existing life.

1848 can be viewed in a similar way, with society crumbling and the people feeling a need to gain comfort away from the real world. So perhaps the people wanted to believe in Davis's book (p. 35), just as their Roman ancestors needed to believe in St Augustine's *The City of God*. And, hey presto, a new offshoot of religion is born. Spiritualism, rather than being the result of sudden supernatural happenings, met a cultural need.

The Medium

WHAT IS a medium? Did the practice of mediumship suddenly begin in 1848? Certainly not. Mediumship seems to be older than history. Every primitive culture has had those people who claim to communicate with the Divine and the spirits of the dead. In times past we knew them as wizards, oracles, medicine men, shamans, witch doctors, mystics, prophets or fortune tellers.

I. Lewis, in his book *Ecstatic Religion*, argued that spirit possession was a belief of pre-literate cultures. The cults that accepted it were, he suggested, 'deprivation cults' – they were a means whereby women and other down-trodden individuals could grasp status and self-esteem. This certainly ties in with Spiritualism, both in terms of feminist esteem and of the rebirth of spirituality in an increasingly secular world. But what about the psychology of the individual medium? Is there a single factor that links all mediums?

Conan Doyle highlighted one possible link when he noted that most mediums were women. He thought that women tended to have more intuitive and mystical minds than men but lacked high intelligence, because in the mid-nineteenth century they were not educated to the same standards as men. And 'Great intellect stands in the way of personal psychic experiences. The clear state is certainly most apt for the writing of a message.'

This is a valid point. Few of the better-known mediums could be classed as intellectual. Home was exceptionally naive; Palladino would cheat at a whim; Stokes described her talent so simplistically – 'They just talk to me.' With the exception of Garrett, they never tried to intellectualize their abilities. Home thought the spirits lifted him. End of story. No questions. No doubt. Plain and simple acceptance, as if sheer, non-questioning belief allowed the ability to flow.

Mental instability has also been offered as an explanation of mediumship. The main evidence here is schizophrenia, where visions and voices in the head manifest – two of the classic mediumistic talents. And there is evidence to suggest a degree of mental instability in mediums. Time after time mediumship can be seen as the result of insecurity in early life, a well-attested precursor to mental instability. Home was thrown out by his father at an early age and was finally brought up by an aunt in America; throughout his life he had many debilitating episodes of tuberculosis. Florence Cook, when an adolescent, ripped off her clothes in public, claiming it was the spirits who did it. Palladino's mother died shortly after her birth, and her father was murdered when she was twelve, her talents manifesting the following year. Two weeks after Garrett's birth both her parents committed suicide. She went to live with an uncle, who also died when she was young. Her first 'vision' was shortly after his death, when he appeared before her.

We can imagine such people clinging to the visions they have, finding comfort in them and refusing to question their reality.

But we can, of course, also see them as brilliant and intelligent manipulators, imbued with the American entrepreneurial tradition that had become well established in America during the 1840s. Indeed, a Mrs Hayden, one of the first mediums to cross from America to Britain, shocked the British public in 1852 by charging for her services.

The trickery involved in mediums' performances certainly supports this view of them. Houdini produced a long list of fraudulent practices exposed by him. They included scanning society pages for births, deaths, marriages and engagements; checking court records for information on property and mortgages; employing pickpockets to rob clients; and bribing lift boys and porters for domestic gossip. Some mediums even 'planted' clerks in businesses and hotels who secretly opened clients' mail. Even today the occasional medium is discovered to have had the waiting room wired, so that she or he can listen in to conversations before the seance. Anything to gain information that could later be regurgitated as a spirit message.

During the nineteenth century, in the heyday of physical mediumship, the then fashionable voluminous skirts were found to be most suited to hiding various objects to be materialized from the other world. And, in the more sophisticated world of the twentieth century, many mediums can be seen to be indulging in what is termed 'cold reading'.

Typical of possible cold reading was a recorded sitting by the American 'psychic to the stars', Peter Hurkos.

Hurkos: 'One, two, three, four, five – I see five in the family.'
Sitter: 'That's right. There are four of us and Uncle Raymond, who often stays with us.'

And almost exactly the same question to another sitter:

Hurkos: 'One, two, three, four, five – how many people are in the family, sir?'

Sitter: 'Six.'
Hurkos: 'Five besides you.'
Sitter: 'Yeh.'

What if there were only four in the family, including the sitter? There are many ways out of that one. A dog, a budgie, a cat. No pets? Then has someone died recently? A good bet. Why else would they be visiting a medium?

Anyone with a little understanding of human psychology can dupe a sitter into believing they are getting answers from the afterlife, when in fact the answers are being provided by themselves. This is especially feasible when the sitter, by virtue of visiting the medium, wants to believe. The same trick is used by your average fortune teller.

I well remember a friend of mine visiting a fortune teller and being totally convinced – until I explained some of the methods used. For instance: 'You wish to advance your status, but money just falls through your fingers.' This was spot on. But what was my friend wearing for the sitting? His clothes were fashionable, but cheap brands. Obvious conclusion: he's in a low-paid job but likes to look his best. Hence, he overspends on his dress, and aspires to greater things.

As we saw earlier, one evident area of trickery is the materialization of spirit guides. Cook's Katie King was almost definitely good old Florence dressed up. Sir William Crookes admitted that of some one hundred mediums he investigated all indulged in trickery at times, as so obviously did the otherwise 'genuine' Palladino.

However, while many mediums were certainly frauds, such trickery does not necessarily involve conscious fraud.

First of all, there is the lack of motive. Fraud is a crime committed for financial gain. But very few mediums have become rich. In America in the nineteenth century the average payment for a sitting was a dollar – five dollars was exceptional. Clearly not a fortune. Today, in Britain, most mediums are equally poorly paid. Fraud for financial gain just does not make sense. But then, if a medium's trickery is not conscious fraud, what could it be?

What do we now know of the medium? There are strong hints that, at some time in their life – usually childhood – there has been a degree of mental instability. They find solace in the visions manifested during their instability, and so construct a belief system in the visions. This allows a degree of their mental instability to remain with them, giving the impression of naivety in later life.

When the medium performs, at times she or he offers valid information from the afterlife which gives the sitter comfort. This usually, but not exclusively, happens in a trancelike state when the medium is 'possessed' by a spirit guide. Alternatively, at other times the medium speaks a great deal of twaddle, indulges in obvious trickery, and even dresses up as the spirit guide she claims to be able to manifest. How do we get such conflicting attitudes in the same individual?

We have seen how mental instability can lead the sufferer to find therapy through dissociation of the 'self' by manifesting multiple personality. As to the trance-like state that leads to possession by the spirit guide, we must remember that a trance is nothing more than self-hypnosis. And during such a state, past-life regression may be achieved, or possession by an apparently different personality.

As to the trickery, we must remember Christine Beauchamp's mischievous personality, Sally; or Christine Sizemore's mischievous and sexual personality, Eve Black. The latter, in particular, loved role play and dressing up. So we must ask the question, was the 'spirit guide' Katie King an actual spirit, or the mischievous, fragmented personality of Florence Cook?

As Eileen Garrett wrote in her autobiography, *Many Voices*, concerning her two spirit guides: 'I have maintained a respectful attitude towards them. I have never been able wholly to accept them as spirit dwellers on the threshold which they seem to believe they are.' Garrett long held the conviction that they were nothing more than split-off aspects of her own mind. And we must also bear in mind that, when not performing, most mediums live perfectly normal, sane, family lives. When not at work, it is the host, the person herself, who is in charge. Through long association with their fragmented selves, they have learnt to control the 'demons' within.

Applying theories of multiple personality to mediumship means that a single psychological anomaly can be seen to explain two supposedly separate supernatural phenomena. In both reincarnation and Spiritualism, we have identical mechanisms at work.

The Split Brain

HELENA BLAVATSKY was born in Russia in 1831. An obese lady with a strong will, she toured the world before arriving in America about the time of the proliferation of Spiritualism. She appeared to be a natural medium and soon became famous, eventually founding the Theosophical Society, which survives to this day. But a disgruntled employee finally showed evidence of fakery and she was discredited.

However, she wrote two lengthy books – *Isis Unveiled* and *The Secret Doctrine*. In them she spoke of receiving messages from the mahatmas of Tibet, who passed on to her the secret of life. The books themselves were said to have been written by the mahatmas, through Blavatsky. They dealt with the illumination of man's mind by the incarnation of human entities from prior worlds and the revolution through reincarnation of the early races of man up to modern times and proposed a cyclical universe – ours being one of an endless series – powered by karma. The first 'root race' of mankind was fire mist; the fourth lived on Atlantis.

Clearly the philosophy is debatable. But what is to be made of the claim that the mahatmas communicated through Blavatsky, as though she were possessed by them? As we saw with Doris Stokes, such possessions can even appear as if another voice is invading the mind. Indeed, how close is this invasion to the conversion of St Paul, where, in a vision, Jesus asked him why he was persecuting him? The British serial killer Peter Sutcliffe, known as 'the Yorkshire Ripper', claimed to have heard a similar voice, urging him to kill prostitutes. Believers in UFO cults speak of voices warning of the dangers of scientific advancement. Could it be the same form of invasion which deludes mediums into believing that the communications they receive come from beyond the grave?

The most logical explanation of such mind invasion is delusion. Sutcliffe had to find justification for his murders. St Paul was, until his conversion, a persecutor of Christians. Could it have been his guilt complex? With Helena Blavatsky, I feel it was a vivid imagination working on an eccentric personality.

Blavatsky's particular talent was automatic writing, a form of dissociation achievable in a trance. One of the first recorded automatic writers was Anna Windsor in 1860. Having no control over the activities of her right hand, which she eventually referred to by the name 'Stump', she involuntarily wrote a number of prose pieces and poems.

At about the same time, American Spiritualist Judge John Worth Edmonds claimed that his automatic writing was due to the spirits of the philosophers Francis Bacon and Emanuel Swedenborg. However, the writings lacked the genius which would have been expected from such notable intellectuals. Indeed, the researcher F.W.H. Myers, who studied some fifty incidences of automatic writing, considered the works poor and certainly not evidence of survival of the soul.

William James, the American psychologist and philosopher, eventually put his finger on the most probable explanation for the talent. To him, automatic writing was a means of gaining access to the unconscious. Rather than coming from outside agencies, the writings could better be seen as a fragmentary element of the writer's creative urges. And such urges do not necessarily have to come from automatic writing. Consider, for instance, the abilities of Saint Louis, Missouri, housewife, Pearl Curran.

In 1913 Curran began experimenting with a Ouija board. Having had little success at first, she was astounded one day to find herself spelling out the message: 'Many moons ago I lived. Again I come. Patience Worth my name.' During subsequent sessions, Worth disclosed she was an Englishwoman born in 1649. A spinster, she eventually moved to America, where she was massacred by Indians. However, Worth had literary aspirations. Between 1913 and 1922 she provided for Curran some two thousand five hundred poems and six full-length novels among other shorter pieces. Through most of this period the works were spelled out on the Ouija board, but eventually Worth possessed Curran and dictated them to her. Several of the novels became bestsellers.

Given what we now know of the abilities of the mind in manifesting cryptomnesia and dissociation through multiple personality, it becomes more logical to agree with James that the unconscious of the individual is involved. With Curran, it was not Patience Worth who had literary aspirations, but Curran herself. And she is not alone.

London housewife Rosemary Brown has had no formal musical training. Yet she has produced recordings considered to have a fair degree of musical merit. But, she claims, the works are not her own. She simply writes down the scores as dictated by the spirits of great composers such as Beethoven or Liszt. Critics consider that if the compositions are really those of the great composers, then in the afterlife their abilities are in decline. The more reasonable assumption is that Brown has talent, and the scores are creations of her own unconscious – another example of dissociation of the personality.

Science is today beginning to offer clues to the physiological root of dissociation of the personality. In the mid-1940s, surgeons began to look at the possibility of restricting the 'electric storm' that attacks the brain during an epileptic fit by separating the brain into two halves, thus restricting the physiological effects of the fit. Higher brain function in human beings is carried out within the exceptionally large cerebrum, which lies just behind the forehead. The cerebrum is in two halves – the left and right cerebral hemispheres – connected by the *corpus callosum*, a motorway of some eight hundred million nerve fibres. If the *corpus callosum* is cut, the brain is effectively split in two.

During the 1960s, after a period of experimentation on monkeys and cats, the first operations on humans were carried out. One of the principal researchers into the effects of the operations was Roger Sperry of the California Institute of Technology. What researchers most wanted to know was whether the patient would continue to be a fully functioning, thinking individual. At first it appeared this was, indeed, the case. Then more intricate tests were carried out.

The first hint that the operation could impair the co-ordinated function of the brain came when a patient bumped into a table on his left side, but had no idea that he had done so. Somehow, the information concerning the accident did not register in the brain. To gain further understanding, Sperry began to blindfold patients and ask them to identify the objects he placed in their left hands. They were unable to do so. But if the object was named, and the patients asked to use it, they could. For instance, if a pencil was placed in the left hand, the patient couldn't recognize it. But if asked to write, he proceeded to do so, knowing a pencil was in his hand. It soon became clear that the split-brain patient no longer had awareness that could be classed as whole. The 'self', it appeared, had disintegrated.

Before long, it was understood that the left and right cerebral hemispheres had different functions. For instance, it appeared that the left hemisphere controlled motor functions of the right side of the body, and the right controlled the left side. Then it was discovered that speech, writing and calculation were the almost exclusive preserve of the left hemisphere, while the right hemisphere was best for noting shapes and perceiving emotion.

It seemed from all this that the two hemispheres viewed the world from different perspectives. In a real sense, the 'self' was no longer an absolute whole, but a system of two complementary conscious outlooks. A human being had two selves. In the left hemisphere logical processes predominated, while the right hemisphere was the seat of emotional qualities and creativity. We each, it appears, have a scientist and artist within us.

Similar tests were performed on people who had not had the operation, and it soon became apparent that in the split-brain patient the differences in activity are simply amplified. We all, in our daily existence, use two complementary mind systems.

Through this split-brain research, we can begin to understand our personalities and characteristics. In normal life, logical processes need to be maintained. Hence, the logical left hemisphere is our main 'self'. It is the left hemisphere that gets us up in the morning, that allows me to sit here mechanically typing. However, when those uncontrollable emotional urges rise into the mind, then the right hemisphere gains dominance, suppressing our logical faculties.

Similarly, in exceptionally creative individuals, such as the novelist, musician or artist, the right hemisphere is dominant. Their emotions usually overpower their logic and they may even appear eccentric. The modern British writer Colin Wilson has dubbed this interaction of logical and emotional impulses the Laurel and Hardy effect. If you get up and notice it is raining, you have made a logical, left-hemisphere observation. But you don't want it to rain. Hence, right-hemisphere emotion rises to add depression to the logical deduction. Stan has over-reacted to Ollie.

However, at times the interaction between left and right hemispheres can be more disturbing. During one experiment with split-brain patients, red or green lights were flashed into the left eye. Because the right hemisphere controls the left eye, logical function was not involved. The patient could not tell which colour light had flashed and could only make a guess. Some patients, if they guessed wrong, then suffered tiny muscle contractions, as if the right hemisphere had heard the wrong answer and was communicating the fact.

These and similar tests suggest that the right hemisphere operates autonomously and separately – an extreme illustration of this being a woman who tried to strangle herself with one hand while the other defended her. Hence, it has been suggested by some researchers that an autonomous right hemisphere could appear to communicate with the left hemisphere (the normal, everyday self) and give the impression of a voice. It would also be possible for emotional fragments of the right-hemisphere personality to seize control of the individual by overpowering the logical processes of the left hemisphere.

Such theories allow for Doris Stokes to hear voices in her head and for Florence Cook unconsciously to role play with her created spirit guide, Katie King. And still there is nothing of a supernatural flavour occurring.

Transference

WE CAN now see that Helena Blavatsky and Pearl Curran were not 'invaded' and given words from outside sources, but were simply taken over by their unconscious creative impulses through right-cerebral-hemisphere dominance. However, this explanation cannot account for all the information received by a medium. Consider, for instance, the medium Cora Richmond.

Richmond gave 'trance lectures'. At her performances she would ask the audience to select a jury, which would then choose a topic – any topic – for her to lecture on. Many sceptics considered her lectures somewhat boring, but audiences often found them of great interest and were impressed by her knowledge. Assuming that the lectures contained facts she did not herself know – which seems likely seeing she had no control over the topic – where did her knowledge come from?

The London-born medium Coral Polge is a psychic artist. She sits in front of audiences and draws portraits from the impressions she receives. Out of some forty thousand drawings, few have not been recognized. However, it has been noted that not all the portraits are of the dead. Occasionally she draws people who are still alive. When this happens, the portrait is of the subject when much younger, at the time when last seen by the member of the audience who recognizes the portrait. It is as if the portrait is produced from the audience member's memory of the subject. Which gives us a strong hint as to the source of the information.

The Irish poet W.B. Yeats once attended a sitting with the medium Geraldine Cummins. She told him a story from the spirit world. Yeats found this fascinating – she was narrating the plot of the book he was working on at the time.

These examples suggest the source of the information to be the mind of the client or, in the case of Cora Richmond, the sum total of the collective minds of the jury (in picking a subject, the jury would be likely to pick a subject they were conversant with). In a word, we seem to be dealing with telepathy.

However, a telepathic message is normally perceived as a short burst of information that 'infiltrates' the mind, not as a body of information so detailed and complete that it can fill a lecture or be the basis for a portrait. Further, there is a great deal in the literature of Spiritualism which conflicts with the telepathy theory.

Edgar Vandy died in a swimming pool in August 1933 in Sussex, England. The inquest on his death recorded a verdict of misadventure, deciding that, although no one actually saw the accident, he had struck his head on the bed of the pool. However, his brother, George Vandy, wasn't satisfied that all questions had been answered. In desperation, he decided to ask Edgar himself, by consulting a medium.

George had consulted mediums before and was a member of the Society for Psychical Research. So he used an assumed name, to prevent the medium gaining information about him in orthodox ways.

The medium in question was Frances Campbell. During the session, although she failed to find out the cause of Edgar's death, she came up with some remarkable facts about Edgar, George himself and the third brother, Harold. Most of these facts were known, even if only as obscure memories, to George, hinting again at telepathic contact. But one session produced a piece of information unknown to George; the medium asserted that there was a cigarette case hidden in Edgar's bedroom, in a chest of drawers. Sceptical, because Edgar had been a non-smoker, George nonetheless checked and found, where the medium had described, not a cigarette case but an aluminium soap box almost exactly the size and shape of a cigarette case.

Assuming that this was a genuine phenomenon – and there is no reason to doubt it – then the telepathy explanation is blown. This information was not in the client's mind. It came from other sources. And there are many hundreds of other anomalies such as this, arguing against telepathy. What, then, does this mean in terms of mediumistic talents and, more broadly, of reincarnation?

With both phenomena we seem to be dealing with the invasion of the mind by some form of personality or outer influence. This influence usually bears some form of link with the medium, or host. If we return to reincarnation, Mary Lurancy Vennum gleaned the information about a family friend's deceased daughter. During hypnotic regression, the past lives recounted are usually based on previous fictional input. With mediums, the information concerns the client who is present at the time.

One of the most compelling episodes giving credence to this idea concerned Uri Geller. In 1974 the researcher Andrija Puharich published his book, *Uri: a Journal of the Mystery of Uri Geller*. In it he describes the time when Geller went into a trance-like state and a 'voice' spoke from above his head and explains that Geller had been trained by 'space intelligences' to prevent man from plunging into catastrophe.

The first impression the reader will have is to brand Geller a nut. However, this is only part of the story. In 1952, long before meeting Geller, Puharich consulted a Hindu psychic called Dr Vinod who, in a trance, took the voice of one of 'the Nine' – super-intelligences who had been keeping a kindly eye on man for thousands of years – who were aiding human evolution. Three years later Puharich met another psychic in Mexico who also spoke of 'the Nine' and even continued the original message passed on by Dr Vinod. Even after Puharich's split with Geller, various psychics continued to pass him messages from 'the Nine', eventually sending him on a series of bizarre missions around the world. 'The Nine' eventually advised that Puharich's work had averted world catastrophe.

As well as being a reminder to researchers not to become too involved, personally, in the work they do, we can see that 'the Nine' were nothing more than a space-age cultural interpretation of Helena Blavatsky's mahatmas, and are most likely an expression of unconscious fears, in this case caused by the intrigues of the Cold War. But most important is the procedure by which a whole host of mediums found communality in the client.

So what is really involved in such phenomena, if, as already explained, telepathy doesn't seem to fit in its classically understood form? Obviously it has to be assumed that the information is taken selectively from some other source. The source being the client's mind does not always seem viable, as seen with George Vandy, so 'from the grave' suddenly seems credible, except that Puharich's 'Nine' would seem to be extraterrestrial intelligences.

Which all prompts the question, are we really dealing with anything of a 'personal' nature in such invasions, or would we be better off thinking of reincarnation and mediumistic talents as the retrieval of information from a source as yet unknown, with the client acting as a 'trigger' for the selection of such information, in the same way as we can access computer memory?

If we can accept this as feasible then, as with our study of reincarnation, we could simply be talking of retrieval of information from my suggested memory shop. As we extend our survey of the paranormal to the arena of ghosts, we should keep this question very much in mind.

Ghosts

I saw a ghost at Bethune. He was a man called Private Challoner who had been at Lancaster with me, and again in F Company at Wrexham. When he went out with a draft to join the First Battalion he shook my hand and said: 'I'll meet you again in France, sir.' He was killed at Festubert in May and in June he passed by our C Company billet where we were just having a special dinner to celebrate our safe return from Cuinchy. There was fish, new potatoes, green peas, asparagus, mutton chops, strawberries and cream, and three bottles of Pommard. Challoner looked in at the window, saluted, and passed on. There was no mistaking him or the cap-badge he was wearing. There was no Royal Welch battalion billeted within miles of Bethune at the time. I jumped up and looked out of the window, but saw nothing except a fag-end smoking on the pavement. Ghosts were numerous in France at the time.

SO WROTE the British poet Robert Graves, in his book *Goodbye to All That*, concerning an incident during World War 1.

Equally disconcerting was the apparition seen one day by the nineteenth-century American novelist Nathaniel Hawthorne.

The reading room of the Boston Athenaeum was a sombre, gentlemanly place. Quieter than a library, speech was unheard of, the clientele preferring silent relaxation to shed the stresses and strains of the day. Hawthorne was a regular visitor, as was Dr Harris, an elderly clergyman. Told of Dr Harris's death, Hawthorne was saddened, especially as Harris had seemed perfectly all right earlier that day, sitting in the reading room. The following morning, Hawthorne again visited the reading room, and was surprised to find Dr Harris seated in his usual place. Unwilling to break the convention of silence by talking to Harris, Hawthorne simply stared, amazed. As he did for weeks afterwards, as Dr Harris continued to occupy his seat, the others in the room oblivious to Hawthorne's vision.

Such experiences are common. In a poll conducted in the 1980s by the University of Chicago's National Opinion Research Council, 42 per cent of the adult population reported they had seen some form of apparition. Classically understood as the spirits of deceased persons trapped in earthly existence, ghosts are usually perceived as solid, just like you or me, although occasionally they can be viewed as transparent or ill defined. And their manifestation can often be accompanied by smells, voices and a sudden drop in temperature. While sceptics ascribe ghosts to simple hysteria, storytelling or that which is found at the bottom of a beer barrel, others are loath to discount their existence.

Robert Graves wrote:

> I think that one should accept ghosts very much as one accepts fire – a more common but equally mysterious phenomenon. What is fire? It is not really an element, not a principle of motion, not a living creature – not even a disease, though a house can catch it from its neighbours. It is an event rather than a thing or a creature. Ghosts, similarly, seem to be events rather than things or creatures.

Indeed, for as long as man has left record of his existence there has been evidence of his belief in life after death. Archaeological evidence is rife with tombs from the world over where wealth has accompanied bodies. Ancient Egyptian religion was mainly based on such a concept; the dead took with them into the afterlife not only wealth but food. From Homer's *Iliad*, through Shakespeare's *Hamlet* to Dickens's *A Christmas Carol*, ghosts have proliferated in literature. Even in the modern day, writers such as American horror-fiction author Stephen King keep the belief alive; his novel, *The Shining*, is a modern reworking of the classic haunted-castle story.

Britain, sometimes known as the ghost capital of the world, has an estimated ten thousand regularly haunted places. The Tower of London has, it is reputed, no less than thirty ghosts, including King Edward V, Anne Boleyn, Lady Jane Grey, Sir Walter Raleigh and Guy Fawkes. Sightings are said to continue to the present day, with some fourteen reported since the early 1970s. Royal palaces have their fair share of ghosts, the most disturbing perhaps being that of Catherine Howard, fifth wife of Henry VIII. Arrested at Hampton Court for having sexual relations prior to marriage, she escaped her guard and ran down a gallery, now known as the Haunted Gallery. Caught, she was dragged away screaming and beheaded in February 1542. Many claim to have seen the ghostly re-enactment of her flight. Although it would be perhaps wise for her not to vary her route if she ever appeared on 26 February. If she did, she might well bump into Sir Christopher Wren, often observed running up and down the stairs on this anniversary of his death.

The sea has its fair share of apparitions. One story tells of the seventeenth-century Dutch sea captain Cornelius Vanderdecken. A cruel man who drove his crew relentlessly, he would take great risks during storms, daring the elements to take him. Once, while sailing from Batavia to Holland, he was stuck for nine weeks in a storm off the Cape of Good Hope. Eventually he cursed God, giving a vile oath that he would round the Cape if it took until Judgement Day. Suddenly a 'radiant being' materialized on deck. Vanderdecken cursed it and shot at it. In retaliation the being promised that Vanderdecken would never see port again and condemned him to sail the seven seas for all eternity as a portent of disaster. Thus was born the world's most famous non-human ghost – the ship, the Flying Dutchman.

Most ghosts are said to be harmless – but not all. A violent English ghost is said to haunt 50 Berkeley Square, London. It dates back to when a Mr Dupre confined his insane brother in an upstairs room. The brother continued stalking the house even after his death. In the same house is also said to be the ghost of a Scottish child, frightened to death by a servant, and another of a young woman who threw herself out of a window to escape being raped by an uncle. Inevitably, the house was left vacant, but one Christmas Eve a sailor and his companion spent a night there to keep warm. After seeing a 'shape', the sailor jumped to his death from a window. Another man died in terror in the house, and when the eighteenth-century man of letters and politician Lord Lyttleton spent a night in the house, he fired pistols loaded with silver coins, making the 'shape' disappear. This experience gave him the idea for his classic story, 'The Haunters and the Haunted'.

We are right to be sceptical of such tales, and to regard them as infantile superstitions satisfying a need within the human psyche to be frightened. However, similar ghost stories continue to be told in modern times, by perfectly rational individuals. Typical is the experience of Roy Fulton.

One night in 1979 Fulton was driving home in his van when he stopped to pick up a hitch-hiker near Dunstable in the county of Bedfordshire. A youth aged 19 or 20 opened the door and got in. Roy set off once more, but a moment later, when he turned to look at the hitch-hiker, the youth had disappeared.

How do we account for such experiences? What possible motive could people have today for the telling of such tales? Nathaniel Hawthorne and Lord Lyttleton were both writers – they were in the business of making up stories. The Flying Dutchman is almost certainly a tale based on nautical superstition. But people such as Roy Fulton have absolutely nothing to gain by the telling of such tales. Indeed, in a sceptical world, there is a disincentive due to the ridicule they can sometimes face. And there are hundreds of similar experiences recounted every year. Yet none are as spectacular as the hauntings of Borley Rectory – a house dubbed 'the most haunted house in Britain'.

Before the Reverend Eric Smith moved into the Suffolk rectory in 1928 the building had been occupied by the Reverend Henry Bull and his son,

Harry, an eccentric man who was believed to dabble in things supernatural. Stories of sightings of nuns and coaches and headless men began during this period. Smith – who claimed to be a non-believer in the active supernatural – contacted the London newspaper the *Daily Mirror* when he noticed strange occurrences, and researcher Harry Price was sent to investigate.

Soon Price began to experience bells ringing, footsteps echoing, medallions materializing, keys jumping out of locks and vases smashing. In 1930 the Reverend Lionel Algernon Foyster and his young wife Marianne moved in. Soon Marianne reported messages for help materializing, fires breaking out and furniture sailing through the air. Price was still a regular visitor, and his work made the rectory famous.

In 1956 the Society for Psychical Research published a devastating report, destroying much of the myth of Borley Rectory. Acoustics, wind vortices . . . the list of 'earthly' explanations was endless. Harry Price was a maverick and unorthodox researcher, and the report could have been made principally to discredit him. But a newspaper reporter who saw pebbles fly through the air discovered similar pebbles in Price's pocket. Was Price myth-making through trickery?

The rectory burnt down in February 1939 and was totally demolished in 1944. And although the Society for Psychical Research published their devastating report, this must be countered by the claims in *The Ghosts of Borley Rectory* (1973), wherein the researchers Peter Underwood and Paul Tabori state: 'We believe that the Borley hauntings represent one of the most interesting, most cohesive and varied chapters in the history of psychical research and that they contain, as if in a microcosm, the full range of psychic phenomena.'

Harry Price may well have been vilified by the Society for Psychical Research, but he earned his position in any history of the subject of hauntings by being the first researcher to employ technology in the search for evidence. Indeed Price put together a researcher's kit, which included a camera, fingerprinting materials, thermometer, movie camera, portable phone and telescope.

This tradition is often continued today, with the employment of time-lapse photography, infra-red sensors, tape recorders, heat sensors and geiger counters. This vast array of equipment is left at supposed haunting sites to try to record materializations, voices and changes in atmosphere. However, even if images are caught, they are often discounted. Consider an early, accidental photograph of a 'ghost', taken in December 1891.

Sybell Corbet wanted a photograph of the library of Combermere Abbey near Nantwich in Cheshire. The owner, Lord Combermere, had recently died. However, when the photograph was developed, an image appeared of a figure looking remarkably like Lord Combermere sitting on a chair on the left-hand side of the photograph.

The photograph caused quite a sensation. But Professor William Barrett, who investigated the case, was not convinced. A slow exposure – a full hour – had been required and for part of the time Miss Corbet had left the room. During this time, decided Barrett, someone – a servant, possibly – had entered the room, sat in the chair for thirty seconds or so, noticed the camera and hurried out. Such a short time of occupancy would appear on the developed photograph as a ghostly image.

Do ghosts exist? If they do, are they spirits of the dead, or are there less spectacular answers for such hauntings? One thing is clear. Ghost stories can titillate the imagination to such an extent that people become compelled to believe in them. I always laugh when I remember a conversation between two girls, recounted by researcher Jenny Randles in her book, *Sixth Sense*. One girl turns to the other and says: 'I don't believe in ghosts. But I believe my friend saw one.'

Dreaming

BETWEEN APRIL 1889 and May 1892 the Society for Psychical Research undertook an international survey into the prevalence of ghosts. For their *Census of Hallucinations* they interviewed some 17,000 people, of whom 1,684 said that they had had ghostly experiences. While many of these claims were discounted as the product of illness, a substantial number of unexplained happenings remained.

Surveys such as this have brought out an important fact regarding ghosts. Only a small percentage of hauntings concern the appearance of historic characters. By far the majority of ghosts are not spectacular events as described in the previous chapter, but rather innocuous appearances, by the bedside, of a recently deceased spouse, friend or family member. Such hauntings have come to be known as 'bedroom visitations'. And as to their modern prevalence, in 1971 a paper in the *British Medical Journal* by Dr W. Dewi Rees pointed out that almost half the widowed population of his practice experienced visions of their loved ones, especially in the first ten years of widowhood. Which provides us with an important clue as to what is going on in such hauntings.

Throughout our study of life after death, certain factors have emerged. Cases of reincarnation can manifest during hypnosis. Many psychic manifestations occur following illness or coma, such as Mary Lurancy Vennum displaying odd behaviour after five days of unconsciousness. Mediums operate in a trance. And all these factors constitute an altered state of consciousness, or ASC. But what is the most common form of ASC? We witness it every night when we go to sleep. It is the dream state.

Dreaming is popularly accepted as a plunge into the unconscious during sleep, an interaction with an amazing fantasy world. During the dream we feel emotion and carry out spontaneous actions ranging from harmless twitching to the more extreme talking and walking and, for the male, ejaculation. Heart rates can increase or decrease, and during a nightmare the sleeper can break into sweats. The experience, while bizarre, often confuses the dreamer into believing he is actually awake and experiencing the dream in real life.

Everyone dreams, yet most dreams are forgotten – the remembered dream is the one occurring as the sleeper awakes. And even remembered dreams tend to be forgotten within a couple of minutes. As to the content of dreams, it is generally accepted that they deal metaphorically with the events, issues and people within the dreamer's life, often displaying elements of fear, joy and anxiety to echo the emotional state of the individual.

Over recent years, this analysis of dreams has led to a new form of pseudo-psychology known as dream interpretation. Here, analysts examine a person's dreams in order to highlight symbolic meanings, offering such analyses as a form of divination, showing the dreamer how his unconscious fantasies can direct his future life.

In early times, dreams were thought of as supernatural influences. The ancient Egyptians, Babylonians and Greeks saw them as prophetic. Indeed, one Egyptian papyrus dating from about 2000 BC details dream analysis, discussing various forms of dream association. Even the Bible narrates many dream interpretations, offering prophecies and direction for the dreamer. However, the more sceptical Aristotle dismissed dreams as the product of supernatural influences.

The first logical analysis of the meaning of dreams came in the second century AD with the Greek soothsayer Artemidorus Daldianus, who thought dreams were extensions of whatever activity the dreamer had indulged in during the day. But as Christianity gained popular acceptance the importance of dreams declined, with, by the thirteenth century, St Thomas Aquinas advising that dreams should be ignored.

All that changed in 1900 with the publication of *The Interpretation of Dreams* by Sigmund Freud. The most brilliant psychologist of his day, Freud had one big disadvantage in his work. Hypnosis had become the central element in psychological diagnosis. But Freud was a lousy hypnotist.

Freud came to the conclusion that dreams were the 'royal road' to the unconscious. He argued that events of the day caused 'day residues' to present themselves at night, offering the analyst access to the deep, repressed unconscious, thereby getting to the heart of neuroses by by-passing the lying conscious mind. Using the method of 'free association' which he had devised, he would let the patient become relaxed, thus allowing the mind to wander. In this state, the patient would begin to discuss his dreams and move on to ideas and emotions within the dream. Such analysis disclosed the true nature of the neurosis by moving from the recollected dream, which Freud termed the 'manifest content', to the unconscious thoughts and wishes hidden in it, the 'latent content'.

In the early stages Freud believed that dreams were tied in with wish-fulfilment allied to emotional reactions to infancy. But he later modified his views, arguing that dreams could be repetitive elements of recent trauma.

Freud's most famous pupil, Carl Jung, furthered our understanding of dreams. To Jung, dreams offered information regarding the 'self' in order to offer guidance. Such guidance caused 'individuation', allowing the individual to become whole. In this way the conscious and unconscious engaged in dialogue with each other. Only through dreams could a person really understand his life, for the symbols surfacing in the unconscious during dreaming represented the true arbiter of our state of mind.

The theories of Freud and Jung are important to an understanding of ghosts. They tell us that at night our unconscious mind infiltrates and takes over the psyche, exhibiting bizarre and emotional characteristics. During the dream state we are predisposed to 'see' a deceased loved one. Our mind is perfectly attuned to their presence.

That is theory. But what has experiment told us about the state of dreaming?

In the 1950s a team of researchers led by Nathaniel Kleitman of Chicago began to investigate dreaming in the laboratory. Observing people in sleep, they identified two specific sleep patterns – REM sleep (rapid-eye-movement sleep), when bursts of eye activity were detectable under the eyelids, and NREM sleep (non-rapid-eye-movement sleep).

Intrigued by these two distinct patterns, Kleitman began waking people immediately after a period of REM sleep, which could last for up to 20 minutes. He found that at these times the sleeper could recall dreams with great clarity. It was eventually accepted that REM sleep was, in fact, dream sleep.

The success of these experiments has led many to believe that it is only during REM sleep that the unconscious invades the psyche. However, this is not the case. In 1962, also in Chicago, David Foulkes concentrated on NREM sleep. Waking people during this sleep pattern, he asked not whether they were dreaming but what was going through their minds. He discovered that these sleepers could often recall far less obvious forms of dream without the imagery – of landscape, for example – commonly associated with the dream state. He concluded that during NREM sleep the sleeper didn't exactly dream but rather indulged in a form of abstract thinking.

Further research into the NREM state led to an understanding of 'night terrors', which usually occur either at the end of sleep or when drifting off to sleep. The sleeper can experience feelings of entrapment, including choking sensations, and may involuntarily sit up and shriek. The unconscious infiltration is usually brief, but of such a subtle nature that the boundaries between sleep and wakefulness are blurred. The individual is quite literally in a limbo land between the two states. At such times, if the person is particularly racked by anxiety, such as how to carry on following the death of a loved one, images of the deceased can impinge upon this limbo land. The resulting visions, occurring as the recipient goes off to sleep, are known as hypnagogic hallucinations; those occurring as he or she awakes are hypnapompic hallucinations. For millennia, however, they have been known by a much simpler name. Ghosts.

Hallucination

TO A widow, a bedroom visitation by her deceased husband is real. She usually discounts angrily the possibility of hallucination. This is natural. The vision is comforting and leaves the widow in no doubt that she is being watched over by her loved one. Such views have been fuelled by thousands of years of cultural belief in the afterlife. But in addition to this belief system, there is the taboo concerning hallucinations in 'ordinary' people. After all, it is madmen who hallucinate. Yet this idea is wrong. The sanest of people can readily hallucinate if the conditions are right.

The Society for Psychical Research realized this very soon after their inauguration. Very early on they undertook an initial investigation of apparitions. Some 5,700 people were interviewed and many had stories to tell. Yet this was not a survey of spirit appearances, for the findings were published under the title *Phantasms of the Living*.

A modern example of this phenomenon was reported by the writer Ted Simon in the British newspaper *The Times* in 1983. Visiting a friend of his mother's near Southend-on-Sea, a seaside resort on the Essex coast, he was unable to get a reply to the door bell. The lights were on in the house so he looked through the window. Sure enough, he could see his mother's friend walking about the house, so he rang the bell again. Still he got no reply, so after repeated ringing he gave up and went to his mother's. From there he telephoned the friend's house, but got no reply. He returned to the friend's house and, seeing her walking in the house, rang the bell once more, again getting no reply. Rather annoyed, he left. The next day he telephoned the friend yet again, and this time received a reply – to be told that he must have been mistaken the day before because the friend had been away from the house all day.

Cases such as this cast serious doubt upon the existence of spirits returned from the dead. The mechanism involved in visions of the dead and visions of the living appear to be the same, suggesting that the sighting of ghosts is a mind-based hallucinatory phenomenon rather than a supernatural visitation. But what exactly is going on when we hallucinate?

An hallucination can be understood as a sensory perception of something that has no external stimulus. In normal perception, we receive impressions through the senses. Such impressions are defined within the mind and we experience sensory inputs of seeing, hearing, feeling, smelling or tasting. In an hallucination, this process seems to be reversed, in that innate impressions within the mind go on to externalize their sensory attributes to the world at large within the experience of the hallucinator.

Typical hallucinatory images are mirages in the desert, when the viewer transfers his thirst for water into an externalized vision of an oasis. Walking through woods at night can confuse the senses, making the viewer frightened to the point that he sees menace in flitting shadows. One variation of the hallucination is the illusion. Here, external stimulus is present, but the viewer misinterprets what he sees, changing the experience into an incorrect vision. Two personal recollections highlight such experiences.

I tend to leave a light on in the landing when I go to bed, allowing semi-light to filter into the bedrooms. One night, when I was getting into bed, I noticed a massive beetle scoot across the eiderdown. I immediately turned on the light and the beetle turned into a piece of black fluff. My expectation, born from my initial fear of a beetle on the bed, fooled my mind into 'seeing' a beetle move.

Stories of such innocuous occurrences can be told by most people. The second incident, concerning my wife, was slightly more disconcerting. After the birth of our first child my wife suffered from severe post-natal depression during which she heard voices and experienced strange reality shifts. One night she threw my son at me because he had suddenly grown horns. Luckily I caught him, and my wife recovered.

These experiences give a glimpse into the state of mind of the hallucinator. My wife was depressed and not co-ordinating with the outside world as she normally would. I was simply tired when I saw the 'beetle'. At such times our senses become lazy and an incorrect analysis of external stimuli can easily occur or the mind can even create externalizations when no stimulus is present. Such hallucinations are usually fleeting because outside stimuli continue to bombard our minds, causing us to re-appraise what we see. Once such re-appraisal is complete, the hallucination vanishes, leaving rather boring reality.

Similarly, disturbances to the brain can cause hallucination. The delirium tremens of an alcoholic is a prime example; an incapacitated brain produces hallucinations of the proverbial pink elephant. Hallucinogenic drugs produce a similar effect. Electrical stimulation of the temporal lobes has also proved successful in bringing on visions.

All these prompters of hallucination involve a withdrawal from the normal appraisal of sensory input. In 1954 researchers at Canada's McGill University began experiments in sensory deprivation itself. Subjects were immersed in covered tanks of water at body temperature. They were naked except for a mask over the head, and absolute silence was maintained. After a time, purposeful thinking became impossible, to be replaced by, first, personal fantasies, and eventually externalized hallucinations. The conclusion was that continuous sensory input was vital to calibrated sensory systems. When the input is reduced hallucinations are an inevitable outcome, regardless of the prior state of mind of the subject. And a widow mourning her husband's death has reduced her concentration on that sensory input and has become more involved in internal and conflicting emotions.

Children, it seems, are natural hallucinators. Not yet adult enough to wish to calibrate their senses, their minds are full of adventure and fantasy. Many children worry their parents by speaking of imaginary friends who to them are real. Sometimes children's hallucinations can be quite frightening to all concerned.

When my eldest son was four years old going to bed suddenly became a traumatic experience for him. After several nights of difficulty in getting him to go to his room I talked to him about his fear. He eventually explained that there was a lion in the room, and he was frightened of it. Of course, to me the lion didn't exist, but the trauma exhibited by my son made it obvious that this was more than a mere creation in his mind in the classic sense. And to tell him that he was talking rubbish would have simply led to more trauma. So I looked around the room. Among the pile of soft toys in the corner I noticed a knitted Davy Crockett doll. In the half light its colour and fringes resembled a lion. I spent several minutes getting to know the 'lion' and transferring my natural father's authority on to it. In this way I convinced my son that I could control the lion. Then I told it to sit on the pile of toys, and proceeded to tell it off for frightening my son. I now told my son I was going to take the lion away. I picked it up – 'it' of course being the Davy Crockett doll – and my son watched me go outside the house and put it in the dustbin. Later I threw away a new jumper of my son's with a large picture of a lion on it – no doubt the root of the hallucination. He was never bothered by lions, or any other bedroom visitor, again.

Perhaps the most fascinating case of hallucination ever recorded concerned not a child but a mother of three children – the subject of the book *The Story of Ruth*, by psychiatrist Dr Morton Schatzman.

Ruth was a twenty-five-year old American living with her husband, Paul, and three children in England when her problems began. As a child she had been abused by her father, and at one point he had attempted to rape her. An alcoholic, her father had regularly been in various prisons and mental institutions. However, until a year after the birth of her third child, Ruth had coped with her past quite well. But, fearing for her sanity, she eventually consulted Schatzman, who had set up the Arbours Crisis Centre in 1971.

Initially, Ruth presented various symptoms associated with mild neurosis, but Schatzman soon elicited the fact that her real problem was that she was stalked by her father. This was impossible because, although her father was alive, he lived in America.

It soon became apparent that Ruth lived with an hallucination of her father. He would appear when she was in bed or simply sat about the house. He once appeared when she was having a bath, and Ruth asked him to pass the towel. One of the most unnerving appearances was when he sat at the dinner table during a party, following the various conversations.

To Ruth the apparition was real in every way. She could walk round him, 'count his teeth', smell him and hold conversations with him. At times he wasn't content simply to appear before her. In bed with her husband one night, his face superimposed itself on his, putting Ruth off having sex with Paul. During one consultation with Schatzman, her father superimposed himself on the psychiatrist.

In spite of these bizarre hallucinations, Schatzman was convinced that Ruth was not unbalanced in herself, and decided the best form of therapy was to teach Ruth to master the hallucination. Eventually she was successful to the point of being able to conjure up her father at will and to gain control over him.

However, in the course of this therapy she also discovered that she could naturally hallucinate. One night, staying away from home in a hotel, she missed her husband, so she hallucinated his presence in the bed and had satisfying sex with him. On boring car journeys she would conjure up friends and hold conversations with them.

It is estimated that as many as four per cent of the population have the capacity to recreate hallucinations as vivid as Ruth's. Drs Sheryl Wilson and Theodore Barber of Cushing Hospital, Massachusetts, decided to see if people claiming fantasy-prone imaginations could readily hallucinate. They enlisted 27 fantasy-prone volunteers, plus a control group of 25 'normal' people. All the fantasy-prone volunteers proved able to hallucinate, regularly experiencing both hypnagogic and hypnapompic visualizations.

Now that we have seen how prevalent hallucination is, and how easily it can be achieved in sane people, we must ask what exactly an hallucination is. And in order to answer the question we must first decide what constitutes the reality outside our minds against which hallucinations seem so strange. For instance, is reality, and our memory of it, an exact, unchanging thing?

If you keep a diary, then some time during the day you will write up the events of that day. In doing so, you assume that you are writing up facts. But between the event and the recording of it in your diary time has elapsed during which knowledge of the event has been committed to memory. So just how reliable is this process?

You can test your memory quite easily. Switch on a cassette recorder and record a spontaneous conversation between yourself and a friend. Afterwards, write down what you and your friend said. Then play back the cassette recorder and see how accurate your memory really is. The result may surprise you. And comparing what you thought you said with what your friend thought you said may surprise you even more.

Usually this experiment tells us two things. First of all, personal memory is not as infallible as we think. And second, your friend may have a totally different view of reality to you. Without the cassette recorder, such discrepancies in our personal view of reality lead to argument over who said, or didn't say, what.

You could argue that this is solely a fault of our memory. But it could equally be something more subtle. If a man suddenly stops in the street and looks up at a roof, within minutes he will have turned into a small crowd, all looking up, wondering what he is staring at. Then if, for some reason, the man says, 'Did you see him?' you can guarantee that someone will say yes, even though there is no one on the roof.

The question must be asked, did that someone really see a man on the roof, or was he simply duped?

Suppressing logic for a moment – and in considering hallucination logic often needs to be suppressed – let's suppose that he did see a man on the roof. After all, any policeman will be able to tell you of incidents when numerous witnesses have given varying accounts of the same event. Who is to say which witness got it right? Did any of them get it right? Or had they all been partially deluded by their own prejudices?

Gestalt imagery is a perfect example of this form of reality-bending due to our personal prejudices. The classic example is the familiar picture of a white vase on a background of black. Depending on how you view it, it will appear either as a vase or as two heads facing each other. The Necker cube is another example. Here a two-dimensional drawing of two transparent three-dimensional cubes is used. The word 'love' is printed in the middle of the first cube, and the word 'hate' on the second. Depending upon your emotional bias at the time, either word can appear to put itself on the front or back of each cube.

We generally discount this effect as optical illusion, but we must be careful not to discount the emotional, inner bias responsible for the effect. And there is a much more ominous example of this form of reality shift within art.

Painting was revolutionized during the Renaissance with the discovery of perspective geometry. This was the first truly scientific understanding of distance, with man realizing that if he put his thumb to his eye it could appear bigger than a building. This discovery caused a fundamental change in painting. Renaissance painting became clearly three dimensional, as compared to pre-Renaissance art, which consisted of two-dimensional images.

With perspective geometry, the way man viewed his surroundings changed completely. And this change represents a total, cultural shift in the way reality was observed.

But how could such an incredible change have come about? Surely what we see as reality is reality as it really is?

Well, not quite.

The physical mechanisms of our sensory organs merely pass patterns of information to the brain. All that the retina records is a blur of colour; it is our mind that introduces logic to what we see. And as our logical process is inevitably tainted with our own prejudices, emotions and thought patterns, what we see is not necessarily reality, but our own deluded view of how we assume that reality to be. And the plot thickens.

As we shall see later in this book, knowledge of the subatomic world tells us that 'matter' does not exist. The reality that we call 'physical' appears to be nothing more than subtle energy patterns within the quantum field. So what we see not only depends on our personal delusions, but also upon some cosmic illusion we call 'matter'.

Reality, as we know it, is not a hard, scientific fact. Reality can best be seen as a process of understanding by the individual, dependent upon how his mind views it. And in the light of this, perhaps the best understanding we can come to regarding hallucination, such as our fictitious man on the roof, my 'beetle', my son's lion, Ruth's father and the widow's visualization of her deceased husband, is to class hallucination as a manifestation in consensus reality of a personal nature, and not a view existing in the minds of the majority. It appears that reality, like time, is relative to the observer.

Hauntings

A FULL AND complete understanding of the fantasy-prone mind can lead us a long way to accepting that ghosts are, in fact, psychological rather than supernatural phenomena. The anomalous effects of dreaming and hallucination can be extreme. Expectation, for instance, when combined with an emotional state, provides a receptive mind for ghostly phenomena.

Consider Private Challoner's appearance before Robert Graves. Graves had just returned from action and was enjoying a rare luxurious meal. Tension and fear were giving way to a contentment not felt for a long time. Briefly, perhaps unconsciously, Graves recalls that Private Challoner should have been there – and the fantasy-prone mind fulfils his wishes.

So, too, Nathaniel Hawthorne. In a place of deep relaxation, where sensory input is reduced because he is not permitted to communicate with others in the room, his sadness at the bereavement triggers his fantasies and provides the ghost. Intrigued by the vision, he wants to see it again and again – and the mind obliges.

Well-known haunting sites such as Hampton Court and the Tower of London offer similar possibilities. Visiting such places, you experience more than just bricks and mortar. You walk through history. Centuries of encul-turation invade your mind, turning your thoughts to past events within those walls. The effect can be similar to an altered state of consciousness. And, again, the fantasy-prone mind comes to the fore and offers you a taste of what really happened – and Sir Christopher Wren runs up the stairs.

It seems to me to be proven that all ghosts can be explained by the mechanics of hallucination, but there are many cases of haunting that don't ideally fit the idea of images and visualizations rising purely from the personal mind.

Take, for instance, the experience of British heating engineer Harry Martindale, recorded in the book *Strange Happenings* by Paul Bannister.

Martindale was working in the cellar of the Treasurer's House in the northern cathedral city of York, one day in 1953, when he heard 'a sort of tinny trumpet call'. He looked round – and a Roman soldier walked through the wall carrying a trumpet, and disappeared through the opposite wall. He was followed by another Roman soldier on a pony and a column of up to sixteen dismounted Romans. Dressed in the normal skirts and leather helmets of Roman times, they had short swords and long spears and carried round shields. As to their demeanour, Martindale described them thus: 'They sort of shuffled along dispiritedly.' He also noticed that, apart from when walking through a trench dug in the floor, they were only visible from the knees upwards, as if they were walking on ground over a foot below the existing floor.

Martindale, a stolid, usually unimaginative kind of person, who later became a policeman, fell off his ladders and cowered in a corner, and was still edgy when, a few days later, he told a local historian of his experience. The historian was fascinated, mainly because an old Roman road was buried underneath the cellar where Martindale had seen the soldiers. However, the incident was dismissed as pure imagination because Roman soldiers, it was well known, did not use round shields.

That would have been the end of the matter, except that seven years later two archaeologists witnessed the same apparition, complete with round shields. Research disclosed that, at about the time the Sixth Legion moved out of York in the fourth century, it had been reinforced by auxiliaries, who carried round shields.

This case is one of the most fascinating hauntings in the history of psychical research. Working alone in a dark, historic cellar might be enough to cause the fantasy-prone imagination to produce the hallucination, but several factors are of note. First of all, we have two testimonies of two separate but identical appearances. Secondly, the detail of the round shields was unknown to any contemporary at the time of Harry's sighting. And, thirdly, the visualization can be traced historically to the Roman evacuation of York. This haunting is not a personal event. It contains detail that could not have existed in Harry Martindale's mind. The appearance of those soldiers cannot be explained within any form of known psychology. So, is it possible that those Roman soldiers really were spirits?

Spiritualists would say yes. To them, spirits are real. They appear because they are trapped on an earthly plane. Usually they do not know they are dead, or are reluctant to leave, feeling themselves robbed of life. However, the founders of the Society for Psychical Research began to offer slightly more scientific theories to account for hauntings.

F.W.H. Myers considered hauntings to be 'a manifestation of persistent personal energy'. Writing in his book *Human Personality and its Survival of Bodily Death* (1903), he theorized about '. . . some residue of the force or energy which a person generated while yet alive'. He noted that ghosts had no consciousness as such, and were simply re-enactments of events performed in life. Such energies formed a 'phantasmogenic centre' which could be picked up by those with psychic abilities. Basically, a form of telepathy passed between the dead and the living.

Fellow founder Edmund Gurney tended to agree with Myers, both believing that while the apparition was produced by personal hallucination, the information leading to the apparition arrived in the mind of the viewer by some form of ESP from beyond the grave. As to hauntings where two or more people view the apparition, Gurney argued that the psychic viewer transmitted the information to others through telepathy.

G.N.M. Tyrrell furthered such theories in 1943 in his book *Apparitions*. He argued for the existence of 'idea patterns'. The hallucinated apparition was the result of a two-part drama. In the first instance, the viewer received information through ESP, his mind becoming the 'producer'. Then an other-worldly 'stage carpenter' came through the mind to add props, providing the actual hallucination.

These early theories were as fanciful as blind acceptance of spirits. To them was added, in England in 1921, an inspired idea produced by a man on a hill taking in the view.

On the 30th June 1921, Alfred Watkins, a Herefordshire brewer with an interest in ancient relics, was riding his horse on the hills near the village of Bredwardine when he noticed something intriguing in the valley below. The countryside seemed to be covered in straight tracks – and these tracks seemed to link together old churches and other monuments, such as standing stones.

Armed with the idea that similar tracks might exist throughout the country, Watkins began to research Ordnance Survey maps. He became convinced, and argued, in his book *The Old Straight Track*, that straight tracks, which he called leys or ley lines, existed throughout the country and that they constituted an elaborate network of prehistoric trade and religious routes connecting sacred sites.

Most archaeologists are sceptical of the existence of leys, pointing out the flaw in Watkins's original research – that he didn't take into account the different time periods of history from which the sacred sites came. Yet a later researcher, John Michell, went on to offer evidence of 22 leys connecting 53 megaliths in Cornwall alone. However, while Watkins never thought of leys as anything other than geographical routes, he had opened up a totally new sphere of research – into 'earth mysteries'.

Such research began when it was noticed that some leys seemed to come in pairs, called aquastats. Why would our prehistoric ancestors have bothered with such double ley formations? A retired solicitor and amateur dowser called Guy Underwood came up with what he thought to be the answer. Dowsing at many stone circles, he noticed that his dowsing rod often showed two parallel lines of energy leading away from the megalith, as if there was some kind of underground magnetic force that permeated the earth in straight lines.

This interesting discovery resulted in leys being associated with earth energies. The natural conclusion to this idea was that prehistoric man knew of such energies and enhanced them by building tracks above them and erecting sacred sites such as standing stones at certain nodal points where the energies were most powerful.

Later researchers added to the mystique of earth energies by pointing out that many hauntings and other phenomena occurred at points where two or more leys crossed. So could such energies lead to psychic events? In 1977 researcher Paul Devereux founded the Dragon Project with the specific task of investigating ancient sites such as standing stones. Research followed two disciplines. On the one hand the sites were tested by various psychics and dowsers; and on the other, scientific analysis was undertaken by the use of various geiger counters, ultra-sound monitors and other equipment. Although results have been sketchy, anomalous phenomena have been recorded, leading Devereux to suggest the existence of a form of planetary intelligence, which he calls 'Earthmind'.

Beliefs in such energies exist throughout the world. Amerindians had similar routes and sacred sites connected by what they call spirit paths. In South America there are many similar intricate networks, the most famous constituting the Nazca Lines of Peru. But nowhere is the belief in such energies more prevalent than in the East, where we find the ancient discipline of *Feng shui*.

Feng shui means wind and water and is a mystical form of understanding of the harmonies between the earth and man. Health and luck are defined by the placing of homes and buildings according to the natural landscape and harmonizing them with the universal life principle, known as *ch'i*. *Ch'i* exists in all things and flows through the earth. *Ch'i* itself is composed of a female component, yin, and a male component, yang. The balancing of yin and yang is the central aim of *Feng shui*.

Even today, buildings are positioned in many parts of the East in line with *Feng-shui* principles, which can even dictate the layout of furniture. Disturbances in *ch'i* result in bad luck and ill health. And one important spin-off of *Feng shui* is the existence of numerous Dragon Paths throughout the East.

Such Dragon Paths seem to reflect the existence of leys. Indeed, if such earth energies really do exist, then it would be natural for all our ancients to have realized this and appreciated such energies in custom and culture, as our standing stones seem to suggest. However, it is here that common sense intervenes to suggest caution.

It is logical to assume that if earth energies do exist they would be uniform throughout the earth. Yet, although leys are perfectly straight, Dragon Paths abhor straight lines. In every case they meander. Indeed,

Feng shui exponents point out that straight lines are not only detrimental to *ch'i*, but they channel a destructive energy known as *sha*. To build at the end of a straight line – as is the case with leys and standing stones – is to invite disaster.

These significant cultural anomalies seriously erode the possibility of earth energies being realized by the ancients. This is not to say that some form of earth energy doesn't exist. But the distinct enculturation employed in leys and Dragon Paths suggests that leys and Dragon Paths are more a social construct than a grid of energy. They are simply a human system by which we appreciate the strangeness of our relationship with the earth.

But if this is so, how could the Dragon Project have recorded strange, anomalous behaviour at standing stones? If they are no more than human constructs, how could the slightest evidence have accumulated concerning such phenomena?

Let us consider a possibility. Prehistoric Britons believed that some strange energy was at work, channelling through the Earth and psychically affecting man. Over the centuries, particular locations of great veneration, such as Stonehenge, began to focus such phenomena. In celebration, the area became a shrine, and further veneration was poured out within it.

How different is this scenario from a person visiting Hampton Court and being affected by the historic enculturation of the location? Could it be that the ancients were similarly disposed to the fantasy-prone imagination, their expectation bringing forth the visualizations so many still associate with standing stones today? And an expectation which caused the members of the Dragon Project to create such anomalous behaviour themselves?

Psychometry

DURING THE 1830s an American professor of physiology called Joseph Rhodes Buchanan had a chance meeting with Bishop Leonidas Polk, who mentioned to him that he could detect brass by touching it, even in the dark, because it caused a metallic taste in his mouth.

Buchanan, intrigued by the bishop's remark, decided to test further the powers of human senses. For his experiments he selected a number of students who seemed to have highly developed sensibilities. He found, among other things, that they could detect emotion through touch. Typical was the 'morbid impression' reported by one student when he touched another's stomach. The second student proved to be suffering from a stomach complaint. One of Buchanan's best sensitives was a man called Charles Inman, who, when handed four letters, was able to talk about the character and emotions of the writers as if he knew them personally.

Buchanan was a serious scientist. Although he carried on with his researches into the strange talent he seemed to have discovered, he feared ridicule by the scientific community. Hence, it wasn't until 1849 that he published his findings in his book, *Journal of Man*. The ability to sense the history and associations of objects he named 'psychometry', meaning 'the measure of the soul of things'. He theorized that the information was conveyed through emotions somehow recorded on objects by those previously associated with them.

An English immigrant to America, Professor William Denton, read Buchanan's book and began his own experiments. He found that his sister, Ann Cridge, was so good at psychometry that she could even describe the physical characteristics of correspondents from their letters.

Denton was a geologist, so he had the idea of wrapping rock samples in paper and asking Ann to hold them and speak about the samples. Ann first analysed a piece of limestone, covered in fossil shells, from the banks of the

River Missouri. Ann sensed that the rock came from a river and described very accurately the location it came from.

Next Denton offered her a fragment of volcanic lava from Hawaii. She saw '. . . an ocean of fire pouring over a precipice and boiling as it pours. I see it flow into the ocean, and the water boils intensely.' She also 'saw' sailing ships, leading Denton to conclude that Ann had visualized a volcanic eruption on Hawaii in 1840.

Ann Cridge offered much evidence for the existence of psychometry, and Denton's wife and son both went on to become sensitives. Denton theorized that psychometry was a '. . . mysterious faculty which belongs to the soul and is not dependent upon the body for its exercise'.

Ideas such as these had a marked effect on the founders of the Society for Psychical Research. Most prominent among them was the English physicist Sir Oliver Lodge, who thought a phenomenon similar to psychometry could account for hauntings. If events could be somehow 'recorded' in a stone, then why not in a specific environment, such as a haunted house? Could an emotional event be held by its surroundings and replayed from time to time as a haunting? In his book *Man and the Universe* (1908) he wrote:

> On a psychometric hypothesis the original tragedy has been literally *photographed* on its material surroundings, nay, even on the ether itself, by reason of the intensity of emotion felt by those who enacted it; and thenceforth in certain persons an hallucinatory effect is experienced corresponding to such an impression.

The English philosopher Henry Price went further. He postulated the existence of a 'psychic ether' which existed beyond space and time. This ether 'recorded' emotional events, which carried on their existence in a timeless dimension. Margaret Murray, a British anthropologist best known for her work on witchcraft, went on to qualify the tape-recording hypothesis for hauntings by surmising 'a form of photograph' caused by light on the air itself.

A further variation was offered in 1963 by the British archaeologist turned psychical researcher Tom Lethbridge. He suggested that nature generates fields of static electricity, particularly near running water, and that these fields are capable of recording the feelings of people. As every person also has an electric field, if someone enters a natural field – which Lethbridge called a 'ghoul' – the feelings could be transferred to the newcomer; hence the fear, or other emotion, we feel in certain locations. Furthermore, the process may work in reverse. The newcomer's strong emotion could flow into the ghoul and in its turn be imprinted on the location.

Robert Morris, the first incumbent of the Koestler Chair in Parapsychology at Edinburgh University in Scotland, once decided to test the 'emotional tape-recording' theory in the field. He took a dog, a cat, a rat and a rattlesnake into a room where a murder had been committed. The dog snarled and refused to go in. The cat leapt up on to its owner's shoulder. The rat didn't seem to mind that much, but the rattlesnake immediately adopted its attack posture.

These fascinating theories would certainly offer an explanation for Harry Martindale's Roman soldiers and the hauntings at Hampton Court and the Tower of London. But somehow they just don't seem to fit in with common sense. It seems ludicrous to suggest that a stone or a room could have a memory, and static electricity has been studied enough to cancel out any such possibility as that suggested by Lethbridge. So what is to be made of the tape-recording theories?

Consider the following anecdote. In 1923 an international conference into psychical research was held in Warsaw. The Polish clairvoyant Stephen Ossowiechi was attending, so the researcher Dr Eric Dingwall decided to stage a test. He sent a message in a well-wrapped package to a Polish researcher who then monitored the success of the clairvoyant attempting to identify the message within.

Dr Dingwall had drawn a picture of a flag with a bottle in the top left-hand corner. Under this was the date, 22 August 1923. The clairvoyant received the unopened package, sealed in three envelopes, and drew a flag with a bottle in the top left-hand corner. Underneath, and slightly to the right, he placed the number 1923.

A classic example of psychometry?

No. A classic example of clairvoyance. In fact all the classic cases of psychometry I have described could also be classic examples of clairvoyance. Stated simply, there is no difference. Until, that is, we bring politics and reputations into the equation.

America in the 1830s was a hotbed of materialist thinking. Industrialization was under way, and in the west the Amerindians were beginning to be wiped out as settlers went on to their new life. These dual impulses had had a profound effect on Joseph Rhodes Buchanan, the discoverer of psychometry.

Industrialization and materialism led to a rejection by the American intelligentsia of all forms of supernatural influence. Clairvoyance, in particular, because Amerindian tradition was steeped in its practices, was scorned as simply a form of 'Indian' culture, a primitive belief. While these taboos didn't particularly affect the population in general – as Spiritualism testifies – they were powerful in the academic world. Professor Buchanan would have faced ridicule had he declared a belief in clairvoyance.

Buchanan had to propose, for the phenomenon he had discovered, an explanation other than clairvoyance. So he came up with the concept of psychometry. But in devising the concept, a subtle transition occurred.

Psychometry is the sensing of impressions contained within an object. Clairvoyance is popularly understood as the 'seeing' of internal or external visions, or the sensing of images – the word is derived from the French for 'clear seeing'. The American psychologist Lawrence LeShan defines it best when he speaks of 'sensory reality' (our normal sensory input) and 'clairvoyant reality'. In the latter, reality is lifted above the normal senses into an interconnected world where everything is in sympathy with everything else. In this analysis you could say that the personal mind interconnects with a wider universal mind. In clairvoyance the personal mind is the important element; it goes out to 'see' things. In psychometry we find the reverse, with the impressions of an object entering the mind.

Psychometry does not exist. It was a subtle manipulation of clairvoyance to gain respectability for its practice. And if this is so for psychometry, then it is also the case with the tape-recording theories of hauntings, which are only valid within a psychometric hypothesis. But if the theory of psychometry was merely a reversal of the idea of clairvoyance, then maybe hauntings can make sense if we reverse the tape-recording theories and look at them in the context of clairvoyance.

Take the medium who knew of the existence of an aluminium soap box in Edgar Vandy's chest of drawers. The fact that she incorrectly identified the soap box as a cigarette case strengthens the case for clairvoyance, in that she made a simple 'visual' mistake, as if she had 'seen' inside the chest of drawers.

Looked at from the point of view of clairvoyance, the source of information contained in a haunting is not a tape recording in a stone or location. It directly enters the observer's mind, with the stone or location acting as an 'agent' that prompts the filtering-in of the information.

In looking at the problem in this way, we are remarkably close to an explanation of reincarnation and mediumistic talents, when, in an altered state of consciousness, the mind grasps 'information', such as the knowledge of the presence of a Roman road, from a single source as yet unknown.

Basically, the location acts as a 'trigger', providing similar communality with the agent as seen in mediumistic talents (communality with the client) and past-life regression, where the memory recall of a novel read can 'trigger' the manifestation of the past life through role play. The only difference is that, in a haunting, the information is not retained in the mind of the individual, but played out before him through a form of hallucination. And as for the source of the information, we are back to my memory shop.

MIND OVER MATTER

Magical Belief

MANY PATTERNS seem to exist in all cultures through all times, although quite often they are hidden by changing conceptions. Take, for instance, Moses, the Hebrew lawgiver, and the German-born American physicist Albert Einstein, both of whom had inspired ideas. We tend to separate them into Moses the prophet and Einstein the scientist, but this separation may not be valid. Perhaps we are simply using different cultural 'tags' to describe them, because our cultural world view has moved on and we no longer assume that inspiration comes from God.

Looking at patterns hidden by cultural change in this way could give new insights into psychology. For instance, we are all aware that when, at the race course, we 'will' our chosen horse to win, we are actually trying to influence it by magic.

Many people carry with them lucky charms, and fear disaster if they forget them. And lucky charms are not always the obvious ones. I once knew an asthma sufferer who seemed to suffer severe attacks only when he realized he had forgotten his inhaler.

We can laugh at lucky charms if we wish, but by carrying objects that boost our security and confidence we can retain our general wellbeing. And if we forget to carry them, we may psychologically deflate to the point of bringing on negative values within our mind and, with the asthma sufferer, body.

This all suggests that magic is still important to us even though we live in a sceptical age. Our ancestors were more accepting. Magic has quite a history. Where it began is shrouded in the shadows of the past, although it is suggested that Stone Age cave drawing is evidence of magical ritual, an attempt to capture the 'soul' of the beast upon which the hunters preyed. It could be that magic is an area of history vital to any understanding of the human psyche.

Today 'magic' suggests a trickster on a stage conning us with sleight of hand and illusion, but this is a recent concept. Magic, in its true, older meaning concerns the pursuit of knowledge of the world and the universe; it is an attempt to unravel the mysteries of life. It is also the use of powers to change the reality of the world to the benefit of the magician. As the sixteenth-century German alchemist Paracelsus, the father of modern chemistry, wrote: 'Magic has power to experience and fathom things which are inaccessible to human reason. For magic is a great secret wisdom, just as reason is a great public folly.'

This says it all. To the magician, rational experience is just one interpretation of life – and a narrow, myopic one at that. To the magician anything was possible. Life and matter could be directly affected by thoughts.

Such interaction often involved malediction, or cursing, when the magician tried to cause harm to another human being. The ritual usually involved the creation of an image – a clay doll or wax figurine – invested with the properties of the victim. Usually pieces of nail or a lock of hair would be included in its making. The idea was that whatever misfortune befell the image would fall also upon the victim.

In the mid-1930s, American journalist William Seabrook documented two famous instances of supposed magical interaction, both in France. The first involved a pianist, whom Seabrook called Jean Dupuis, who joined a rather dubious magical circle. When he quarrelled with other members they decided to destroy his ability to play the piano. They produced a doll and baptized it with Dupuis' name. They placed the doll's hands in a vice, which they tightened each day. Then they began to suggest to Dupuis that his hands were becoming less dextrous. As a result, he became anxious and his performances suffered as a result. A few days before a major concert, Dupuis received an anonymous letter describing the ritual magic that was being used against him, including details of the doll and the vice. The concert was a disaster – Dupuis' performance was so awful that he ran out in shame.

I doubt, in fact, whether magic, in its classical sense, was being used here. We need nothing more than psychology to explain Dupuis' reaction. Few people would be able to remain totally sane and confident under such psychological warfare. In a real sense, the doll and ritual were irrelevant to the outcome. But Seabrook's second story is perhaps more intriguing.

A young mechanic called Louis was dating a young girl whose grandmother was known in her peasant region as a witch. The grandmother took an intense dislike to Louis and one day they quarrelled, almost coming to blows. Louis set off to walk home along a mountain path, while the witch set off in another direction, chanting an incantation against him. Louis did not arrive home. A search party finally found him almost paralysed and entangled in the bushes at the side of the path. He seemed to have had a stroke, although a doctor later diagnosed him as totally fit.

Seabrook, intrigued by this incident, immediately raided an old wine cellar where the witch practised her magic. He found a model landscape, complete with thorns and briars, and within it a doll in the image of Louis. He showed the doll to Louis, but the mechanic refused to believe that magic was involved and still claimed that he had simply had a stroke.

I am very sceptical of this story. The witch could hardly have had time after the argument to make a model landscape and carry out a magic ritual. If a malediction was involved, it must have been pre-planned. More probably, some form of psychological suggestion was involved. Or Seabrook was the victim of collusion, in order to 'prove' something he was known to be interested in.

However, such anecdotes do tend to distort the practice of magic. We hear of white magic and black magic, as if there are two distinct types. This is nonsense. There can be good or bad people, but most practitioners of magic will tell you that it is simply a tool, neither good nor bad. A gun can be used to protect or to kill. It is the person who uses the gun who defines the morality of its use. In a more sceptical and trivial world, the most-used magic involves love ritual, where the practitioner attempts to gain the love of the desired one. But perhaps the most widespread magic is practised throughout the Western world in churches on Sunday mornings, when worshippers put their hands together to pray for God's supernatural intervention to affect the outcome of a friend's illness.

Many readers will be appalled that I ally magical ritual to God. Yet intrinsic to magic is the belief that magical ability can be achieved through making contact with deities. Just which deity is to be contacted seems to be dependent upon the cultural inheritance of the adept attempting union. Indeed, the most unlikely entities can be conjured up by the magician.

Take, for instance, the case of the gunsmith-cum-magician Thomas Parkes from Bristol in the southwest of England in the 1680s. Parkes asked his vicar, the Reverend Arthur Bedford, if it was lawful for a Christian to raise spirits and converse with them. Bedford said it was not, whereupon Parkes proceeded to tell him that he regularly conjured up entities in the shape of little girls approximately eighteen inches high. They would play about within a magic circle and spoke in the voice of an old woman. Bedford at first doubted Parkes' sanity, but eventually became convinced that he was sane – and told him to abandon such practices immediately.

The rest of the story offers a warning for anyone who dabbles in magical practices without knowing what they are doing. Three months after first speaking to Bedford, Parkes approached him again. By now he wished he had heeded the vicar's advice. He had attempted to conjure up a further entity that could be used by him for his own gratification. The entity duly appeared, but was followed by unwanted and uninvoked spirits of bears, lions and serpents. Parkes was terrified and, according to Bedford, from that day until his death, he was constantly ill and repentant of his sins.

Anyone thinking of experimenting with the craft should remember the two laws of magic, which are as old as history itself. First, do not use magic to harm others, for whatever harm you do to another will come back thrice upon yourself. And, second, the rule which I doubt has been bettered by any religion since its founding: Do as you will; but let it hurt no one.

History of Magic

T HE FIRST well-documented magician was Simon, sometimes known as Simon Magus. Mentioned in Acts, he practised magic in Samaria in the first century AD. He was said to be able to make himself invisible, walk through walls and fire, turn himself into an animal and fly. Sentenced to death by Nero, he saved himself and became a court wizard.

He is said to have come to a sticky end in a magical duel with St Peter. Many believe that Simon Magus was really Simon the Gnostic, leader of a heretical Christian sect. This is feasible if one compares the ideals of magic with the beliefs of Gnosticism.

We know of Gnosticism mainly from the discovery, in Egypt in the 1940s, of the Nag Hammadi Scrolls. They are thought to have been buried in the second century AD, hidden at a time when the Gnostic heresy was being brutally repressed. Among the many texts included in the Scrolls were: The Gospel of Thomas; On the Origin of the World; The Apocrython of James; The Gospel of Truth; The Exegesis on the Soul; The Sophia [Wisdom] of Jesus Christ; The Apocalypse of Adam; The Thunder; Perfect Mind.

Inspiring titles, one and all. So what is their philosophy? The Gnostic believed in the 'gnosis', or knowledge – a secret truth. Tobias Churton, in his book *The Gnostics* (1987), says:

At the very heart, at the 'root' of the Gnostic is the 'Living Jesus'. That is what it means to 'know yourself'. The Gnostic knows that he or she is a spiritual being, 'of one substance with the Father'; for what the orthodox say of Christ, the Gnostic is free to say of himself.

He continues:

The Gnostic clearly distinguishes himself from the great mass of human beings . . . 'They have always been attracted downwards' (Book of Thomas the Contender). Such people were described as 'hylic', that is 'material'. This means that there is none of that divine light within them which longs for union with the Father. It is the guiding dynamic of gnostic thought that divine light has become imprisoned within the material world . . .

Later he says:

The gnostic Jesus comes from the spiritual world within and above, appearing to those who are awake. To those who are not, who do not have the gnosis, He is merely an image made of flesh. Flesh of itself is without life. It is part of the world. To the Gnostic, the world of material perception has become an image and is no longer subject to its control. . . .

The Gnostic clearly believed in a higher, non-material truth; a wider consciousness not trapped within the body and not dependent on what the person could rationally see and feel. And it is this higher consciousness, an ability to transcend mere matter, that lies at the heart of magic.

So the Gnostics were suppressed – everyone could not be a potential Jesus, said orthodox Christianity – and the Dark Ages followed the fall of Rome. Then, slowly, Christianity grew to reign supreme once more. And nowhere is this transition from paganism to Christianity better understood than in the character of King Arthur's mythical wizard, Merlin.

Most of what we know of Merlin comes from the writings of a Welsh cleric, Geoffrey of Monmouth, writing in the twelfth century. Usually described as a wise old man with a long white beard, Merlin is most likely a composite of various magical influences prevalent in the fifth century. According to Geoffrey of Monmouth, Merlin was the result of a seduction of his earthly mother by a 'spirit', who is usually referred to by Christian legend as the Devil himself. His later consort was Viviane, also known as the Lady of the Lake. The pair are thought of as the male and female principles of the cosmos, similar to yin and yang.

At first a force fighting against the works of Jesus, Merlin is later portrayed as discarding his powers of the Devil but retaining his magical abilities in order to further Christianity. He is said to have arranged for the appearance of King Arthur by orchestrating the seduction of his mother Igraine by Uther Pendragon. The story of Arthur pulling the sword Excalibur from the stone comes from a later work by Sir Thomas Malory written in the fifteenth century.

Merlin could disappear at will and had the ability to cast the most extreme spells. However, he was eventually tricked into disclosing his magical knowledge to Viviane, who went on to use the knowledge to trap and imprison Merlin in a magical place. When Arthur missed him, he sent Sir Gawain to find him. Merlin told the knight – from a cloud of smoke – that he would never again be seen; Arthur should no longer seek him but should search instead for the Holy Grail.

There is a great deal of historical truth to be found in the legend of Merlin. Remembering that all we know of him came from later Christian writers, we can see the Dark Ages' rejection of paganism as Christianity comes to the fore. King Arthur himself can be seen as initially a paganized individual. He sees the light, and goes on to be the complete embodiment of Christianity. Finally, to seal paganism's fate, Merlin is betrayed by his own power, and goes on to validate the Holy Grail – the true symbol of Christianity as the right way – as the only course for noble men. And again Christianity is seen to suppress other forms of belief.

In the fifteenth century magic re-enters the realms of chronicled history and literature with the man known as Faust. We have no definite knowledge of Faust performing magical feats, but hearsay gives us some examples – such as the time he vowed to a churchman that he would make pots fly up his kitchen chimney.

Martin Luther, the founder of Protestantism, believed that Faust had made a pact with the Devil. In 1507 Johannes Tritheim, a known scientist of the day, offered a slightly different opinion: 'The man of whom you wrote me, who has presumed to call himself the prince of necromancers, is a vagabond, a babbler and a rogue.' Faust was immortalized by the great German poet and sage Goethe in his drama *Faust*, of which Colin Wilson wrote, in his book *The Occult* (1971):

> Goethe's *Faust* can be seen to be the greatest symbolic dream of the west, since it is the drama of the rationalist suffocating in the dusty room of his personal consciousness, caught in a vicious circle of futility. . . . Faust's longing for the 'occult' (meaning hidden) is the instinctive desire to believe in the unseen forces, the wider significances that can break the circuit.

Faust's sudden appearance on the officially recognized scene came at the beginning of the Renaissance. It was the time of the inspired artist who asked deep questions – questions that often criticized Christian orthodoxy and which began the intellectual battle that resulted in the decline of a popular God. This process 'gave birth' to Faust. And it was helped by two opposing trains of thought.

Luther condemned Faust's demonic practices. But Luther was the man who split Christianity, beginning the Reformation. It was a period very similar to that of the Cold War in this century. It was a time when the theologies of both sides – Catholic and Protestant – dug in and waited to take the strain. It was a time when any dissent was stamped on. A Faust didn't suddenly appear. He had always been around, but now, suddenly, he had to be exposed; and in being exposed he was recognized.

It was also a time of a new spirit of scientific enquiry. Material sciences were being born. Galileo's and others' theories were making supernatural explanations redundant. Faust had to be exposed and dealt with.

So it was science and the Church that were jointly responsible for the revival of magical tradition. It was their condemnation which brought magic to popular attention.

And another ancient system of knowledge was already beginning to bubble to the surface. This was the Jewish system known as the Cabala.

Initially an oral, esoteric tradition, the Cabala – which means 'that which is received' – is thought to originate from the writings of one Rabbi Akiba ben Joseph, who was put to death by the Romans in about 135, in his *Book of Creation*. Further insight into the tradition was offered by the Spaniard Moses de León, in his *Book of Splendour*, written in the thirteenth century. The Cabala revolves around the diagram known as the 'tree of life', which highlights the ten 'emanations' of God and the relationships between them.

Leading the initiate along the path to a true understanding of God and the universe, the Cabala deals with beliefs in a hidden reality that can only be opened up to those who deal in mysticism and ritual study. Through such study the Cabala attempts a reconciliation between contradictions such as an unknowable God and a God who makes himself known; between a God who is intrinsically good, and his creation which allows evil to thrive; between an infinite God and a finite, and doomed, world.

The Cabala had a great influence upon both Jewish and Christian mysticism during the Renaissance, and from then until the early nineteenth century. It was considered by many scholars to be the true Jewish theology. And it is easy to see why. For in many ways the Cabala echoes the beliefs of Gnosticism, arguing that the orthodox view of God was not the only emanation, and underneath normal reality there was a hidden knowledge, similar to Lawrence LeShan's 'clairvoyant reality'. However, while the Cabala annoyingly refused to go away within 'official' religion, the idea of a hidden reality and many aspects to God found acceptance also in the occult fraternity – in particular by the German scholar Cornelius Agrippa, who incorporated the Cabala into his own philosophy.

Cornelius Agrippa was born in Cologne in 1486. He studied law, philosophy, medicine and languages. In 1509, after travelling widely throughout Europe, he settled down as a teacher at Dôle in eastern France. However, his increasing interest in the Cabala drove him out of favour and he spent his last years travelling once more and turning towards theology. There are several stories of his magical exploits, but he is best remembered for his treatise *On Occult Philosophy*. Agrippa foreshadowed psychiatry with his belief that fantasy and imagination had power over passions, changing our perception of physical things. But above all, he believed that magic had nothing to do with the Devil, but with obscure abilities of the mind. To him there was a real possibility of a union between human consciousness and the Godhead which is the centre of all things.

On Occult Philosophy became a bible to a particular breed of scholar over the next hundred years or so. One of these was the English mathematician and astrologer Dr John Dee. Born in 1527, the son of a minor official at the court of Henry VIII, Dee was accepted for Cambridge University by the age of fifteen. Possessing a fanatical thirst for knowledge, he became an assistant professor at Trinity College by nineteen and was eventually to amass a library of no fewer than four thousand volumes – over three thousand more than the library at Cambridge held at the time. After more studies, at Louvain and Paris, the twenty-four-year old Dee returned to England, only to be thrown into prison for casting a horoscope for Queen Mary which she didn't like. Finally released, it was he who chose, on astrological grounds, the day for Queen Elizabeth's coronation.

He eventually settled down to a quiet life in the country, where he could devote himself to learning. Although he lived to the age of eighty-one, he could still write: 'All my lifetime I had spent in learning . . . and I found that neither any man, nor any book . . . was able to teach me those truths I desired and longed for . . .'

Dee eventually searched for these great truths by communication with angels. This he did with the help of a somewhat disreputable occultist called Edward Kelley. And, if his records of the manifestations are to be believed, Dee not only communicated with but recognized the angels with whom he spoke.

After Dee's time rationalism became the order of the day. The Age of Enlightenment banished not only the occult, but, increasingly, religion itself. Magicians continued to appear, but the official record speaks of them only as charlatans – which perhaps they were. And the official record, perhaps deliberately, suppressed the fact that some of the greatest minds harboured occult tendencies. For instance, it is rare to read that the German astronomer Johannes Kepler, who devised the laws of planetary motion, was a mystic; or that the English physicist Isaac Newton spent most of his life writing alchemical texts; or that Descartes, the father of modern philosophy, believed the pineal gland, often called the mystical third eye, to be the seat of the human soul.

Yet as the nineteenth century dawned, magic re-entered our cultural history. Vital to this process was the English occultist Francis Barrett, who, in 1801, published his magical textbook, *The Magus*. Following its success, Barrett became so confident about his magical abilities that he advertised for pupils for his esoteric academy, set up to investigate 'the hidden treasures of nature.' Little is known about this academy, but among the subjects thought to have been taught were natural philosophies and the Cabala, supposedly advancing a whole host of occultists 'far upon the path of transcendental wisdom.' It is even believed that Barrett began a secret tradition of occult practices within Cambridge University that continued through the nineteenth century and well into the twentieth. Whether this is right or wrong, there is no doubt that Barrett injected a new lease of life into occult practices, with magic circles opening throughout Europe. But what was really responsible for this occult revival?

The Enlightenment had failed. Materialist philosophies, which had held such hope for the civilizing of man, had been shattered. 'Liberty, Equality, Fraternity' had, just over a decade before publication of *The Magus*, dropped France into the bloodbath of its revolution. As *The Magus* was published Napoleon was consolidating his power, ready to throw Europe into bloody turbulence, and forging the continent into the nationalist nightmare that would continue to haunt history. The great materialist intellectual adventure was in tatters, and the people longed for a different route to knowledge and enlightenment.

One such person was the sickly but highly intelligent youth Alphonse Louis Constant, better known as Eliphas Lévi. Born in Paris in 1810, by the age of twelve he had rejected materialism and gone in search of the spiritual. At first he thought of the Church, where he was taught by Abbot Frère Colonna, a tutor at the seminary of St Nicholas du Chardonnet, who believed the world was heading for a great spiritual awakening. Lévi was at first impressed by Colonna's vision. But the Abbot's attacks on demonic forces awoke in Lévi a thirst to understand them. He left the Church and discovered the Cabala and the Tarot, eventually combining the two into a joint system.

Of particular interest to Lévi was the relationship between the microcosm and the macrocosm, a relationship – 'As Above, So Below' – said to have been defined by the mythical ancient magician, Hermes Trismegistus. In order to learn more of the relationship, and its relevance to the Cabala, Lévi is said to have three times raised the spirit of the ancient Greek magician Apollonius of Tyana.

Lévi wrote two highly regarded books on the occult – *Dogma and Ritual of High Magic* and *History of Magic*. By his death in 1875, he was honoured by hundreds of occultists throughout Europe who openly mourned his passing.

Of the many occult societies that sprang up after Lévi, perhaps the most famous is the Hermetic Order of the Golden Dawn, founded in 1888 by three occultists – Dr William Wynn Westcott, S.L. MacGregor Mathers and Dr William Robert Woodman. A repository for all manner of study, it was chiefly concerned with 'rejected knowledge' – those areas of thought disdained by the establishment because of their demonic or supernatural qualities.

The Golden Dawn owed much to Freemasonry. Hence, the order was highly ritualized with a hierarchy of ten ranks and three orders. The central purpose of any member of the order was to 'obtain control of the nature and power of my own being.' Attracting such eminent members as the poet W.B. Yeats, the order seemed set for a long existence. However, it existed for little over fifteen years. It pulled together a mishmash of egoists and was never far removed from anarchy and power struggles.

The disintegration of the Golden Dawn highlights a problem with the occult that exists to this day. Unlike organized religion, there is no absolute ancient creed behind occult ceremony. The occultist is free to idolize and invoke any of a whole host of godheads. Further, to be an occultist is to reject existing knowledge. It takes a particular form of egoism to do this. The combination of egoism and personal choice in deity veneration usually leads to veneration of a deity that echoes the personality of the particular occultist. In this psychological environment it is so easy for the occultist to believe he *is* the particular deity. As a result, in many organized occult societies, uproar breaks out, guaranteeing disintegration of the society.

One occultist who attempted to take control of the Golden Dawn was the infamous Aleister Crowley. Dubbed 'the Wickedest Man in the World', Crowley was born in England in 1875 to parents who were members of the fundamentalist religious sect the Plymouth Brethren. Rebelling against the repression of his upbringing, he went to Cambridge, but dropped out before taking his degree. He joined the Golden Dawn in 1898, quickly rising to the top of its hierarchy. Taught by MacGregor Mathers, Crowley became a much respected magician, but as the two men began to argue, rumours circulated of a psychic battle between them, and finally Crowley was expelled from the Golden Dawn.

A writer of erotic poetry, Crowley became deeply involved in sex magic, taking a string of women and indulging in what he termed the 'serpent Kiss', where he used his teeth to draw blood. William Seabrook told of perhaps the only known feat of magic attributed to Crowley, when the magician began walking in step behind a passer-by. Suddenly Crowley buckled his knees and the man also collapsed to the ground. Sadly, Seabrook never researched the incident to the point of discounting the possibility of the 'act' being staged with an accomplice.

In 1903 Crowley married Rose Kelly. A year later, Kelly received a message from the astral plane instructing her to contact the Egyptian god Horus. Crowley ritually invoked Horus's spirit messenger, Aiwass, whom Crowley decided was his 'true self'. Over the following three days Kelly dictated the words of Aiwass, and the result was Crowley's *The Book of the Law*, which included the perversion of occult law known as the Law of Thelema: 'Do what thou wilt shall be the whole of the law.'

Aiwass went on to declare Crowley a prophet for the coming Aeon of Horus, the third age of humanity. In 1920 Crowley had a vision of a hillside villa while driving in Italy. This resulted in the setting up of a colony of sexual magic in Sicily known as the Sacred Abbey of the Thelemic Mysteries. The sexual excesses reported there resulted in Mussolini expelling him.

Among his many works, *Magick in Theory and Practice* is said by some occultists to be a major work on ceremonial magic, with him changing the spelling to distance himself from stage magic. Crowley died in 1947 following years of ill health and drug dependency.

Aleister Crowley severely damaged the public perception of magic, guaranteeing the accusations of fraud and sexual perversion that still dog occultism today. And while I agree that Crowley was an egoistic sensational-ist, and most likely a complete charlatan, it would be instructive to look at Crowley in the light of his times.

The religious repression within which he was brought up was so extreme that his mother christened him 'the Beast', believing him to be the Antichrist. The chances are that Crowley was simply hyperactive, but the naming made such an impression upon him that he called himself the Beast of the Apocalypse. This was the inheritance he took with him to adulthood thanks to his 'godly' parents.

And into what form of society did Crowley grow? He thought himself to be a great erotic poet. When he was twenty, another great erotic poet was sentenced to imprisonment in Reading Gaol for, indirectly, homosexual conduct. That poet was Oscar Wilde. And like Wilde, Crowley entered the spirit of revolt against Victorian values that were to lead to an age known as 'decadence'. It is therefore perhaps wrong to remove Crowley from this time. There were many others like him, the only difference being that Crowley allied his decadence to magic. Indeed, as for the sexual attitude of the time, it must be remembered that even academe was taking an interest, with the sexual theories of Sigmund Freud.

Crowley was a monstrous man. But much of his decadence must be seen as a result of his society rather than his magical beliefs. Indeed, a contem-porary of Crowley was offering a much more refined form of occultism in Russia.

Just when Georgei Gurdjieff was born is unknown, but it is believed to have been some time in the 1860s. Brought up in a small Russian village, his first employment was as a spy and adventurer. But after beginning a quest to know the 'whys' of life, he went on to rock occultism to its foundations with his liberation philosophy, known as the Work. During the 1920s he went on to devise techniques of group therapy that form the basis of much of psychoanalysis today.

Gurdjieff argued that human beings are machines run by forces over which we have no absolute control. As such, even when awake, people are really asleep. In order to awaken, people must work hard to break out of their normal unconsciousness and reach the true consciousness that lies within them. Gurdjieff taught a number of teachers, whom he called the Men Who Know, and sent them out to begin schools where students could reach such self-realization. Such a state would be reached by a number of 'shocks', changing the person's pre-conceived ideas of the 'self'.

To Gurdjieff the universe was governed by two cosmic laws – the Law of Three and the Octave. The former controlled the universe, while the latter was a number of stages of human development which must be gone through to achieve self-realization, as if going through the notes of the octave. In previous times, this knowledge had been known to the fakir (who went through torture to gain insight), the monk (he reached insight through emotion and faith), and the yogi (who meditated his way through his intellect). Gurdjieff argued for the Fourth Way.

The Fourth Way rejected the requirement to suffer either physically, emotionally or intellectually. Rather, through a series of exercises such as hard physical labour, discipline and complicated dance routines, the students worked on themselves as they really were, attempting to harmonize their energies and wake themselves up.

In 1922 Gurdjieff left Russia and soon settled down in France, where he opened the Institute for the Harmonious Development of Man. However, many of his students rejected him and he eventually gave up teaching, spending the rest of his life in writing.

In actual fact, Gurdjieff did little more than turn an esoteric philosophy, rather like Buddhism, into a twentieth-century form, re-devising the complicated rituals and spells of magic into a form of ritual amenable to the twentieth-century mind. Even his Octave can be likened to the Buddhist striving for Nirvana. But Gurdjieff allows us to look at the practice of magic in a way far removed from those early adepts who dabbled in the 'supernatural'.

Archetypes

THE HISTORY of magic seems to contain many contradictions. The Gnostic speaks of the living Jesus being within him. Dee documents his communion with angels. The Cabala tells us of an almost multi-faceted God. Agrippa denies such supernatural realities and elects for magic being grounded in a wider, hidden consciousness, which Gurdjieff seemed to validate in his philosophy.

Crowley is perhaps the most interesting figure regarding such contradictions. One the one hand we can see him as a charlatan, yet his apparent other-worldly communications seem to hint at the supernatural. But Colin Wilson obviously saw in Crowley a more subtle interaction when he wrote:

> What Crowley realised instinctively was that magic is somehow connected with the human will, with man's *true will*, the deep instinctive will. Man is a passive creature because he lives too much in rational consciousness and the trivial worries of every day. Crowley, with his animal instinct and his powerful sexual urge, glimpsed the truth expressed in Nietzsche's phrase, 'There is so much that has not yet been said or thought.'

So is magic a descent into the supernatural or, more realistically, an interaction involving human consciousness? Are the entities manifested within the realm of magic real spirits, or human constructs?

One thing is abundantly clear. If a supreme deity, or god, does exist, then there can only be one. But, having said that, we are faced with the sheer multiplicity of supernatural systems – the deities of ancient Egypt, Greece and Rome, the Norse and Celtic mythologies, the One God and attendant angels of the monotheist.

The sheer number of contradictory superbeings evoked by the adept makes a total farce of the whole concept of the supernatural. Unless, that is, we bring into the equation the cultural and traditional biases of the particular believer, and the way his prejudices can cause a shift in his reality. If we do this, the contradictory deities can maybe be seen in a new light.

To explain what I mean, consider one of the greatest intellectual debates of history – a debate that brought science out of religious dogma some four hundred years ago.

Prior to the birth of modern science, the Aristotelian Cosmology, which spoke of a stationary earth as centre of creation, was accepted as a literal fact. In this system, the sun orbited the earth. Copernicus, Galileo and Newton eventually destroyed this fallacy by proving that, in fact, the Earth moves and orbits the sun.

Here we have two completely contradictory systems, and at first it is easy to say that the people who thought the earth stood still were little more than crackpots. However, as the Viennese-born philosopher Wittgenstein has noted, whether the earth stood still or orbited the sun the effects – in our observation – would have been exactly the same. Regardless of which was true, the sun would still rise and set.

If we apply this cultural interpretation to the conflicting deities, we can come to the conclusion that the particular deity witnessed by a member of a specific culture is dependent not on a fundamental reality, but on what the observer's culture and beliefs had suggested he would see.

Hence, be it a Catholic witnessing the Virgin Mary, or an adept invoking the spirit of Beelzebub, the mechanics of the manifestation become identical.

In this way, we can come to the conclusion that Agrippa could well have been right when he decided that magic was a property of human consciousness, the deities being nothing but inventions of the adept's mind. However, to leave it there is to say that every magician who attempts to invoke deities, or influence reality with their help, is nothing more than a crackpot. I don't, for a minute, believe this to be the case. For instance, the deities may well be psychological inventions, but not necessarily of man as an individual. Rather, they could be creations of mankind as a whole.

Carl Jung realized the potence and existence of psychic images and symbols with his theory of archetypes. Archetypes, manifesting within myth, dreams and folklore, he saw as universal symbols – mental images passed on through inheritance from our primeval past. Such theorizing became the rockbed of his theory of a collective racial unconscious to which we can all connect, and such a theory can be seen as useful in terms of the possible existence of deities invoked through magic.

Although Jung identified many archetypal images within the psyche of his patients, his first introduction to them occurred at the age of three, when he had a profound dream of a dark opening in the earth and a myriad of pagan god symbols. Following this dream, he began to realize that he had two personalities. The first was his normal self, but underlying this was a personality he thought of as a wise old man who personified the whole experience of life. The old man lived outside his personal mind, he later theorized, and was, in fact, an archetype. He named him Philemon, and as Jung grew older, Philemon increased his dominance over Jung himself.

In Philemon we can see the beginnings of a psychologically produced entity, based upon Jung's cultural beliefs. But, of course, what we can actually see happening is an interaction of the left and right cerebral hemispheres. If Jung had been a medium as opposed to a psychologist, Philemon would have eventually become Jung's spirit guide, with the emotional right cerebral hemisphere gaining prominence over the more logical left hemisphere. Indeed, several past-life therapists have theorized that such archetypes are at the root of past-life manifestations.

Principal among Jung's archetypes were the Sage, the Hero, the Earth Mother, the Child, the Judge and the Trickster. These six collective traits were not seen as images but as outer influences upon the psyche. They are not formulated personas, but urges that lead the individual through life by communicating with the conscious. In other words, we are all conditioned by them, but in the rational individual their interaction is so subtle that the urges which drive us are seen as personal to the individual rather than existing 'outside' the psyche. However, in the delusions of the schizophrenic, or in trance states, these images can be identified as exhibiting form. They exist in an hallucinatory reality. So could the entities evoked by an adept be nothing more than an hallucinatory archetype?

The beauty of the archetype is that it exhibits characteristics of the human psyche, while being adaptable to the individual's cultural beliefs. The Hero is the embodiment of supernatural beings from the Greek Hercules to the Norse Thor. The Earth Mother can be identified in deities such as the Greek Demeter and Gaia and can also be seen as taking form in the Christian Virgin Mary. The Sage is usually seen at the top of the deity hierarchy, embodied in the Greek Zeus or Roman Jupiter. When Michelangelo wanted to give form to God for the Sistine Chapel, he chose the Sage, and we invest our wisest humans with the image, be they Moses, da Vinci or Einstein. (Although Einstein recognized relativity when he was a young man, our culture requires his genius to be seen as age-old wisdom.) As for the Trickster, the most vivid image in Western culture is that of the Devil himself.

Of course, Jung's archetypes are not proven, and have constantly been attacked by academe. Their existence eats away at the validity of the self, which, as I noted earlier, is seen as essential to human intellect and society. But shortly we will go in search of the mechanics of such archetypal hallucinations, and highlight new insights into consciousness in doing so. But first we must ask whether, in contemporary society, we are really as divorced from the influences of a psychologically based form of magic as we believe.

Magic as Routine

A MAN'S twenty-first birthday party can be a peculiar thing. It is a coming together of the celebrant's family and friends, in which the cultural and generational divide collapses. The coming of age of the celebrant – his transition from youth to man – is celebrated by the elder partygoers by a return to boyhood and the drinking of much alcohol. A good time is had, involving much back-slapping and congratulations for the celebrant's success in reaching a new phase in his life.

Of course, this new phase of life is a purely human construct. Biologically the new man is no different, and any psychological change can be explained purely by the new place he has in a sociological context. In a real sense, the celebration is irrelevant, other than in terms of the social and cultural importance we place upon it. He has simply proceeded through a rite of passage.

In most societies this rite of passage is a religious event. Typical is the Jewish bar mitzvah, steeped in religious tradition. In fact, most societies celebrate four rites of passage – birth, transition to manhood, marriage and death – and all were born from religious processes and mankind's submission to the laws and morals of a supernatural deity.

The Western world is increasingly seen as a secular society, the popular God banished as an archaic superstition. Yet still our major festivals and holidays are regulated by the old Christian calendar, the most popular being Easter and Christmas, which celebrate respectively Christ's crucifixion and resurrection and his birth. The year in which we presently live is devised according to Christ's birth, and while the year itself is an astronomical calculation of how long it takes the earth to orbit the sun, the week is based on the six days of Creation and the Sabbath.

Such celebrations and rites of passage were initially instigated for an important reason. They gave a society a purpose which led to orderliness.

Without such orderliness, chaos and unrest would be the order of the day. However, while Christianity is popularly seen as the originator of such practices, they are in fact much older.

Typical is Christmas, where the culinary festivities may include the consumption of the Yule log. Yule is the pagan winter solstice. The log is from Norse tradition – a log found in the forest was ceremonially burnt in order to use its light and heat to fight the forces of winter and darkness, thus reminding the people that the cold, barren earth would soon be transformed by a more amiable climate as winter receded.

Easter has similar pagan origins. It is not known when Christ was crucified. So why is Easter celebrated when it is? Christ's crucifixion and resurrection are symbols of renewal. What was dead has suddenly sprung to life once more. Christ was dead, and suddenly he lives again. However, pagan societies celebrated a similar process at springtime – the time when life once again sprouts from the earth. By placing Christ's death and rebirth at this time, Christian authority is placed over pagan tradition. The name 'Easter' itself is derived from the pagan god Ostera.

The Christian dominance over pagan rites and festivals is best seen in the Eucharist itself. Re-enacting the Last Supper, at which Christ blessed and offered bread and wine as symbolic of his flesh and blood, every Sunday Christians partake in a symbolic re-enactment of the most ancient pagan rites involving cannibalism and the blood rite.

The importance of such rites and celebrations was to celebrate the power of a deity. Such ceremony was not instigated to mark an event. Rather, the ceremony produced the event. It was the result of a pact between a human society and that society's godhead. In observing the laws and morals imposed by the godhead, the member of a society, or the society itself, was blessed with a divine intervention, creating the rebirth of life at spring-time, or literally turning a boy into a man. By taking part in such rites and celebrations a society took part in a magical rite.

Looking at human society and culture in this way, we can see not only how important magic was in the prehistoric past, but how important it still is even today. After all, what do we tell our children about how Santa Claus comes down the chimney? By magic, of course.

All societies have had a particular person, usually known as a shaman or witch doctor, who channelled magical abilities from the godhead to the society. And although the magician is no longer important to our society, the priest still carries out tasks similar to those of the pagan shaman. All religious societies live in a dualist culture. They live by two separate trains of thought – pragmatism and mysticism, the practical elements of life and the higher supernatural order. Such duality is expressed in a society's establishment. In pagan times we had the chief to deal with normal life, and the shaman to interact with the supernatural. In Christian hierarchy, this can be seen in the king and barons, and bishop and priests.

In order to fulfill his role of liaison with the supernatural, the shaman and priest engage in higher ritual. The priest's higher ritual involves additional prayer and preparation, the most obvious example being the blessing of the bread and wine. But for the shaman, or today's magician, the ritual is far more spectacular and involved.

Magical ritual came to be recorded in grimoires – elaborate textbooks of ceremonial magic. One of the earliest grimoires is ascribed to King Solomon, who was thought to have immense magical powers.

Although all grimoires are different, the rituals they describe are nearly all based upon a three-stage procedure used to invoke entities to do the adept's bidding. The first stage is the preparation of the materials required for whatever spell is to be cast. It is here we find instructions concerning, for example, the gathering of toad's legs, collected under a full moon on a Tuesday. This stage also involves the preparation of magical weapons such as the wand.

The second stage involves the preparation of the magician's mind. It is generally accepted that this is done in order to attain an altered state of consciousness, and involves fasting, chanting, meditation, dancing, sleep deprivation or the taking of narcotic substances.

Once these two stages are accomplished, the third stage is the ritual itself. This usually takes place within a magical circle, guarded by magical symbols in order to protect the magician from unwanted demons that may materialize. From the protection of the circle, he will burn incense and utter the required incantations, thus completing the process of ritual.

In a modern, sceptical world such practices have become the subject of ridicule – and it is easy to see why. It seems ridiculous to believe that the collection of bits of toads and a drop of blood from a magpie collected during particular atmospheric conditions can have any bearing at all upon ceremony. But this is to miss the point of what is going on.

The central purpose of magical ritual is to unite the macrocosm, or deity, with the microcosm, or magician. In doing so, the magician invokes supposedly awesome power, achieved by years of practice and dedication. It is therefore logical to assume that to achieve success, a formidable and, most importantly, difficult process of preparation and ceremony must be entailed. Consider a soldier in training. He undergoes immense physical preparation with marching and physical exercise. He learns how to clean and prepare his weapons. He has to sleep out at night in all weather to prepare himself for the physical torture of war. Then there is the discipline. He must learn to obey orders without dissent and become part of a macrocosmic whole – his platoon.

What the soldier is doing is echoing magical ritual. Like the instructions in the grimoires, much of his physical and psychological preparation seems stupid. Doing fifty press-ups for being last in a two-mile run is illogical, but teaches the soldier the importance of physical perfection. Being told off for walking on the grass is ridiculous, but it hones the mind towards obedience. Hence, when the soldier goes out to enact the ritual for which he is trained – the fighting of a war – the apparently stupid preparations he has worked through pay off by making him physically and emotionally ready.

Seen in this context, the preparations for magical ceremony are not the ends, but the means to an end. The more difficult and illogical the act, the greater the discipline achieved, and the more likely a successful outcome.

In psychological terms, the preparations for magical ritual can be understood as a form of cleansing of the mind in order to interact with reality in a more positive way. Which was, of course, the philosophy behind Gurdjieff's Fourth Way. And, looking at the preparations in this way, we can perhaps see the importance of magical ritual even in modern society.

Every morning my first hour of the day tends to be identical. I get up at the same time and do the same things in the same order. The remainder of the day may be very different from other days, but that first hour is almost always the same. It is my 'routine'. But what happens if, for some reason, my routine is disturbed by, for instance, sleeping in or receiving an early morning phone call?

You can almost guarantee that the remainder of the day becomes a catalogue of disaster. And I don't simply mean disasters caused by me, such as pouring tea into the breakfast cereal. The car won't start, or the train is late, or the traffic jam is twice as bad, or the secretary calls to say she is ill, or a labourer drops a brick on my head, or my mother-in-law turns up. Basically, we say it has been 'one of those days'.

I doubt if I know anyone who has not mastered some form of routine. And I doubt if I know anyone who doesn't have their day drastically changed by an interruption to their routine. This is because the interruption has knocked the mind out of equilibrium. The peace of mind has gone. Concentration on life has been stripped away.

Looked at in this way routine becomes identical to magical ritual. In the modern world magic has been perfected rather than abandoned. It has been perfected to such a degree that we hardly notice it, yet it is essential to the fundamental order we take as normal life. So perhaps magic is not a dead superstition, but could be alive and well in the form of routine.

Entities

IN THE 1880s, American physiologist William Carpenter from Boston carried out an experiment in hypnosis which has entered the annals of psychology. He hypnotized a student in Washington DC and then asked him if he would like to speak with Socrates. Getting the answer 'yes', he told the student that Socrates was present and ready to converse. Only the student, though, would be able to hear Socrates' side of the conversation so Carpenter asked him to repeat aloud what Socrates said.

The student and 'Socrates' went on to converse for two hours. This whole experiment was conducted in front of an audience, which included the then sceptic Thomson Jay Hudson, who later wrote that the thoughts that came out of this conversation would have 'formed one of the grandest and most coherent systems of spiritual philosophy ever conceived by the brain of man.'

Later, when Spiritualists in the audience decided they were seeing proof of life after death, Carpenter summoned up for the student a philosophical pig to discourse on the Hindu belief of reincarnation.

This, and hundreds of documented cases like it, suggest that while in an altered state of consciousness we can invoke personalities, or even deities, from our unconscious. Often the personality manifested has a level of intelligence far greater than that of the invoker – like Socrates in the Carpenter case. This suggests that the manifestation comes from a source greater than the observer (when it is a visual hallucination, from clairvoyance) or listener (when it is the hearing of voices, through clairaudience).

While studying patients in the 1960s who were suffering from hallucinations, the American psychiatrist Wilson Van Dusen categorized two types of hallucinatory influence. He called them 'lower' and 'higher' order hallucinations. In the lower order he found stupidity and repetitiveness. They were, basically, delusory influences, most likely manifested by a disturbed mind.

But he recognized the higher hallucinations as being symbolic, religious, supportive and instructive.

Could such higher hallucinations be caused by higher, outside influences of a greater intelligence than us mere mortals?

Disregarding the obvious metaphysical repercussions of such entities for the time being, there is an apparent stumbling block to this idea in that science, as presently understood, disallows mind invasions from outside the personal mind. Understanding of mind can only be grasped within an understanding of an autonomous 'self'. Contemplation can only come from the individual experiencing things. Mind is nothing more than a chemical reaction of the physical brain. So it is impossible for a mind creation, such as 'Socrates', to come from anywhere except the individual's mind.

But does this argument necessarily hold up? We all understand the idea that we have a mind, but few of us have the slightest notion of what 'mind' involves, or how it has consistently failed to be understood in terms of science, philosophy or religion. Up until the seventeenth century, a largely religious intelligentsia thought of mind as nothing more than our ability to choose between God and the Devil, good and bad. Mind was nothing more than an expression of free will. That part of us which transcended the body was known as the soul – a supernatural element that survived death.

In the early seventeenth century, academe began to take notice of the relationship between mind and the physical body. The philosopher René Descartes described the physical body as a simple machine, with mind (which he still termed the soul) lying outside the body and beyond understanding by science.

Identifying the body as a simple machine was a natural progression of the times. The Industrial Revolution was about to break out, and many previously repetitive tasks were already being replaced by mechanization. To class the body as similar to such machines appeared logical. However, religion still held sway in overall academe. Hence, when the physician Julian de la Mettrie suggested, in the 1740s, that maybe the mind was also a machine, he was hounded out of his practice.

By the nineteenth century such a view was no longer laughed at. The German physiologist Franz Joseph Gall took the world by storm in the early years of the century with his suggestion that you can identify a person's personality by studying the bumps on the head. Such cranial development, argued Gall, reflected the development of particular areas of the brain. Gall went on to categorize the areas of the brain responsible for specific human traits such as vision, emotion and speech.

'Phrenology', as Gall called his new science, has been well and truly repudiated today. But, as is often the case with pseudo-scientific ideas, a large degree of common sense resides within it.

In the 1920s it was discovered that the brain produced electrical activity that could be picked up by monitors attached to the scalp. By means of these electroencephalographs (EEGs) science learnt of electrical patterns within the brain which changed to reflect the conscious state of the individual. Waking and sleeping have their own peculiar electrical patterns, which at times can go haywire, as happens during an epileptic fit.

The existence of such electrical activity seriously eroded the dualist view that mind and body were separate. Mind was increasingly being seen as a physical consequence of brain activity. And in the 1940s this view seemed to be confirmed by a new understanding of memory.

The American neurosurgeon Wilder Penfield discovered while treating epileptics that electrical stimulation of particular areas of the brain produced distinct memory sequences, offering further argument that mind was a consequence of brain activity. But, more than this, Penfield's work suggested that a localized area of the brain did, as Gall suggested, control related mental function.

These ideas were rationalized by Canadian psychologist Donald Hebb, who argued that the brain contained neurones which were interconnected and formed patterns of impulses. These neural circuits could be modified by experience and thus produce memory. Most neuroscientists and philosophers accept that understanding of Hebb's neural pathways will eventually lead to a total understanding of the mind. The prevalent view within academe to this day is that mind is a physical outcome of a physical brain, specific to the individual, and that certain areas of the brain control particular traits of the person.

However, even as such theories were being postulated, a contemporary of Penfield's was coming to a different conclusion concerning the localization of traits within the brain. American neuropsychologist Karl Lashley surgically removed particular areas of the cortex of rats to see if the removal would destroy the rat's memory of how to negotiate a maze. He discovered that memory was not lost but reduced, dependent upon the amount of cortex removed.

This suggested that, while sensory and motor functions of the brain (such as sight and physical body function) may well be localized, memory exists not in specific areas but within the whole brain, as if in a memory field.

Lashley's work never gained prominence and still tends to be ignored today. The main reason for this is that a 'field' theory for mind complicates Hebb's neural-connectionist hypothesis. Scientists like to keep things simple and straightforward. And nowhere is this more so than in the recent ideas of Francis Crick, the joint discoverer of DNA.

In his *The Astonishing Hypothesis: the Scientific Search for the Soul*, Crick points out that not the whole brain is involved with mind. Much of the brain deals with motor function. However, rejecting any ideas about mind being outside the brain, he suggests that a specific element of the brain produces mind – an element that is a connection of 'awareness neurones'.

The discovery of this 'awareness neurone' will, says Crick, answer the mysteries of mind. We don't need anything more than such an element. His argument here is that the higher functions of the mind can be seen as the result of the combination of billions of smaller, simple cells.

This idea is attractive, and finds an analogy in society. A grouping of people is nothing more than the coming together of many individuals. However, the interaction of the people produces a higher product known as culture.

In a real sense, Crick can be seen as attempting to explain mind in terms of the coming together of simple elements which, by the very fact of coming together, produce something more potent. But sadly, in terms of real science, there is a flaw in this argument. Fundamental to it is the observable fact that when higher animals appear to be aware of the outside world their neurones oscillate in unison. The whole argument rests upon this starting point. The problem is that there is no guarantee that neuronal oscillation is fundamental to the explanation of mind. And if the starting point is irrelevant the argument is invalid.

That the answer to mind is to be found in the brain is today widely accepted in scientific circles, and, consequently, society as a whole. For instance, the philosopher Daniel Dennett agrees, in his *Consciousness Explained* (1991), that the understanding of the brain will lead to a total understanding of mind. The problem of consciousness will eventually go no deeper than that of motor function, or breathing.

Robotics researcher Hans Moravec goes further in his book *The Mind Children* (1990). He argues that the brain is nothing more than a digital computer. In a matter of decades we will be able to download our mind into a computer in order to attain immortality.

However, one scientist is beginning to challenge the simplicity of the neural-connectionist hypothesis.

With his books *The Emperor's New Mind* and *Shadows of the Mind*, the mathematician Roger Penrose has greatly unsettled the scientific community. Famous for his earlier work on black holes, Penrose argues that consciousness must be taken into the physical equation of the universe. He associates the mind with the puzzling quantum characteristics of the universe.

At present, neurones are seen as switches, the state of the switch facilitating neural connectedness. However, a neurone is not the simple construction it was once thought to be. A neurone has a cytoskeleton, or inner structure, consisting of a latticework of protein rods called microtubules. A hollow cylinder 25 nanometres across, each microtubule is built from strands of the protein tubulin, which seem to behave as tiny switches in their own right.

Looking at this inner sanctum of the neurone, Penrose has noted that the microtubules are just the right size to amplify subatomic effects. Penrose thus suggests that quantum characteristics could lie within consciousness.

So the standard view of mind, expressed in the neural-connectionist hypothesis, is not cast in stone, but has quite a reaction brewing against it.

Gerald Edelman, who won a Nobel prize for his work in immunology, stresses the dynamic creativity of mental processes, allying them to an evolutionary model which makes the machine analogy an error. While he accepts that science may eventually gain a form of understanding of mind, he doubts that an ultimate explanation of a human individual can be grasped by science. The Austrian philosopher Karl Popper tried to inject a bit of common sense into the debate by pointing out it was possible to be a dualist without believing in God. But the neurophysiologist Sir John Eccles argued against the idea that a purely materialist explanation of the mind is achievable. We only seem to be heading that way because the materialists control academic appointments, funding and publishing, thus suppressing contrary opinion. Indeed, he argued that advances in neuroscience so far are perfectly compatible with the existence of a non-physical mind.

However, we seem to have a paradox here. If neuroscience, including the neural-connectionist hypothesis, is not wrong, how can it possibly be compatible with a non-physical mind? But really there is no paradox at all. What we must do is simply understand the prevalent scientific and philosophical idea of reductionism, which states that any system is best understood in terms of its basic parts. Hence, having identified the neurone, there is no need to look deeper. If a theory can arise from understanding the action of the neurone, that is satisfactory to science.

With such a reductionist outlook, the scientist is excused from the deeper conceptual issues involved in mind research. It stinks too much of metaphysics and implications of the existence of God. Better to leave that kind of stuff alone. It degrades the intellect, hammers at the door of the 'self'. It could even lead to a world where there is more than science.

We have come to the crux of the problem. Science works with the material universe – with that part of existence that can be termed physical. It has no other function. And the neural-connectionist hypothesis must be seen in this light. It simply explains the physical, banishing anything else out of existence. Neural activity is seen by science as the cause of consciousness. But it can also be seen in another, equally important, way, outside the scientific paradigm. Rather than being the cause of consciousness, neural activity could equally be seen as the physical effect of a working mind. In other words, they've found the car, but not the driver. They are not interested in the driver. But, sadly, without a driver, a car won't go.

Penrose has, in effect, looked for the driver. And what he may have discovered is that the driver is not the individual but the totality of the universe. In other words, something from outside the personal mind may well have an effect upon the mind.

We can now look at the 'Socrates' manifested by Professor Carpenter's student, and, indeed, the entities manifested by the magician, in a new light. Whether science likes it or not, there is a possibility of outside influences invading the mind. Whether their neurons oscillate in time with the entity is irrelevant to the fact that brain research cannot disprove their existence.

Entities, hallucinated higher intelligences, Jungian archetypes – call them what you will. A collective racial unconscious is not out of the question. And neither is my collective memory shop. And if it exists, then within it would be the memory of Socrates and his entire philosophy. And there too would be the memories of other people, philosophies and mythologies from the Virgin Mary to Beelzebub (not to mention all the personages referred to in our survey of life after death), no doubt affected by personal bias, but existent all the same. And, surprisingly enough, one of the arch reductionists – Francis Crick himself – could well have proved the existence of a possible contributory mechanism through which a collective unconscious could work.

Consciousness

THERE IS one important influence outside the individual mind which science has been unable to banish adequately. Instinct. In its classical form, instinct is animal behaviour that is not learnt by experience. It was at first seen to be a kind of innate control. Indeed, in the Middle Ages St Thomas Aquinas was quite clear that instinctual behaviour is not free but regulated by nature.

As the more rational philosophers moved into academe, beginning their construction of the 'self', instinct proved an obvious problem. Arch-materialist philosopher John Locke, who devised a mind model based purely on experience, had to admit, in his *Essay concerning Human Understanding* (1690), that there was: '. . . an uneasiness of the mind for want of some absent good . . . God has put into man the uneasiness of hunger and thirst, and other natural desires . . . to move and determine their wills for the preservation of themselves and the continuation of the species.'

For the early rational philosophers, God still existed, so they could attribute instinct to him and give no further thought to the subject. But by the early eighteenth century God could no longer be used as a repository for those bits that didn't quite fit the intellectual model. Hence, Francis Hutcheson, Professor of Moral Philosophy at Glasgow, argued that instinct was the element of a life form that produced an action prior to thought of the consequences. Such an idea can be seen in action on both animals and humans. Whenever we place ourselves in danger we seem to react quickly and without thought. Touch something hot, and we 'instinctively' pull our hand away, suggesting that we have a motivational urge beyond thought processes – in this case obviously geared to a survival urge.

The nineteenth-century rationalists coped with instinct in a subtle way. William James, the American philosopher and psychologist, saw human nature as a combination of blind instinct and rational thought. However, to

Sigmund Freud, instinctual behaviour was at the heart of humanity. Life was a battle between two predominant instinctual drives – the sexual instinct, or urge towards pleasure, and the ego instinct, which strives towards self-preservation. From the 1920s onwards, Freud regarded the two basic drives, rather differently, as the sexual instinct and the death instinct. The clash between these dual instincts was, he thought, the root of psychological disorder.

A different form of understanding of instinct came with Erasmus Darwin, the English poet-physician, who argued that animals could reason. This led him to theorize that animals developed habitual behaviour because of the stability of their environment. At the time there was no scientific model with which to test his theory. But this all changed with Erasmus's grandson, Charles Darwin. In his *Origin of Species* Darwin saw instinct as complex reflexes made up of inherited behaviour, and thus subject to natural selection. In this view, instinct becomes a product of both inheritance and environmental influence.

Konrad Lorenz, the Austrian authority on animal behaviour, modified this view some hundred years later by bringing genetics into the equation. Animal behaviour, he decided, included a number of fixed action patterns that were, in the main, genetically determined. He postulated that such patterns of behaviour were due to 'action-specific energy'.

Sadly, however, this was the last innovative theory about instinct. The self had gained prominence and the possibility of innate abilities, or human action being decreed other than through environmental stimulus, was shunned. These ideas have never been disproved. They are simply frowned upon. They don't fit. They've been sucked into the intellectual black hole. The orthodox mind model ignores the existence of instinct, sealing the fate of scientifically accepted outside influences. Yet where does instinct come from? Where *could* it come from? The most likely donor is, of course, the individual's parents. In other words, instinct could well be hereditary – because we now know that the person we are is based principally on heredity.

The scientists Crick and Watson proved this in 1953 with the discovery of deoxyribonucleic acid, or DNA. DNA molecules are paired in the cell as two long chains wound around each other in a double helix. Each molecule is a blueprint for the reproduction of another. The molecule simply uncoils one of its chains which carries the genetic information for the new cell.

Is it possible for instinct to be inherited through DNA? Up until the time that scientists shunned instinct, that is clearly the way all the theorizing was heading. Indeed, instinct seems the predominant influence in animals. The whole animal kingdom is thought to be regulated by instinctual drives. However, some life forms react in a most peculiar way.

One of these strange life forms is the slime mould *Dictyostelium discoideum*. When faced with lack of food, its forty thousand separate and identical cells can come together to form a sausage-shaped slug called a grex, which then travels in search of food (at a speed of one millimetre per hour). When it has found it, it reverts to its original composition.

Here we have simple cells which can act instinctually to change their function. We might go further and say, without going too far out on a limb, that in coming together as a grex this slime mould is exhibiting not only instinct, but consciousness – and consciousness without the specialized formulation of a brain.

This suggests strongly that cellular constructions can contain, and pass on through heredity, the fundamentals of consciousness. In turn, this provides a scientific explanation of the collective unconscious. Thoughts are passed on to the individual's offspring, giving everyone access to a communal ancestral consciousness. And whether you believe we came from Adam and Eve or the primeval slime, we all trace our ancestry to a single source. And if instinct – a mind phenomenon – can be passed on by hereditary means, then why not other mind phenomena, such as consciousness and memory itself?

Some modern scientists are already coming to terms with these new concepts. Principal among them is American anaesthesiologist Stuart Hameroff, whose ideas led Roger Penrose to suggest a quantum influence within consciousness. Working at the University of Arizona, Hameroff and others have suggested that a rippling effect within the microtubules which exist within the cytoskeleton of the neurone (see p. 106) could in reality constitute a form of biological computer, where a cell is able to trigger an on/off switching process in its neighbour. Hameroff is convinced that microtubules are essential to an understanding of consciousness.

But a neurone is simply a cell, and the cytoskeleton construction exists within all cells, not just those associated with the brain. So Hameroff's ideas allow a form of consciousness in all biological matter – it is not necessary to have a brain to attain consciousness. Hameroff has noted that even single-cell life forms appear to be able to 'learn'. For instance, the actions of the single-celled paramecium suggest that it can learn how to negotiate a maze.

Such theorizing opens a path towards a radical shift in our understanding of consciousness and memory, offering a foundation upon which a theory of a wider non-material consciousness may be built. This could well be the gnosis, or knowledge, attained by the magician – his occult (meaning 'hidden') reality.

But even if this new view of consciousness could account for phenomena such as deity manifestation, hereditary remembrance or Jungian archetypes, we are still a long way from explaining the total psychology behind magic. Two questions immediately present themselves. Why do we now see the wider reality of deities as 'hidden'? And how did occult deities gain such importance in the first place?

A clue to the understanding of these processes is provided by Colin Wilson, the British writer on philosophy and the occult. Fundamental to Wilson's thinking is the belief that man has a restricted attitude of mind which he calls 'close-upness'. Man has a very small view of reality; he sees the world from a worm's-eye view and is unable to complete a world picture in his mind. This is due to man's need to concentrate. Basically, if man had a wider view of reality in normal life, he would be flooded with so much meaning that concentration would be impossible.

This close-upness causes a natural state of 'upside-downness'. It makes people suffer the delusion that the trivia of life are important. Negative values impinge upon the intellect and values are turned upside-down. Hence, boredom results in further boredom, rather than giving people the impetus to rise out of their lethargic state and grasp meanings within the world.

Wilson finds justification for this theory in the split-brain concept. Since logic is required for concentration, modern man is open to left-brain dominance. However, there are times when right-brain dominance takes over, and when this happens man experiences a bird's-eye view, when the world holds greater meaning. Wilson calls this state Faculty X; it is the route to occult vision.

Wilson may well have hit the nail on the head when he says we experience close-upness because of our need to concentrate. The mind has two distinct parts – the conscious and the unconscious. The immense memory recall shown in hypnosis suggests that the mind registers every perception it makes. However, the mind also acts like a sieve, diverting information not required for normal life to the unconscious.

The best way of noticing this is to go into a quiet room with a ticking clock. At first you notice the ticking, but after a while this irrelevant information is relegated to the unconscious and you no longer hear it. However, should the clock suddenly stop, this information is deemed to be of relevance, and you notice, consciously, that the clock has stopped.

We can thus suggest that concentration alone is not the reason for our worm's-eye view, but rather the sieving of information that is deemed of no importance to our conscious life. And this, perhaps, is the result of an evolutionary process.

Evolution theory has a hard and fast rule. Stated simply, it is that we only have, we only evolve, what we need for survival. And this could well be true, not only for our physical traits but for consciousness too.

Take the frog. It is now known that the frog's conscious perception is only of shadow and light, enough to give it the ability to catch food, but no more.

Now let us assume that we had total consciousness – the ability to perceive everything there was to perceive. What would our life be like?

The British astronomer Sir Arthur Eddington described perfectly the dilemma of a physicist with total perception of the information available within reality entering a room:

In the first place, I must shove against an atmosphere pressing with a force of fourteen pounds on every square inch of my body. I must make sure of landing on a plank travelling at twenty miles a second round the sun – a fraction of a second too early or too late, the plank would be miles away. I must do this whilst hanging from a round planet head outwards into space, with a wind of aether blowing at no one knows how many miles a second through every interstice of my body. The plank has no solidity of substance. To step on it is like stepping on a swarm of flies. Shall I not slip through? No, if I make the venture one of the flies hits me and gives a boost up again; I fall again and am knocked upwards by another fly; and so on. . . .

He concludes that it would be wiser to be an ordinary man and simply walk through the door.

This gives a possible indication of what consciousness and, by definition, life, is. A rock is simply a rock. It does nothing of its own volition. If it flies through the air, it does so because something has thrown it. A rock is 'dead' because it has no will of its own, and therefore no consciousness. It has no innate purpose.

Life, on the other hand, has purpose. It has devised a form of will of its own, and to do so it has grasped consciousness. However, at a subatomic level, there is little difference between a 'dead' lump of granite and a 'living' kidney. But, at a cellular level, the kidney has developed purpose.

We can provide a rough analogy by going back to the grex. As a slime mould, its purpose is simple. Like a rock, it isn't really bothered if an aether is blowing through every interstice of its form. The information doesn't affect it one way or the other. But a slug wouldn't be able to perform if it was aware of this aether. Hence, its consciousness begins to filter out this information, and suddenly, attaining close-upness, each cell transforms from an identical non-entity into a specialized life form, as if its microtubules have inputted a new program. Literally, by sieving information from reality out of its conscious, it has furthered its grasp on conscious existence, or life.

Life, therefore, could be understood as a 'grasping' of close-upness; the ability to sieve information out of conscious existence to the point that the level of information is so low as to allow the understanding of innate purpose.

Psychological Evolution

NO ONE knows exactly how it happened. Neither do we know why, or even when, it happened. But at some point in our evolution an ancestor picked up a branch, a stone or a piece of old bone and used it as an extension of his own physical ability – in other words, as a tool or a weapon. Realizing that it was useful, he kept it and eventually fashioned it for greater effect. Man had begun to understand technology. He had begun the process that has led to the microchip.

We call the discovery of the microchip the beginning of the information-technology revolution – and for a very good reason. Increasing technology provides an increase in perceived information. Hence, when our ancestors picked up that branch, or stone, or bone, man began to create his own information. For the first time on planet earth, information not restricted to an instinctual, or natural, impulse had been created. This was, of course, a great evolutionary leap. So what happened?

In order to survive – to concentrate his thoughts on a particular issue such as using his tool or weapon – man had to again increase his close-upness by diverting more and more unrequired information to his unconscious, developing, along the way, the specialized fields we live by today. Thus, to stop information overload, and the difficulties it would cause us in trying to concentrate on particular issues, we have a very narrow conscious, and, seemingly, a vast unconscious.

However, as this state of close-upness is man-made, it could be argued that it is not fundamental to nature, in that no other species has this information-technology requirement for close-upness. So it is possible to argue that, at times when the amount of man-made, external information is cut off from consciousness, our mind could revert to its pre-technological state.

This fact is clearly indicated by hypnosis, where external information is cut off and our conscious is flooded with unconscious information, to the extent that, under hypnosis, some people have remembered exact texts previously read. However, as we have seen, hypnosis is not the only time when external information is cut off. It is cut off also when we go to sleep, involving dreaming and, at the borders of sleep, hypnagogic and hypnopompic hallucinations.

If such experiences are the result of a mind cut off from technological, or man-made, information – and our study of hallucination showed that all people suffer such images if deprived of outside information – then it is valid to say that pre-technological man lived in this state, regularly experiencing his contemporary and ancestral memories in his perceived reality. In other words, in our distant past, man had a wider consciousness which involved his 'seeing' – his perceiving – his dead ancestors, or, at least, memories of them.

A lecturer at Princeton University, Dr Julian Jaynes, caused a storm of protest in 1976 with the publication of his book, *The Origin of Consciousness in the Breakdown of the Bicameral Mind*. The heart of his book is his observations on ancient writings such as the Old Testament, the Epic of Gilgamesh and Homer's *Iliad* and *Odyssey*. He observed that the authors of such books appeared to have no form of self-consciousness. 'Iliadic man,' he wrote, 'did not have subjectivity as we do; he had no awareness of his awareness of the world, no internal mind space to introspect upon.'

What Jaynes is saying here is that Iliadic man had no substantial personal mind. Decisions, actions and impressions were the product of some entity higher than the mind of the individual man, as if they were somehow 'controlled' by superior thought patterns.

Jaynes came to the conclusion that any decisions that Iliadic men came to were due not to their own consciousness but the hearing of voices in their heads. These voices were appreciated as instructions from their gods. And, in a way, even today this idea can be seen in religious people. A devoted priest has a 'calling'. A man is saved from death, not by the surgeon, but by God.

Religious people act in this way because they believe that the spirit of God is all around and within them. Hence, as in the confessional, God acts as their conscience. And this is exactly what can be inferred from what Jaynes says of Iliadic man. But we can now, perhaps, see why.

Iliadic man came shortly after the birth of city-based civilization in Greece, in a period of technological advance. His consciousness was undergoing dramatic evolutionary change as he was swamped by man-made information. (You could even argue that, as in the split-brain concept, his left, logical brain was fiercely overpowering a previously predominant instinctual right). With more new technological information than he could comfortably process his close-upness grasped him tightly, but his pre-technological consciousness was still there.

Hence, his ancestors would still be seen and heard in perceived reality – understood now only in terms of clairvoyant and clairaudient spirit guides and magically produced entities – but his advancing close-upness would make it difficult for Iliadic man to understand just what he was perceiving.

Prehistoric man had no such dilemma. His cave paintings show that his spirits were benevolent and helpful. But Iliadic man's spirits were frightening. And, because they were, Iliadic man would become subservient to them.

Further, it is more than likely that when man's mind began to really grasp purpose from his technological consciousness, the first glimmerings of such consciousness would come via the symbolic route of ancestral, archetypal memories. Basically, purposive consciousness would first come through Iliadic man in such a way that it caused his ancestral memories to play psycho-dramas in his perceived reality, giving apparent outside authority to his actions.

Hence, the Ten Commandments came from God rather than man, and the Old Testament tells us quite clearly that 'there were giants in the Earth in those days.'

In Mesopotamia, civilization and, by implication, technology, came earlier than to the Greeks and Hebrews. It is therefore logical to say that Mesopotamian consciousness evolved earlier too. The Assyrian king, Tukulti-Ninurta I, had built, around 1230 BC, a stone altar with a king kneeling before an *empty* throne of his god. Human consciousness had made the gods redundant. Close-upness had filtered this no-longer-required information out of normal existence. And as if to show, without possible doubt, that the gods of the ancients were remembered historic characters rather than mere mythologies, in the nineteenth century the German archaeologist Heinrich Schliemann discovered Troy with nothing but the works of Homer to guide him.

Thus we have a possible answer to the enigma of how the gods gained prominence over ancient man's life and why we no longer normally see them today. They have been locked within our deep unconscious, experienced as archetypal images of an hereditary collective unconscious; locked away together with our no-longer-understood instinctual drives – themselves banished by our new-found technological consciousness.

But it leaves us with yet another enigma concerning magic. For if the gods were memories of people who once lived, they performed some amazing feats – not least flying through the air upon chariots, or even parting the Red Sea.

Biblical Miracles

O NE OF the powers attributed to magicians is the ability to affect reality in a physical way, such as making pots fly up chimneys without the use of hands. And the gods were said to have similar abilities.

Of course, many tales of godly demonstrations of this power can be discounted as the result of faulty observation or because they rely on a supernatural explanation for something that is now known to have a simple scientific explanation. For instance, consider possible alternative scenarios for many of the miracles described in the Old Testament.

The first truly spectacular miracle of the Old Testament is the destruction of Sodom and Gomorrah. God is said to have destroyed the cities because the inhabitants were 'great sinners'. 'Brimstone and fire' were rained down on them.

Sodom and Gomorrah are thought to be two of five cities close to the shore of the Dead Sea – Bab-edh-Dhra, Numeira, es-Safi, Feifah and Khanazir. These cities were destroyed around 2350 BC, and three of them show signs of destruction by fire. This is, of course, strong evidence to support the myth. But what really happened?

The Dead Sea lies in a rift valley, in an earthquake zone. So could the cities have been destroyed by an earthquake? One thing in abundance in the region is bitumen, and it is not inconceivable that it could ignite during an earthquake, causing 'brimstone and fire' to rain down. And although there is no definite evidence of an earthquake at this time, the fire damage is highly suggestive of it.

The story also speaks of Lot's wife turning round to watch the destruction as the Hebrews are 'deserting' the cities, and God turning her into a pillar of salt. The Dead Sea has a high salt concentration which, over the millennia, has caused numerous pillars of salt to rise. So we can envisage a situation where, running from an earthquake, a woman falls, possibly unconscious, and her husband looks back and, in his superstitious way, observes a pillar of salt standing where, a moment earlier, she had stood.

Alternative scenarios like these can be offered for other miraculous Biblical happenings.

The greatest set of miracles in the Old Testament revolves around Moses. Through Moses, Jehovah called down on Egypt the Ten Plagues, to convince the pharaoh that he must release the Hebrews. First, the Nile is turned into blood. This is followed by invasions of frogs, mosquitoes and flies. Then the cattle perish. There is an epidemic of boils on men and beasts. Severe hail falls. There is a plague of locusts. Darkness falls for three days so that no one can move. And, finally, all the first-born of Egypt die.

So what is to be made of the Ten Plagues?

First of all, the Nile can appear to turn into blood. But what is really happening is that it is polluted by the red soil washed down from the highlands of Ethiopia. This regularly happens between July and the following March. A particularly bad pollution would cause an abundance of frogs to leave the Nile in search of shelter. The brackish ponds left as the waters recede following their annual flooding at the time would be ideal breeding grounds for mosquitoes and flies. They, in turn, would pass anthrax to the cattle, and as anthrax can also be caught by men, they too would come out in sores, or boils.

Although rare, it is not unknown for the Nile region to suffer extreme weather conditions in January, usually resulting in downpours of hail. These are accompanied by strong winds, which can blow swarms of locusts into the area from the Sudan and Ethiopia, where they are a regular pest. If the winds become strong enough they can create a 'khamsin', a sandstorm so bad that it shuts out the light, which can last for days, severely restricting all movement.

The ancient Egyptians were totally dependent upon the Nile valley, and the coming together of Nile pollution and severe weather conditions would have resulted in starvation and deaths. And the ancient Egyptians considered the first-born to be the most important of their offspring. They would lament his passing the most. And, given the famine, is there any wonder they didn't mind getting rid of the Hebrews – so many extra mouths to feed?

But the famine passes and Egypt becomes strong again. Pyramids are left unfinished, and the Egyptians decide to get their slaves back. Rameses leads an army of chariots to recapture them. But, according to the Old Testament, Moses parts the Red Sea, allowing his people to walk safely to freedom, the waters then washing over the Egyptians, killing them.

First of all, the name 'Red Sea' could be a misunderstanding. The Hebrew term was *yam suph*, which translates as 'Reed Sea' or 'Sea of Marshes'. Before moving out into Sinai the Hebrews would have had to pass close to the region around Per Rameses, a region of sweetwater lagoons and papyrus swamps. The significance of this is that people travelling on foot with minimal possessions would have had little difficulty negotiating this region, whereas an army of chariots would immediately have become bogged down, eventually sinking into the mud.

Admittedly, this scenario is not as spectacular as the 'Red Sea' version, but, let's face it, short stories turn into taller ones even today.

The final truly earth-shattering miraculous happening of the Old Testament concerns the fall of Jericho. On the seventh day of marching round the city, Joshua ordered the trumpets to play and the walls came tumbling down. The city was then routed.

First of all, it is known that the city of Jericho did exist in very early times. The incident has been dated to about 1200 BC or to about 1400 BC. If we accept the later date, then archaeological evidence rules out the existence of high walls. But at the earlier time Jericho was a major centre. What is more, there is evidence to suggest that the city was destroyed about this time. But was it destroyed by trumpets?

The Old Testament gives us one very important fact. It tells us that a few days prior to coming upon Jericho, Joshua walked over the Jordan River 'on dry land'. How is this possible?

The River Jordan, like the Dead Sea, lies in an earthquake zone. And one peculiarity of an earthquake in this region is that it is often preceded by mudslides which dam the Jordan, as last happened in 1927. So it is highly likely that Jericho was, in fact, destroyed by an earthquake, and that the Old Testament story records the mudslide and the inevitable earthquake damage to Jericho's walls. The fact that Joshua's forces encircled the city and then waited indicates that they were conducting a siege. The earthquake was a most timely event – perhaps even an expected one. Joshua could have known that a mudslide was a precursor of an earthquake.

So we are left with the possibility that these biblical miracles resulted from natural phenomena. With Moses we have unfortunate weather patterns in Egypt followed by an ill-advised pursuit over marshy ground. And with Jericho as well as Sodom and Gomorrah, we have earthquakes which, to this day, are classed as acts of God. But does this suggest that the writers of the Old Testament were conning us?

No. We must simply remember that the Old Testament was written in the age of superstition, where everything that happened was inextricably linked with the supernatural. And, bearing in mind my words on an evolved consciousness, it could be argued that God was, in fact, with the people at the time, in the form of ancestral memories and voices heard in the head.

Stripped of superstition, even the greatest miracles can be seen in logical terms. Natural causes are not the only explanation. Hypnotically induced psycho-drama can also account for many seemingly supernatural phenomena.

A case in point is the researcher who was lucky enough to witness the fabled Indian rope trick. Throughout the incredible performance he took pictures with his camera, but when they were developed he was mystified to discover that neither rope nor boy had left the ground. It was nothing but a brilliant illusion.

But there remain, even today, well-researched cases of mind-matter interaction that hint strongly at magic – both controlled and uncontrolled. And none are more impressive than the many outbreaks of activity ascribed to poltergeists.

The Poltergeist

M RS H. WAS a single parent who lived in a council house in Enfield, North London, with her four children. However, in August 1977 a new occupant moved in with them. At a time when the family was experiencing psychological turmoil, they suddenly found themselves living with a poltergeist – and a poltergeist that stayed with the family for fourteen months.

One of the best-documented poltergeist outbreaks ever, its phenomena included rappings on the walls, spontaneous combustion, the movement of furniture, mysterious voices and even human levitation. One professional photographer actually caught a curtain twisting into a spiral on film and much of the voice phenomenon was recorded. In all, investigators gained testimony of strange happenings from over thirty witnesses, including social workers, reporters and the police.

Many critics of the case put the phenomena down to trickery on the part of the children – especially Janet, who was eleven when the phenomena began – but the principal investigators, Guy Lyon Playfair and Maurice Grosse, had a different story to tell in their book, *This House is Haunted*.

Playfair and Grosse – both seasoned members of the Society for Psychical Research – claimed success in communicating with the 'entity' by means of a code of raps. Further, a visiting medium confirmed that Janet was somehow a 'focus' for the spirit. At first claiming to be an occupant of the house thirty years previously, the entity eventually manifested a voice, claiming to be one Joe Watson. Later it claimed to be Bill Haylock, an occupant of a nearby graveyard. Eventually a Dutch clairvoyant was successful in easing the situation and the phenomena ceased.

Just as disconcerting as the Enfield case were the phenomena surrounding one Esther Cox, reported by Walter Hubbell in his book, *The Great Amherst Mystery*. In 1878, in Amherst, Nova Scotia, strange happenings began to occur shortly after seventeen-year-old Esther had been led, at gunpoint, into woods by her boyfriend, Bob MacNeal. He tried to rape her, but fled when they were disturbed. Soon afterwards rustling noises were heard in the Cox family house; later Esther's bedclothes began floating around the room, furniture moved and small fires broke out.

More frightening still was the physical effect on Esther. Her body inflated like a balloon; only after a bang like a thunder clap did she return to normal. Esther even received mysterious messages, written on the wall. Typical was, 'Esther, you are mine to kill.' The phenomena eventually ceased after Esther was imprisoned for arson after a barn burned down.

What are we to make of episodes like this? In other words, what is a poltergeist? The term is German for 'noisy spirit' and the poltergeist appears to be an unknown force that can throw this and that about the place, making a general paranormal nuisance of itself. Documented cases go back to the ninth century and encompass the globe. One of the earliest cases is recorded in the chronicle *Annales Fuldenses* of 858 AD. This concerned an 'evil spirit' which threw stones and made walls shake in a farmhouse at Bingen on the Rhine.

Many people mistake outbreaks of poltergeist activity for hauntings. But Harry Price graphically made the distinction in 1945:

> The poltergeist is mischievous, destructive, noisy, cruel, erratic, thievish, demonstrative, purposeless, cunning, unhelpful, malicious, audacious, teasing, ill-disposed, spiteful, ruthless, resourceful and vampiric. A ghost *haunts*; a poltergeist *infests*.

The poltergeist seems adaptable to technology, showing signs of being intelligently controlled. Consider an outbreak in a lawyer's office in Rosenheim, Germany, in 1967.

For many weeks drawers flew out of desks, light bulbs exploded, pictures rotated on the walls, fluid spurted out of photocopiers and a telephone ran up a large bill by continually ringing the speaking clock, apparently without human aid. Indeed, during one period, the speaking clock was continually rung so fast that a human being could not have dialled quickly enough.

Some forty persons witnessed the phenomena, including telephone engineers and physicists from the Max Planck Institute. No physical cause was ever discovered, so Germany's then leading parapsychologist, Dr Hans Bender, was called in. In no time at all, he associated the phenomena with a young clerk called Annemarie Schneider. Confirmation of her association with the poltergeist soon came. When she left the job, the phenomena ceased.

In the late 1970s, parapsychologists Alan Gauld and A.D. Cornell analysed a total of five hundred poltergeist infestations dating back to 1800 trying to find and classify the characteristics of the phenomenon. They discovered that 64 per cent of cases involved movement of small objects; 58

Carl Gustav Jung (1875–1961). Student of Freud and ground-breaking psychoanalyst, his identification of a 'collective racial unconscious' revolutionized our understanding of the paranormal. (*Mary Evans/Sigmund Freud Copyrights*)

Virginia Tighe became the centre of the reincarnation controversy after being hypnotically regressed by Morey Bernstein, manifesting the past life of Irishwoman Bridey Murphy. (*Associated Press*)

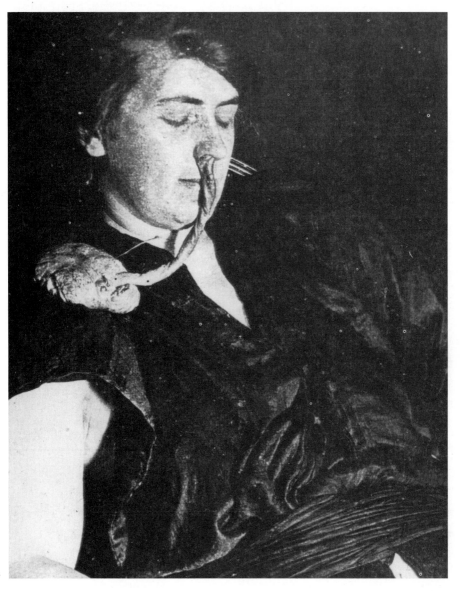

Mrs Mina Crandon, who became famous as 'Margery the Medium', issuing ectoplasm from her nose. Spirit guides were said to manifest from this strange substance. (*Mary Evans/Harry Price Coll., Univ. of London*)

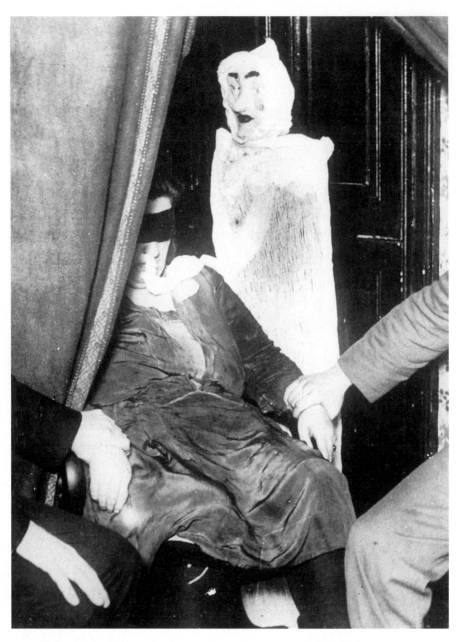

The medium Helen Duncan, pictured here with her spirit guide, Peggy, was prosecuted for fraud. It is easy to see why. Nevertheless, believers thought Peggy was genuine. (*Mary Evans/Harry Price Coll., Univ. of London*)

The medium Helena Blavatasky went on to found the Theosophical Society. She claimed she could communicate with the mahatmas, mankind's secret masters. (*Mary Evans Picture Library*)

Borley Rectory in Suffolk, made famous by the ghost hunter Harry Price, was for years dubbed the most haunted house in Britain. (*Mary Evans/ Peter Underwood*)

Is this a ghost in the library of Combermere Abbey? More logical explanations exist for the image of a legless man in the chair on the left of this photograph, taken by Sybell Corbet. (*Mary Evans/Society for Psychical Research*)

Were Stonehenge and other monoliths built on nodal points of strange earth energies? Many researchers believe so, and it is through such energies that ghosts are sometimes thought to appear. (*Michael J. Stead*)

Charlatan or magician? Aleister Crowley became the most controversial figure in Western occult practice, considering himself the Beast of the Apocalypse. (*Mary Evans/Harry Price Coll., Univ. of London*)

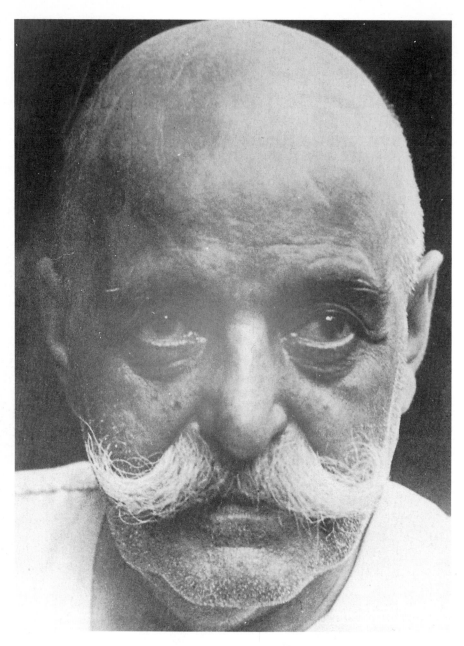

George Gurdjieff formed a system of occult philosophy far removed from the supernatural, hinting at the psychological and mind-based stimuli behind occult powers. (*Mary Evans/The Cutten Collection*)

(*Opposite*) D.D. Home was the ultimate nineteenth-century medium. His ability to levitate was well attested. According to Home, he was lifted by 'spirits'. (*Mary Evans Picture Library*)

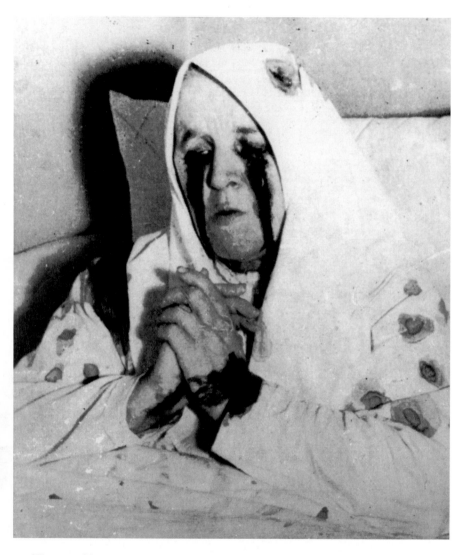

Therese Neumann was deeply religious and used to experience stigmata during Holy Week. Her stigmatism began following a traumatic experience. (*Mary Evans Picture Library*)

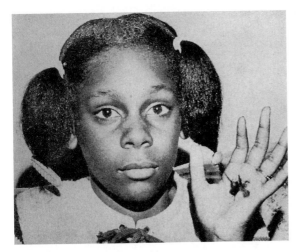

One of the youngest recorded stigmatics, Cloretta Robertson hints at the psychological basis of the phenomenon of bleeding from the palm, imitating church statuary. Crucifixion victims were nailed through the wrist.
(*Fortean Picture Library*)

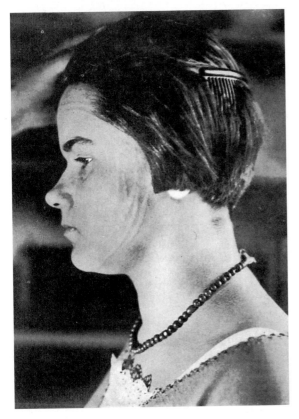

Eleonore Zugun pictured following a poltergeist 'attack'. Are these scratches evidence of angry spirits, self-mutilation or a variation of psychological stigmata?
(*Mary Evans Picture Library*)

J.B. Rhine popularized the term Extrasensory Perception and took psychic research into the laboratory. (*Mary Evans/Society for Psychical Research*)

Dowsing has been practised since the late Middle Ages. Here, a dowser is in search of metal in sixteenth-century Germany. (*Mary Evans Picture Library*)

St Benedict being escorted to heaven by angels. Research into the near-death experience is beginning to show that there may be reality behind such illustrations. (*Fortean Picture Library*)

Charlotte Moberly (left) and Eleanor Jourdain (right) had a strange experience at the Gardens of Versailles. Did they go back in time to the eighteenth century, or did they share a unique hallucination? (*Mary Evans/Society for Psychical Research*)

Many premonitions are said to surround the sinking of the *Titanic*. Did such premonitions really take place, or are they better understood in terms of human psychology? (*Mary Evans Picture Library*)

per cent were most active at night; 48 per cent involved raps or knockings; 36 per cent featured movement of large objects; 24 per cent lasted over one year; 16 per cent involved communication with an 'entity'; and 12 per cent involved the shutting and opening of doors and windows.

Many theories have been offered to account for poltergeist activity. F.W.H. Myers began the debate by pointing out, as Harry Price did later, the differences between the poltergeist and standard hauntings, which involve no physical effects. However, a fellow member of the Society for Psychical Research, Frank Podmore, injected some scepticism into the argument by noting that most outbreaks were faked – usually by stone-throwing children. A case from Windsor, Nova Scotia, in 1906 illustrates the possibilities.

A probate judge, Mr 'X', consulted researchers after experiencing a spate of strange happenings around the town. He had encountered the headless 'spirit' of a man, heard mysterious voices and often seen a barrel rolling about the town. Coins had been dropped in front of him as he went into shops, objects were thrown about in the local restaurant he used, and lamps threw out their bulbs in the barber's shop.

Researcher Hereward Carrington was despatched to investigate. He cleared up the mystery rather quickly. Workers in one factory had rigged up a chair to rock, speaking tubes had been erected, which accounted for the voices, townsfolk had practised and perfected the ability to throw objects without arm movement and an enterprising eight-year-old had rigged a contraption to make objects fly unaided. The whole town had conspired to play a series of practical jokes on the judge.

Another theory not involving the supernatural – the Geophysical Theory – was offered in 1955 by psychical researcher G.W. Lambert. Lambert ascribed poltergeist phenomena to water 'moving in an unsuspected sub-terranean stream underneath the building that is affected'.

A slightly variant example of Lambert's theory occurred in England in January 1979. The residents of the Mount Pleasant Estate in Wisbech, Cambridgeshire were becoming fearful of the vibrations, accompanied by rumbling noises that shook their homes sometimes so severely as to cause ornaments to fly off shelves. Mystifyingly, the bouts of shaking came at regular, short intervals throughout the evenings. However, this proved to be no poltergeist. The air-relief valves had failed in the local sewer system, which, as it approached overload, rumbled and shook. The regularity was the fault of the commercial breaks on television, when the toilets were in greatest use.

However, the Geophysical Theory received a severe blow in 1961. The scene was again England. Alan Gauld and A.D. Cornell borrowed a terraced house due for demolition in Cambridge. Placing a number of objects, and themselves, in the house, they attempted to re-create poltergeist activity with the help of a specially devised vibration machine and a 60-pound demolition hammer. They shook and banged the house until cracks appeared everywhere but, although a couple of objects fell, they were unable to reproduce any poltergeist effects.

The Geophysical Theory was, in effect, dead. So does this suggest that the poltergeist really is a spirit?

In the 1850s a Frenchman called Rivail became interested in the new religion of Spiritualism after witnessing the phenomenon of automatic writing. In 1860 he heard of a particularly violent poltergeist in Paris. Through a medium he learned that the disturbances were the work of a spirit. The poltergeist spirit was summoned, again through the medium, and told Rivail that he was a dead rag-and-bone man who was manifesting through a servant girl in the house. This experience was one of several that convinced Rivail that all poltergeist activity was the work of spirits and he later wrote *The Spirit's Book* under the pseudonym Allan Kardec.

Little did he know that through this he was to be creator of the religion of Spiritism, which still thrives in Brazil. As Spiritism gained prominence in Brazil, its beliefs amalgamated with local religions similar to voodoo.

Guy Lyon Playfair, co-investigator of our opening case in Enfield, went to Brazil in the 1960s to investigate poltergeist outbreaks and, in books such as his *The Flying Cow*, expressed his own belief in the spirit hypothesis. A later meeting between Playfair and Colin Wilson began to convince Wilson that Playfair might well be right. Of most interest was the initial appearance in many cases of inexplicable pools of water. This, apparently, was due to a 'spirit bubble', the first manifestation of the rising spirit.

Wilson became even more convinced after researching a most mysterious poltergeist known as the Black Monk of Pontefract.

It began on a September night in 1966. Most of the Pritchard family were on holiday, leaving only fifteen-year-old Philip and his grandmother at 30 East Drive, Pontefract, Yorkshire. Suddenly a film of white dust descended, covering everything, soon to be followed by the manifestation of a number of pools of water. Then a wardrobe hobbled out of its corner. However, by the time Philip's parents and twelve-year-old sister Diane returned, the phenomena had disappeared. Indeed, there was no more activity for two years. But then all hell broke loose.

Pots, pans, bedding and ornaments began to fly. Furniture moved. A carpet sweeper 'danced'. A roll of wallpaper reared up like a snake. Green foam poured out of taps. And the house began to shake violently from time to time, accompanied by loud, thunderous crashes.

A priest was called to exorcise the house. A candlestick floated before him. He advised there was 'something evil' in the house and left, advising the family to move. One day an Aunt Maude visited. She was a member of the Salvation Army and was convinced the children were playing tricks. To prove otherwise, the spirit levitated a pair of gloves in front of her. Shocked,

Aunt Maude told them to get away. One glove formed itself into a fist and shook itself at her. Aunt Maude began to sing 'Onward Christian Soldiers'. The gloves began to 'conduct' her, mockingly.

Many of the phenomena seemed to be directed at Diane. Several times she was thrown out of bed, and furniture seemed to attack her. One day a crucifix flew off the wall and struck her, leaving a red weal. But most terrifying was the time an 'entity' grabbed her and dragged her screaming up the stairs. Red fingermarks were later found on her neck.

But most disconcerting of all was the shadowy, black figure – the Black Monk – that materialized repeatedly shortly after Aunt Maude's visit. Described as a tall man in a long, black robe, the most graphic appearance was to Philip, who saw it standing behind a pane of frosted glass. Slowly, the Monk disappeared through the floor.

Colin Wilson concluded that the Black Monk of Pontefract, whose activities eventually stopped, was a spirit who had been waiting for the required energy to be present in the house. The energy in poltergeist cases tends to be provided by adolescents. Hence, the Monk appeared first when Philip was going through puberty, and again two years later when Diane was at this stage.

Previously, Wilson had accepted the most prevalent and convincing hypothesis for the poltergeist – that of the unconscious-mind school of thought. A Dr Alfred Winterstein was the first to put forward the unconscious-mind theory for the poltergeist in 1930. Then, in 1945, the Hungarian/American psychoanalyst Nandor Fodor added to this by stating, in *The Journal of Clinical Psychopathology*, that poltergeists were personality fragments.

This is interesting. How similar this sounds to multiple personality. According to Fodor and other researchers since, these personality fragments express themselves best in poltergeist activity whilst experiencing puberty or adolescence. This is the time when life makes little sense, when resentment and confusion can control the mind. Indeed, such an adolescent does seem to exist in most poltergeist infestations. Consider Philip and Diane in the Pontefract case, young Annemarie in the Rosenheim case, Esther in the Amherst case and young Janet at Enfield.

The adolescent is seen as the focus for poltergeist activity. Indeed, Fodor identified the 'focus' straight away when he decided to research the infamous Bell Witch.

The Bell Witch first struck the house of Tennessee farmer John Bell in 1817, when it caused scratching noises on the walls. After this, invisible hands began to pull bedclothes off beds, and human-sounding choking noises were heard. Then the poltergeist began throwing stones and moving various items of furniture.

Not satiated, it began to attack one of Bell's daughters, Betsy. It used to pull her hair and slap her, causing reddened cheeks after the assault. After about a year it developed a voice, uttering such phrases as: 'I can't stand the smell of a nigger.'

The attacks then moved to John Bell himself. His shoes were pulled off and he was struck on the jaw. Soon Bell developed violent convulsions and, after the poltergeist had told him that it would kill him, he fell into a stupor and died. Upon his death the poltergeist filled the house with shrieks of triumph.

Rather than associating such an infestation with a spirit, Fodor identified Betsy as a focus. He suggested that Betsy had been the subject of incestuous attacks by her father, John Bell. Such a victim expresses, first, disgust at herself (the poltergeist attacks her) and then anger at the perpetrator (the attacks move on to Bell).

So what is really happening during poltergeist infestations? Are they fraudulent? Are real spirits involved? Or is some unknown element of the mind at work?

Perhaps we can gain most mileage from looking at the focus. If it is the mind that is involved, how did Betsy manifest 'marks' after being 'slapped'? How did fingermarks appear on Diane's neck if no spirit hand had placed them there? How did Esther Cox blow up like a balloon? And in looking for answers to these initial questions we begin to understand just how easily mind can affect matter – in particular, the adolescent, hysterical mind.

Hysteria

A YOUNG WOMAN – attractive, delicate – overreacts to a stressful situation. A panic grows within her and she begins to scream. Her man – strong, dark, handsome – takes command of the situation. He slaps her and pulls her to him, to comfort, to protect. Her panic is gone. She has been saved from her madness.

This sort of sexist rubbish has been rightly banished to the dustbin of cultural history. Its last home was perhaps Hollywood – in many films the hero was strong and tough while the heroine looked pretty but collapsed into hysteria when the going got tough. But this stereotypical portrayal was no Hollywood creation. The insult to women goes back much much further.

The term 'hysteria' can be traced to the fourth century BC and the father of medicine, Hippocrates. It comes from *hystera*, which means womb. Hippocrates thought that only women could suffer from hysteria and that therefore it must have something to do with the female anatomy. As women had wombs, and men didn't, it was argued that hysteria resulted from the womb becoming detached and moving around the body. The difficulty in breathing during hysteria, which we now understand as a panic attack, was thought to be due to the womb being stuck in the throat.

You would think that such a ridiculous notion would be discarded when rational thought became prevalent during the Enlightenment. Not at all. In 1682 the English physician Thomas Sydenham, one of the founders of clinical medicine, suggested that men seemed to suffer hysteria too. He was virtually ignored – the idea was anathema to male-dominated society. Even when Freud reported to the Vienna Medical Society in 1886 his belief that hysterical symptoms could be experienced by both sexes, the idea was still not well received.

By this time, though, it was accepted that hysteria was not caused by a 'wandering womb'. There were two schools of thought about it. One thought that vapours released from the womb affected the brain – which was why it was only women who suffered attacks of 'the vapours'. The second put hysteria down to 'ovarian pressure' and cured it by surgical removal of the ovaries.

Today it is accepted that hysteria is a problem of both male and female, but the medical establishment is still suspicious of the illness, arguing that hysteria is due to the suggestible mind. The hysteric tends to play to an audience, thus providing the symptoms people expect to see.

Up until very recently the hysteric would simply be told, 'Pull yourself together.' Even today treatment for hysteria usually comes in the form of tranquillizers, which treat the effect while leaving the cause to fester.

Partly because of the attitude of the medical establishment, society at large is still unwilling to recognize hysteria in men. The stiff upper lip is the prevalent ideal of maleness and it denies male tendencies towards hysteria. Moreover, the initial symptoms of the hysterical personality – manipulative behaviour, shallow emotions, fickleness, flirtatiousness, lack of self-criticism and a tendency to overreact to situations in a dramatic way – have all been stereotyped as peculiarly feminine characteristics.

This attitude shows an incorrect understanding of hysteria. It distances an obvious form of neurosis from normal behaviour. Yet most of us, if we were honest, would have to admit that we suffer from one or more of these symptoms.

The more severe hysterical symptoms bite deeply into the mind-body relationship. As hysteria advances, its initial effects are amplified, leaving the sufferer paranoic, anxious and distressed, with feelings of frustration, helplessness and confusion. These are symptoms often manifested by teenagers, the processes of adolescence being very similar to those of hysteria, and can be viewed as a means of escape from an intolerable situation. But the most rational of persons can be affected following the sudden release of pent-up emotions. This is hysteria as we know it best – the sudden explosion of tears or anger, often leading to violence.

Prolonged hysteria, though, is much more ominous. It can seem to imitate physical illness. Well attested are cases of blindness, dumbness, deafness, tremors and paralysis – all just as crippling as their physical counterpart. Indeed, we usually refer to such ailments as psychosomatic illnesses.

The term 'psychosomatic' came to prominence at the beginning of the twentieth century when it was recognized that physical diseases could have a psychological origin. In an attempt to understand what was going on, the German psychoanalyst Georg Groddeck argued around 1923 that the body and mind were creations of a third entity which he called the 'It'. He argued that this third force shaped the physical characteristics of the body, as well as personality and emotion.

The Austrian psychoanalyst William Reich advanced this idea by proposing that all illness was the result of a form of bio-energy trapped behind an outer mask which we impose upon ourselves in order to appear normal within a basically authoritarian society.

Today, psychosomatic illness is just as misunderstood. No creditable theory exists to explain how the mind can affect the body – which it clearly does. The best idea on offer is that somehow our emotions cause the problem.

One obvious reason for the inability of the medical establishment to offer a credible theory is the simple fact that psychosomatic illness contradicts the existing view of mind and consciousness. As we saw earlier, mind is seen as a physical spin-off of brain chemistry. Hence it is impossible that psychological states could affect the body. Yet a growing science and therapeutic method are showing quite clearly the vast extent of psychological control over our physical state of health.

Our conscious mind has evolved to fulfil a single purpose. It is that part of the individual which relates to our external environment, allowing us to interact with society and our physical reality. It is not concerned with what goes on inside the body. If we had consciously to think about breathing or digestion concentration upon life would be impossible.

In order to achieve this state of mind, the body is equipped with two distinct processing systems. In order to control our movement and voluntary physical activities we have a central nervous system. We have a degree of conscious control over this – we decide to walk, for instance. The second system, the autonomic nervous system, is responsible for, among other things, breathing, digestion and hormonal activity.

To the medical establishment, it is impossible to exert conscious control over this second nervous system. It is outside the remit of conscious mentation. However, every time a male gains an erection because of a sexual thought he is consciously affecting the autonomic nervous system, as is a female who delays menstruation because of emotional turmoil.

Dogs are rather clever, too. In 1924, Ivan Pavlov, a Russian physiologist, showed that dogs could be conditioned to salivate on cue. In further experiments he even showed how they could be trained to control their blood flow. Later experiments by Neil Miller in New York showed that small electric shocks to the 'pleasure centres' of rats could condition them not only to salivate but to produce extra urine, speed up their heartbeats, increase their blood pressure and increase body heat in their ears.

Today, mind-body interaction of this kind is used on a daily basis by patients being treated by biofeedback. The method was devised in 1958 by Joe Kamiya, who used an EEG to show a subject when his brain was relaxed, thus teaching him how to recreate the relaxation by conscious control. Biofeedback uses a whole host of monitoring equipment to teach patients how to exert conscious control to cure themselves of all forms of physical disorder from high blood pressure to migraines.

Regardless of what the medical establishment says, hysteria and biofeedback have persistently shown that the mind *can* affect the body.

Stigmata

THERESE NEUMANN was from Konnersreuth in Bavaria. Born in 1898, by the age of twenty she was bedridden, blind and paralysed from hysteria after witnessing a fire on a neighbour's farm. In 1925 her hysterical symptoms left her after she had a number of religious visions. In 1926 she began, regularly every Friday, to bleed from either palm, feet or forehead and to weep tears of blood. The phenomenon continued to occur until her death in 1962, reaching an annual climax during Holy Week.

This is one of the better documented cases of stigmata – the manifestion of the bleeding wounds of Christ. The first stigmatic is thought to have been St Paul, who wrote, in Galatians: 'From henceforth let no man trouble me: for I bear in my body the marks of the Lord Jesus.'

Then there was the case of St Francis of Assisi. The son of a wealthy cloth merchant, Francis was a fun-loving, adventurous soul who enjoyed the good life. In 1202 he was taken prisoner in a war between Assisi and Perugia. Upon his release he became seriously ill, only recovering after great suffering. This illness changed his life. Suddenly he had an interest in the deplorable lot of the poor and later, in the church of San Damiano, he had a religious experience when Christ communicated with him.

By 1206 he had totally cut himself off from his previous connections, publicly stripping himself of his fine clothes and donning rags. By 1210 he was living a life of ascetic poverty, gaining approval for the founding of the Franciscan Order in 1224. Then, while praying on the slopes of Mount Alvernia, he had a vision of Christ's crucifixion, after which he began to bleed. The wounds of Christ stayed on his body until his death two years later. Even walking became difficult for him because the nails used in the crucifixion materialized too, making movement painful.

How real are stigmata? Dr A. Imbert Goubeyre, a French professor, published no fewer than 320 case histories of stigmata in 1894, and this seems to be simply the tip of the iceberg. In many cases, stigmata begin with the appearance of blood which can be wiped away, leaving no wound. Eventually the severity increases with wounds appearing on palms, feet, side and sometimes forehead. Up to one and a half pints of blood can be lost per day and in extreme cases the nails are clearly visible.

Perhaps the most famous stigmatic was Padre Pio who in 1968 was buried in San Giovanni Rotondo in southern Italy after bleeding from hands, feet and side for some fifty years. It began for him in 1918, when he was at prayer shortly after celebrating the feast of the stigmata of St Francis. Born into a peasant family, he became a member of the Capuchin brotherhood, many of whom heard his scream that fateful day. Running to his aid, they found he was bleeding from all five traditional places – wounds that would never close for the rest of his life.

One early member of the Society for Psychical Research rejected outright all evidence for stigmata. To Eric Dingwall, the mystery was easily explained. Looking at cases such as that of St Mary Magdalen de Pazzi, who was said to have become a stigmatic in 1585, he argued that the simple, devout faith of religious ascetics, combined with the masochistic deviancy that can develop from their life style, explained stigmata as simply the result of self-mutilation. This could clearly account for many stigmatics, including St Mary, who was known to punish herself, and her nuns, in a most sadistic manner, including beatings. But it fails to explain cases such as that of Cloretta Robertson.

Ten-year-old Cloretta, from Oakland, California, first manifested the stigmata in 1972. Cloretta was the first recorded black stigmatic, but what makes her unique is that she wasn't particularly religious. But she had seen, a week before the wounds appeared, a television film about the crucifixion.

The case of Cloretta Robertson does, of course, hint at a psychological cause for stigmata. With the deeply religious, asceticism somehow produces the effect; with others, such as Therese Neumann, hysteria seems to play a big part.

What is clear is that stigmatics do not reproduce the actual wounds suffered by Christ. First of all, it is impossible to crucify a person by nailing their palms. Body weight simply rips the hand free of the nail. Crucifixion victims appear to have been nailed through the wrist. The stigmatic seems simply to imitate church statuary, which is interesting when you consider that St Francis became a stigmatic at just the time when Jesus began to be represented in church statuary. Another problem concerns the differing shapes, sizes and severity of the wounds. If these are the true wounds of Christ, then we would expect consistency to prevail.

So it seems that stigmata are expressions of hysteria through religion; the stigmatic is suffering from a psychological disorder that manifests in body change.

Researcher Ian Wilson took much this line in his book *The Bleeding Mind*. He argued that the wounds of stigmata are self-induced by sufferers from stress who, to gain relief from their suffering, turn to prayer and contemplation. He further suggested that elements of multiple personality are exhibited in stigmata.

The psychological hypothesis is neatly illustrated by the case of Elizabeth K. Elizabeth was born in 1902 into a family with a history of neurosis. Disturbed as a child, she received further shock when her mother died when she was six. Intelligent and imaginative, as she advanced in years she began to suffer from shaking limbs and, eventually, periods of paralysis. In 1929 she attracted the interest of the psychiatrist Dr Albert Lechler, who employed her as a servant so that he could keep an eye on her. One thing he noticed was her tendency to imitate other people's illnesses.

During the Easter of 1932 Elizabeth – who was non-religious – saw a slide show depicting Christ's crucifixion, and shortly afterwards she began complaining of severe pains in her hands and feet. Dr Lechler began hypnotic sessions with Elizabeth, concentrating her attention on these pains. Under hypnosis she produced wounds on her hands and feet and cried bloodstained tears.

Stigmata as a psychological disorder associated with hysteria becomes a valid explanation in the light of such cases. And manifestations much like stigmata, but with no religious associations, perhaps strengthen the case.

Professor Oscar Ratnoff of Cleveland, Ohio, and his team have documented over sixty cases of bodily changes associated with emotional distress. One patient began oozing blood from hair follicles on the thigh, though there was no sign of a wound. But the Hungarian poltergeist focus Eleonore Zugun must surely rate as one of the most impressive non-religious stigmatics. At various times during the 1920s her skin exhibited huge red weals, bite marks and swellings in the shape of letters on her body.

We can, of course, easily challenge all this evidence on many grounds, not the least of which is the sloppy scientific procedures used in the early days of psychoanalysis.

But another example, described in the *British Medical Journal* of 23 August 1952, is not so easy to discount.

A teenager who suffered from ichthyosis – a condition in which the skin becomes rough, scaly and evil-smelling – had been twice operated on to ease his condition, but without success. Then he became the patient of a young doctor, A.A. Mason, who had an interest in hypnosis. In February 1951 Dr Mason began a number of hypnotic sessions at each of which he 'suggested' that the layer of skin should fall off one part of the body. Success rates varied with the part of the body, but fell between 50 per cent and 95 per cent.

This doesn't seem all that spectacular – after all, it has long been known that hypnosis can cure skin conditions such as rashes and warts – but ichthyosis is not psychologically based or slight, but a deep-seated, con-genital illness. What Dr Mason achieved could be compared to wishing away a physical scar.

In earlier times such a success would have been attributed to a miracle. Today we know that the answer to Mason's success must lie somewhere within the phenomenon of hypnosis.

Hypnosis

IN TODAY's heady world of stage hypnotism, the practice of hypnosis has been severely degraded in the eyes of the public. We see it as a 'fun' phenomenon and our attitude tends to suppress the important psychological and, indeed, philosophical importance of the mystery.

The word 'hypnosis' comes from Hypnos, the Greek god of sleep. The hypnotic trance is an induced altered state of consciousness, during which the subject is rendered passive and open to suggestions made by the hypnotist. The trance is induced by repetitive stimulus provided by rhythm, colours, movement or sound.

Ninety per cent of people are thought to be open to hypnosis, regardless of age, sex or level of intelligence, although only about four per cent of the population are ideal subjects, able to reach the deep trances where most phenomena associated with hypnosis manifest. Analysis indicates that these tend to be fantasy prone in the first place, and usually enjoy reading novels and escaping into a good story.

The eighteenth-century Viennese physician Franz Mesmer is often thought of as the discoverer of hypnosis, but this is untrue. Mesmer devised the concept of 'animal magnetism' which became known as mesmerism. Animal magnetism was a force that permeated the universe, like a fluid, and an imbalance of it within the body led, thought Mesmer, to illness. By channelling the fluid through himself to the patient by way of laying on of hands, staring, or with a form of wand, Mesmer believed he could regulate the inner balance, providing a cure.

Whilst some of Mesmer's patients would undoubtedly have *become* hypnotized, mesmerism was a means of manipulating an apparent universal force, and not a psychological discipline. However, one of Mesmer's students, the Marquis de Puysegur, is credited with offering the first account of a definite hypnotic trance, achieved by him when he made 'mesmeric passes' over the body of a young shepherd called Victor Race. Victor fell into a trance under which the Marquis could give instructions. Upon waking, Victor could remember nothing.

Although mesmerism was discredited in mainland Europe after a royal commission in France had denounced Mesmer as an imposter, a professor of medicine at University College, London, John Elliotson, became interested in the subject. He was the first serious academic to consider it and he became convinced of its value in medicine. When, though, he delivered a lecture on mesmerism to a silent audience at London's Royal College of Physicians, the medical journal the *Lancet* dubbed him a professional pariah who would strike a blow against medicine. In the end he had to resign his professorship. However, a contemporary of Elliotson's was more successful.

James Braid, a surgeon and physician from Manchester in the northwest of England, also took an interest in mesmerism, but from the start rejected any such force as animal magnetism. It was he who, in 1842, devised the word hypnotism. He saw the trance as a purely psychological phenomenon and used it in a variety of medical treatments, such as speech therapy following strokes. He explained the trance-state as a re-direction of the patient's consciousness to the hypnotist, achieved by tiring the subject to the point of fatigue through repetitive stimuli. Any cures, thought Braid, were the result of the lessening of anxiety in the patient through hypnotism.

However, the first truly phenomenal spin-off of hypnosis came through the work, in India, of the Scotsman James Esdaile. During the mid-nineteenth century, he reported performing over three hundred major operations using hypnosis in which the patients suffered no pain. His operations included limb amputation.

Partly because of Braid's writings on hypnotism, there was a huge revival of hypnosis towards the end of the nineteenth century. But this was not so much a medical revival. Hypnosis became the central tool of the growing practice of psychotherapy, especially after the French neurologist Jean-Martin Charcot had endorsed its use in the treatment of hysteria.

A whole host of therapists turned to hypnosis, and it was during this period that the true strangeness of the phenomenon showed itself. There were graphic accounts of hallucinations, heightened memory recall and post-hypnotic suggestion, where the subjects could be instructed to behave in odd ways when they 'awoke'. However, Freud became a critic of the widespread use of hypnosis. He argued that hypnosis was a fascinating phenomenon but an inadequate tool. It cured the symptoms of mental disorder but didn't allow the therapist to dig down to the actual causes.

Twentieth-century experiments in hypnosis have tended to be inconclusive, but even today academics have to admit that uncanny abilities can be exhibited during trance. Indeed, today we can recognize three degrees of intensity for hypnosis, each of which has its particular characteristics.

In light hypnosis, voluntary muscles can be affected but there is no loss of consciousness and no amnesia.

In deep hypnosis, sometimes called the cataleptic state, the subject is rendered unconscious, voluntary muscles are affected, sometimes causing an increase in strength, and sensory systems seem to break down.

In the somnambulistic state, extremely deep trance is achieved. In this stage the openness to suggestion has cured symptoms of hysterical blindness and paralysis. Operations have been carried out with no visible discomfort. Subjects have been exposed to sharp pins and naked flames without the slightest effect, and leaving no marks or inflammation. And finally, hallucination and immense memory recall have been achieved.

Interestingly, the three stages of hypnosis are mirrored by the three degrees of severity of the epileptic fit, an intermittent disorder of the central nervous system due to the sudden discharge of electrical impulses in the brain. In psycho-motor seizure the effects of epilepsy are slight, causing no real loss of consciousness, but having minor effects on voluntary muscles. In petit mal the sufferer experiences momentary unconsciousness, loss of sensory systems and slight twitching of face and limbs. And in grand mal we have deep unconsciousness followed by confused behaviour. However, during unconsciousness the sufferer produces extreme convulsions with erratically twitching limbs.

Some researchers have speculatively allied such behaviour with the characteristics of the poltergeist. And I certainly feel there is advantage in comparing the anarchy produced in the brain with the poltergeist phenomenon. But such ideas fail to show how an effect within the body can be transferred outside the body. However, there is strong evidence that the hypnotic trance does involve connection with an 'outside' influence.

The successful hypnotic trance requires two essential elements. First of all, the patient must be predisposed to being hypnotized, believing that the outcome will be successful. Second, the patient must achieve a good rapport with the hypnotist. If the two are not in tune trance is difficult to achieve. Hence, it could be argued that fundamental to the successful trance is the transference of the authority of the hypnotist into the mind of the patient.

Such an idea is not liked by academe, for it hints of an invasion into the self of one individual by another. Yet if we return to the case of Dr Mason and his curing of the boy with ichthyosis, we must bring into the discussion a vital fact. Dr Mason didn't know that the disease was congenital. He thought it was more of a psychological nature. In a real sense, it can be argued that his success was due to his belief that hypnosis would work – a belief that was transferred to the patient.

This apparent transference from the mind of the hypnotist to the subject occurs throughout the practice of hypnosis. For instance, past-life regression is far more likely to be achieved if the hypnotist believes it exists. The recent controversy about false memory syndrome – where repressed memories of child abuse surface during hypnosis – is principally associated with therapists who believe child abuse is rampant. Basically, the odds for finding evidence of a phenomenon increase in line with the therapist's belief in the phenomenon.

This all suggests a real possibility of a form of mind invasion going on during hypnosis, hinting at the ability of a mind to infiltrate from outside the individual's brain. So could an understanding of the poltergeist come from this line of thought?

In the 1960s, William Roll, director of the Psychical Research Foundation in Durham, North Carolina, studied over a hundred poltergeist outbreaks. He concentrated on the psychology of the focus and concluded that poltergeist outbreaks are due to psychological disfunction in the focus. Indeed, he put them down to an uncontrolled aspect of psychokinesis – 'recurrent spontaneous psychokinesis'. Roll opened up poltergeist research into a new dimension.

Psychokinesis

IN AUGUST 1971 a twenty-four-year old Israeli called Uri Geller was performing in a disco in Jaffa. His repertoire included bending keys by stroking them and mending broken watches by looking at them. In the audience was psychical researcher Andrija Puharich, who immediately began researching Geller's powers (pp. 54–5). Geller told him that he had first discovered his talent as a young boy.

Geller soon began his incredible career as a superstar by travelling to Germany, where, among other things, he is said to have stopped a cable car in mid-air. Going from there to America, where he was tested by the researchers Targ and Puthoff, he scored exceptionally high in ESP experiments. However, when it came to the metal-bending talents for which he is most famous, the cameras set to record the action always experienced technical problems.

A magician, James 'the Amazing' Randi, added to Geller's problems by inviting him to perform in front of reporters from *Time Magazine*. Geller did so, and the subsequent article severely condemned him, Randi claiming to be able to do all Geller's stunts by trickery.

Geller went to England and, in November 1973, appeared on a television show. He was an immediate success and later letters showed that he had caused cutlery to bend and broken clocks to work in hundreds of homes throughout the country.

No one in the history of the paranormal has caused such a stir as Uri Geller. No true understanding of the subject can be made without taking him into account. Some people have complete faith in him, while others are adamant that he is a fraud. I simply don't know. All I can say is that his sudden appearance in a televisual world, and the exceptionally high profile he created, hyped up with so much showmanship, was guaranteed to make him suspect in many minds, whether he is genuine or not. Whether this is his fault, or the fault of the people who advised him is open to question. But he is destined, due to such a profile, to be treated with more than a little suspicion, particularly in a field where people shout 'Fraud!' before even attempting to get to grips with the subject. However, we can grasp at indications of the state of mind of psychic superstars such as Geller by looking at a phenomenon closely related to metal bending – levitation.

The inexplicable floating into the air of objects and people without physical aid, levitation has a long history of association with mystics, mediums and poltergeist activity. One of the first documented cases involved Simon Magus who, during his first-century AD magical duel with Peter, levitated to the top of the Roman forum. Peter prayed for assistance and Simon fell headlong to his death.

Levitation's association with Christianity is close. In the sixteenth century, St Teresa of Avila could levitate spontaneously during deep prayer. She once levitated over a foot above the ground for half an hour, the experience disturbing her deeply.

Perhaps the most famous Christian levitator was St Joseph of Copertino, a seventeenth-century monk said to be of feeble mind. Born of a peasant family at Apulia, Italy, he spent his early years trying to reach religious ecstasy by self-flagellation, going on to devote his life to prayer. At the age of twenty-two he became a monk and surprised his brothers one morning during mass by floating into the air and landing on the altar, burning himself on the candles. He spent the last thirty years of his life banned from public services because he so greatly embarrassed his brother monks. Witnesses to his levitations included two cardinals and Pope Urban VIII. A fellow monk saw Joseph, walking in the monastery garden, take to the air and fly into an olive tree. Then he was unable to get down until the monks fetched him a ladder. As the levitations were obviously the work of God, Joseph was canonized.

As Spiritualism rocketed to fame in the nineteenth century, Daniel Dunglas Home became perhaps the world's most renowned levitator. His most famous levitation was in 1868 when, in London, he was seen to levitate out of a third-storey window and back into the building through an open window in an adjoining room. Another medium, Amedee Zuccarini, was photographed while levitating nearly two feet above a table.

Eastern mysticism has its fair share of levitators too. The thirteenth-century Tibetan yogi Milarepa used to sleep, eat and even walk in the air while levitating.

These mediums and mystics share a great deal with Geller. They had such a complete conviction in what was happening to them that they rarely questioned the forces involved. St Joseph had, as did most stigmatics, total religious belief. Home had a similar faith in the existence of spirit entities, which he claimed to have seen since childhood. They also tended to be naive. They shut themselves off from normal life and developed complete emotional trust in their abilities. Home never asked for money for his performances. He only asked for a bed and a meal.

Many occult adepts shared a similar trait. Often they were accused of being charlatans not so much because of their activities but because of their general attitude towards life. They tended to class it as unimportant. Social niceties and living by the rules demanded by society were alien to such people.

But why did they act in this manner, as if inviting claims of charlatanism? Perhaps because of their inability properly to concentrate on life. As I pointed out earlier, those who, in pre-history, had access to pre-technological consciousness would be flooded by so much information about the world in which they lived that concentration would be a near impossibility. Hence, we can perhaps identify, in adepts, mediums and psychic superstars, personality traits indicative of people who have access to the wider consciousness through which the paranormal seems to manifest itself.

The phenomenon demonstrated by such skills as levitation and metal bending is psychokinesis, or PK – the ability of the mind to directly affect matter without apparent physical cause. Of course, we can study Geller as much as we like, in the same way as previous scientists such as Sir William Crookes studied Home, and never will even a bit of evidence surface of a scientifically verifiable nature. Performances can never be 'controlled' to the satisfaction of today's scientists. So to test the feasibility of such skills as metal bending, we have to divert to the laboratory.

Professor John Hasted of Birkbeck College, London, carried out such experimentation. With the assistance of various metal benders – usually children – and with the aid of strategically placed electronic strain gauges, Hasted has recorded signals of possible PK being focused on metal objects. Electronic anomalies and physical vibrations have been ruled out as causing the effects, and fraud is virtually impossible in these cases. But this is only the beginning of the story. Hasted has noticed that some metal benders actually change the structure of the metal itself: 'It was as though the bent part of the spoon was as soft as chewing gum.'

The French investigators Crussard and Bouvaist were funded by a metals company; they used hallmarked metal objects, tested microhardness before and after experiments, and analysed the chemical composition of the metals. So this is not a stage show, but well-documented scientific analysis. And their tests showed local hardening in the metals. Hasted, in similar experiments, spoke of properties of hardness similar to 'a strip exposed to crushing by a weight of five tons'. What is more, the pattern of hardening and strain was not consistent with external forces, but with internal metal stress.

Metal bending is, of course, just one area of research into PK effects. Gaining a thirst for understanding of the phenomenon following the PK effects produced by physical mediums, researchers soon descended into the laboratory or environments where 'controlled' experiments could be undertaken. Their work has evolved into two distinct areas of research – macro- and micro-PK experimentation. Macro PK is an 'observable' PK effect upon an object. Micro PK is a subtle effect measurable only against the laws of chance. Any deviation from a chance outcome provides a statistical inclination towards a micro-PK effect.

The first researcher to search for micro PK in the laboratory was J.B. Rhine, working at Duke University, North Carolina. In 1934 Rhine began a statistical analysis to test the claims of a gambler who said he could influence dice to land on specific numbers or combinations of numbers. Early results appeared to show that the gambler was getting results better than chance, suggesting a PK influence upon the dice. But the success soon fizzled out.

Rhine wondered why the effect should disappear. However, his assistant, Betty Humphreys, pointed out that success seemed to be achieved early in a particular experiment, but declined towards the end. Publishing his findings in 1943, Rhine noted this 'decline effect', hinting that micro PK was being manifested, but its effect depended upon the state of mind of the subject. If he became tired or bored, the effect soon disappeared.

Rhine's methods came in for much ridicule, particularly concerning his inability to guarantee that the dice obeyed the laws of chance. Rhine was trying to gain statistical evidence of micro-PK effects from an experimental model that could not be proved to be perfectly following chance probabilities. The PK effect manifested could be seen as a bias within the balance of the dice themselves, cancelling out the PK effect.

This problem was overcome by American physicist Helmut Schmidt in the late 1960s. He asked volunteers to exert mental pressure on coins, to test whether the fall of a coin – heads or tails – could be affected by micro PK. In his experiments he used an electronic coin flipper controlled by the random decay of radioactive particles. This removed the weakness in Rhine's experiments, the radioactive decay being a truly random event, perfectly in line with the laws of chance. Again a small statistical bias in favour of micro PK was recorded, leading Schmidt to develop the random-event generator, in which subjects tried to influence the radioactive decay itself.

Today, one of the leading micro-PK researchers is the rocket-propulsion scientist Robert Jahn, working from the basement of the engineering department of Princeton University. In the Princeton Engineering Anomalies Research Laboratory, or PEAR, Jahn has brought together a small team who work with a whole myriad of ingenious devices to record micro PK. His main weapon is an electrical diode which produces random white noise. Devising the most stringent safety mechanisms to check against fraud, fault and deviations from randomness, Jahn has been running his diode for fourteen years.

The diode produces, one thousand times per second, bursts of white noise. Each burst has either a negative or a positive value. According to the laws of chance, the ratio should be fifty-fifty. Any significant variation from this mean would hint at micro PK. Over the fourteen years up to 1993 Jahn has run fourteen million trials with one hundred subjects and has consistently produced a difference from chance equal to one tenth of one per cent. This is, of course, tiny. But the consistency of the effect adds up to a one in five thousand chance – a significant statistical anomaly.

With such a finding, it would, of course, be assumed that Jahn is hailed as a great scientific trailblazer at Princeton University. But, sadly, he is not. When he went public with his research in 1986 the authorities were horrified and Jahn was demoted.

The behaviour of the Princeton authorities symbolizes the problem of research into micro PK. Nothing has changed since Rhine except the degree of sophistication of the testing. For some sixty years PK has been routinely measured and just as routinely condemned. The tests have shown up undeniable statistical anomalies, but the anomalies are not significant enough to be noticed by the academic establishment. Because no definite theory exists by which the anomaly can be measured, the vast majority of scientists are happy to turn the other way.

The only way this stand-off could possibly be altered would be if a much more significant PK effect was recorded. But because of its very nature, micro PK will go on producing consistently small effects. In other words, micro-PK research is a dead end, and will remain so until such time that a theory is formulated or more significant results are produced which academe cannot ignore. And the most likely way for such evidence to surface is in the research on macro PK.

Macro PK, like metal bending, has produced its psychic superstars. In 1968 Nina Kulagina from Leningrad came to the notice of the West because of her ability to levitate small objects. Equally puzzling was New York artist Ingo Swann, who could affect the magnetic field of a magnetometer. However, such feats suffered from the Geller phenomenon, in that no suitable controls could be put in place to satisfy the scientific community. Nor could the scientist's requirement for repeatable experimentation be met – results even outside the laboratory were haphazard. However, a significant move in the right direction began to be made in the early 1960s.

In October 1961 Professor John G. Neihardt set up the Society for Research into Rapport and Telekinesis (SORRAT) in Rollo, Missouri. The society, with a membership of just over a dozen, simply sat in a room on a regular basis, chatting happily, but with the intention of producing PK. One member, Joseph Mangini, developed a trance-like ability. After a while, the meetings began to produce rapping phenomena. By 1965, after several years of intense dedication, they managed to levitate a small oak table. Gaining confidence from this, they were soon able to levitate a table weighing some thirty-seven kilograms (eighty-two pounds).

Eventually the PK specialist William Cox became involved with SORRAT. He devised a large box with a glass top, which became known as the mini-lab, constructed in such a way that it could not be opened without breaking seals. Various objects were placed inside, and the bottom covered with dried coffee grounds. The box was placed in SORRAT's meeting place. Regularly the coffee grounds were found to be disturbed by the inexplicable movement of objects within the box. During another experiment a stylus, together with a piece of carbon paper, was placed inside the box and the SORRAT members were instructed to try and make it write. Several times the stylus pressed on the carbon, leaving carbon images on the floor of the box. At other times, a pack of cards sorted itself into suits and two solid leather rings linked and unlinked.

These last two effects were captured on film, but when it was shown to researchers in Britain in the early 1980s it was viewed with derision, and SORRAT were labelled as possible fraudsters. However, Julian Isaacs of Aston University, Birmingham, took up the challenge with his own mini-labs, placing them in the homes of known psychics. Again, PK effects were noted but his work was curtailed when he left to live in the United States.

Before Isaacs, Britain's foremost investigator of the effects of macro PK had been Kenneth Batcheldor, a clinical psychologist from Devon. Working from his own living room with friends and neighbours, he experimented with table-tipping. Of course, the slack procedures used by Batcheldor, such as attempting PK in dark rooms, meant that his work could not earn scientific credibility. But with the work of Batcheldor, Neihardt and Cox, certain factors became clear concerning macro PK.

First of all, a good, jovial state of mind was required before PK was achievable. Second, a conviction that PK was achievable was of supreme importance in producing it. And third, when PK was achieved, many group members formed the opinion that a specific entity, or 'agent' had been released, as if they had created a form of poltergeist. During the early 1970s Dr A.R.G. Owen and his wife, Iris – members of the Toronto Society for Psychical Research – decided to test these ideas in Canada by attempting to communicate with an imaginary ghost.

They formed a group to create their ghost. One member wrote its biography; another drew its picture. 'Philip' was a seventeenth-century English aristocrat. He had a mistress who was burnt as a witch and he had a distinguished military career during the English Civil War. He finally committed suicide in 1654, aged thirty.

Then what became known as the Philip Experiment began. Satisfied with their creation, and convincing themselves that Philip existed, the group began to meet in a light-hearted fashion in order to communicate with him. Sat around a table in a typical seance mode, they had little luck at first. But eventually they produced raps. Employing the usual 'yes' and 'no' code, they confirmed that it was Philip they were talking to. However, shortly afterwards, the table they were sitting round began to manifest PK. It jumped up and down in time with the songs they would sometimes sing and once even chased Dr Owen out of the room. It became obvious that the table had *become* Philip. In 1974, table-Philip and the group appeared on Toronto City Television. Table-Philip walked up three steps to the stage.

SORRAT, the mini-labs and the Philip Experiment are the high points of macro-PK research. But, as with micro PK, the effects have been ignored by science. The principal reason for this is the possibilities of fraud within such loose experimental conditions. So in what direction should PK research go in order to provide the definitive proof that is required?

One point that seems to emerge from SORRAT and the Philip Experiment is that PK effects which are slight in an individual are amplified by a grouping. Hence, it seems to me that if the conditions of a macro-PK experiment such as SORRAT could be replicated with a grouping before a random-event generator under strict laboratory conditions, the statistical anomaly of micro PK could be enhanced. Perhaps Robert Jahn should be placing more chairs in front of his electrical diode, inviting a group to concentrate on a task presently undertaken by an individual.

But what about a theory by which PK effects can be measured and understood? No such theory exists. But it is increasingly becoming clear that the answer to this question lies within the very foundations of what we term reality.

The Holographic Universe

W E LIVE in a material world. We strive to own an expensive house and drive a luxurious car. In work we labour to receive financial reward, climbing up the material ladder of success. We live like this because we feel the world is material. We can stamp on a hard earth. We can knock on a hard door. In summer we feel the heat of an obviously physical sun. But if science can tell us anything about reality, it is that the material world is an illusion – a false existence.

Science tells us that we have three known levels of existence. If you look in the mirror, you see yourself – a particular mass of flesh and bone. If you look at yourself through a microscope, you see a different you – a you of molecules, genes and cells. But you also exist on a third level – as the electrical pattern that makes up your subatomic structure. Basically we are all reducible to particles, to universal stardust – and stardust which is far older than you. These particles were first cooked in stars, released as the stars died in supernova. And this world of existence is very strange indeed.

To see just how strange, look at the hologram, which is essentially a descent into the interactiveness of particles.

Holography was invented by Dennis Gabor, a Hungarian-born British electrical engineer, in 1948, but didn't come into practical use until the 1960s, with the development of laser technology. A hologram is a three-dimensional image created by scattering light from a reference object and interfacing it with light from a reference point, both beams hitting a photographic plate simultaneously. Both these beams should come from the same light source. As the two beams are coherent, they form an interference pattern which is recorded on the plate, and produces the hologram.

Light is, itself, an electric field, similar, in terms of physics, to the electric field which creates our bodies. Therefore, by use of lasers, holography becomes a reaction with subatomic structures.

One particular quirk of the hologram is that if part of the information which creates the hologram is destroyed – by, for instance, tearing off a piece of the reference image or photograph – the *whole* information of the source is retained and, as if by magic, the hologram remains whole, the only effect being a slight decrease in the intensity of the image. There is only one credible and acceptable scientific answer to this enigma so far, which is that, in the subatomic field, the part retains the information – the blueprint – of the whole.

This idea suggests that, at our subatomic level, we are made up of information connecting every part of us to every other part. We have an electrical life force – a scientific astral body, as it were. And this further suggests that our widening of consciousness in an altered state of consciousness is a connection with this force – we become interactive with it, at least on a mind level and perhaps on a physical level too.

Many life forms – certain reptiles in particular – share the whole-information peculiarities of the hologram. They have the ability to grow a new limb if the original is cut off. Earthworms are even more spectacular. Cut an earthworm in half and it will form into two earthworms. As with the hologram, the destruction of part of the whole does not destroy the information required to reproduce the whole.

We noted earlier that the frog appears to have a much reduced consciousness. In the light of the above information, this could well be because its close-upness is not generally reduced, but is overly expansive, in that it reacts within an information universe with too much information intake to allow it to concentrate on anything but pure survival requirements. Going back to the earthworm, we could argue that it senses its ability to recreate its form because it has access to a wider picture of its form from the information universe. Basically, it is our physical complexity that has required close-upness to allow us to survive, hence taking away from us, in normal consciousness, the ability to react within the information universe.

Thus, as the frog could well react within the information universe of its perception in a physical way, we, too, could well physically react within the wider information available to us in an altered state of consciousness. Basically, we could become as intelligent as a dolphin, which appears to navigate by sensing and physically reacting within the electromagnetic field.

And here lies a possible answer to the poltergeist and, by implication, magic and PK. In fact, science tells us as much, if scientists would only admit it.

Quantum Theory

NINETEENTH-CENTURY scientists believed that atoms were hard, solid substances like billiard balls. To them the universe was a mechanistic, Newtonian machine, unchanging and predictable. This grounded universal laws in a simple structure, unaffected by man, the supernatural, or anything else. Then, in 1897, Joseph John Thomson, an English physicist, discovered the electron – a subatomic particle of negative charge. Shortly afterwards a New Zealand-born physicist working in Britain, Ernest Rutherford, described the atom as a nucleus orbited by electrons. Later he discovered the proton. Another Briton, James Chadwick identified the neutron, for which he won the Nobel Prize for Physics in 1935.

An atom was now seen to consist of electrons orbiting a nucleus, which itself consisted of positively charged protons and electrically neutral neutrons. If you magnified the atom to the size of earth, electrons would be the size of an average bungalow and the nucleus the size of a cathedral.

Understanding of the atom led Enrico Fermi, an Italian-born nuclear physicist – who later built, in the United States, the world's first atomic reactor – to create artificial radioactivity through neutron bombardment. The age of nuclear power was with us.

But early in the understanding of subatomic construction, a major problem surfaced. Under observation, particles were sometimes seen as waves. This was impossible. Particles and waves were totally different things.

At the turn of the century a German physicist, Max Planck, had observed that hot bodies gave off energy, not in a continuous manner, but in packets, or quantities – hence the term 'quantum'. Following up this work, a French polymath, Prince Louis-Victor de Broglie, came to the conclusion that particles could interfere with each other, forming out-of-phrase waves which produced interference patterns.

The enigma was explained. But, in the process, Newtonian physics and the old theory of waves of energy came crashing down. Waves, which appeared such predictable things, just did not exist in the way we assumed. With the very small, such as subatomic structuring, there was no such thing as predictability. The way we perceived the universe as working was wrong. Man suddenly found he had made the 'quantum leap' from a mechanical universe to something else. But to what?

In the mid-1920s a German theoretical physicist, Werner Heisenberg, formulated his 'uncertainty principle'. He showed that particles could be waves or particles depending on what equipment you used to observe them. If you looked for particles, you would observe them. If you looked for waves, you would find them too. But you could never find both at once. As Sir William Bragg, a distinguished British physicist from an older school, joked: 'Electrons seem to be waves on Mondays, Wednesdays and Fridays, and particles on Tuesdays, Thursdays and Saturdays.' The great Danish physicist, Niels Bohr, who later worked in America on the development of the atom bomb, formulated the principle of complementarity to explain the difficulty:

> The concept of complementarity is meant to describe a situation in which we can look at one and the same event through two different frames of reference. These two frames mutually exclude each other, and only the juxtaposition of these contradictory frames provides an exhaustive view of the appearances of the phenomena.

In other words, given two materialistic views of reality, we must compare the two to decide, ourselves, where true reality resides.

This seems incredible, especially when the idea itself comes from observational science. But not when you understand just what is being observed. For instance, Heisenberg also noted that you could never know both the position and the momentum of a particle. Further, to observe either, you have to shine light on to the particle. In fact you don't even observe the particle. It is too small to be seen. What you observe is the outcome of the observation. But even this is not, exactly, true.

Light itself consists of particles. Therefore, by the very act of lighting a particle in order to observe it, you are bombarding it with particles. Hence, by observing, you are directly affecting the state of the particle. It is rather like two cars colliding. The result of this is that, in observing a particle, you see the result of the observation, and not the true state of the particle.

However, in this Alice-in-Wonderland world of quantum mechanics, it is even wrong to state that this collision between particles is similar to the collision between two cars.

Let us swap the cars for balls.

When two balls collide, they shoot off in a specific direction. However, observation of an electron's orbit around a nucleus tells a different story. One minute it appears to be in one orbit, and the next it fools you by being in a different one. This unpredictability of the movement of electrons has led to a somewhat unorthodox theory.

Basically, when two particles collide – as happens millions of times every second in your fingernail – the mathematics of quantum physics state that there is an equal probability of them shooting off in any of the directions possible. Therefore, in its natural, uninterrupted state, quantum 'reality' is probabilistic, with every outcome of a specific event being as real as any other.

The fundamental building blocks of existence had been locked in a shadowy world of uncertainty. This probabilistic world can best be seen as a field of energy with 'matter' being nothing but stable patterns in a foam-like environment. 'Matter', as such – together with the definite reality it is thought to produce – is an electrical hallucination similar to our holographic image, writ large.

However, the nature of reality as we perceive it is such that when we look into the quantum field we perceive only one outcome. By observing, we grasp definite order from probabilistic chaos. Our view of reality is constituted by human consciousness itself. Our mind is a central factor in quantum physics. Things 'are' only when we see that they are. Existence cannot exist unless there is an observer to observe it.

And from here it is but a short step to theorize that when our close-upness decreases in an altered state of consciousness, then our interactiveness with the quantum field also shifts, allowing us to change probabilities and shift the human laws of nature, thereby utilizing the mind to affect the physical world.

Science does, of course, shun such an idea. But while the idea of the paranormal and quantum physics being related is anathema to the scientist, he can offer no concrete argument against the possibility, only a denial. The evidence of the 'physical' world that is collected by science is reliant on the prevalent 'world view' of how the universe works. Such a view is not a hard, observational discipline, but a series of assumptions concerning how we believe – or even wish – the universe to work. Only the data that fits the world view is accepted. And here lies an important lesson concerning PK.

The world of the particle is locked in uncertainty and probability. No quantum event has ever occurred uninfluenced by man's observation within a scientific experiment. We only assume a subatomic particle exists. It is nothing but an outcome of mathematical theory. Even the fact that our understanding of the particle has led to the microchip is not proof of its existence. Just because something works, it doesn't necessarily mean that we understand how it works.

PK should be seen in a similar way. For it is equally possible that the importance of observation in a quantum event is evidence of a psychokinetic event. It is only our assumed world view that says otherwise; a world view that may have produced an equally magical property – the particle.

Psychodrama

O N HALLOWEEN Night, 1992, a play called *Ghostwatch* was shown on British television. The plot involved a television reporter spending the night in a house infested by a poltergeist, along with the occupants – a mother and two daughters of approximately ten and twelve years of age. The father had recently left the family home, leaving the household in turmoil.

During the night various manifestations occured, including shaking walls, flying objects – including a picture – and inexplicable noises. The older daughter spoke in a man's deep voice and, at one point, became covered with scratches which disappeared a couple of minutes later. She was also caught red-handed banging on the central-heating pipes, faking the rapping sounds within the house.

The family named the poltergeist 'Pipes' and, as the plot unfolded, Pipes was portrayed as the spirit of a previous occupant of the house who was a known child-molester.

As well as being excellent, if ill-advised, entertainment, *Ghostwatch* can be seen as a perfect vehicle for an analysis of poltergeist activity, for, apart from the highly dubious ending, when Pipes moved into the television studio and practically destroyed it, it offered a perfect scenario for the on-going manifestations prevalent in such activity. Indeed, the phenomena highlighted could be classed as mild compared to some hauntings. And against a back drop of such activity we can build a picture of just exactly what is going on.

The scene is set by a household showing signs of anxiety and insecurity following acute family upheaval. The atmosphere is such that this anxiety sporadically erupts into argument. Emotions are high and explosive. Within the household is an adolescent whose confused mind is already psychologically disturbed. The added pressures of family argument and suspicion push the child over the edge, so that she withdraws into herself and approaches an altered state of consciousness. Reality, within the house, is beginning to shift.

The child moves ever closer to being the focus of psychic happenings. During tantrums, sometimes when stomping up and down the bedroom, alone, she begins to throw things. This disturbs the whole family downstairs, who become jumpy – and consciousness is beginning to *communally* change. Fear creeps in and a psychodrama begins to unfold.

The family, as a whole, goes beyond the boundaries of accepted reality and foreboding grows in the dark, lonely nights. Fear produces recollections of a childhood reaction to fear – wetting oneself – and puddles mysteriously appear on the floor. The anticipation of tantrums from the focus produces a climate where the family wait for rapping noises, for bangings-about upstairs – and hear them they do. The poltergeist is present – a product of the communal turmoil of the household.

By now, the adolescent focus is a psychological mess, and her mind is fragmenting into the phenomenon of multiple personality, occasionally displaying a logical outlook, while another personality is mischievous, sneaking into a lonely corner to bang on the pipes, adding to the trauma, to the expectancy, which builds up and builds up until an ornament flies across the room.

The poltergeist is out, present and omnipotent, and it soon seeks to throw bigger things, and pictures fly off the wall.

Should the house have a violent or emotional history from previous tenants, then the communal altered state of the household senses this history via the memory shop, and clairaudient and clairvoyant hallucinatory influences break out. The past seeps into the altered reality, giving the impression that the poltergeist is an actual spirit. The adolescent focus, more disturbed than the rest of the household, is most sensitive to these memories and, as in cases of past-life regression, the fragmented mind forms a specific personality based on the previous occupant. At times, the focus *becomes*, and speaks with the voice of, the previous occupant. But the in-built anger of the focus does not just throw furniture and bully other members of the family. A further fragmented personality is outraged at itself and matter-change attacks the body – stigmata appear.

After several months, the manifestations – this psychological infestation – play themselves out and normality, of a sort, returns.

In all this we have the scenario for the ultimate expression of the paranormal as psychologically based idiosyncrasies of not so much an individual as a community. Nothing of a supernatural nature is occurring, but the intensity of the phenomena results from a communality of minds involving all those present in the psychodrama, encompassing elements suggestive of all known explanations of the poltergeist – the mischievous child, the adolescent focus, and the manifestation of spirit. Reality, as we know it, has been displaced by the coming together of minds, just as SORRAT eventually produced PK as a group, and 'Philip' manifested as a table in similar experiments in Canada. And at Borley Rectory the phenomena changed with the arrival of each occupant, finally turning into classic poltergeist phenomena when a new player appeared on the scene – the researcher Harry Price.

Consider, also, the Black Monk of Pontefract. The initial outbreak occurs when only two family members are present. When the other members of the family, not privy to the poltergeist infestation, return from holiday, they immediately place a psychological calm upon the house, banishing the phenomena. When Diane reaches puberty, the outbreak resumes. But why does it eventually become so nasty? A priest is called to exorcize the house, but leaves, calling it 'evil'. The poltergeist simply co-operates. But, most significant, Aunt Maude sings 'Onward Christian Soldiers'. Happy to oblige, madam! A manifestation of a black monk, a Jesuit – from an order that wears black and whose members are known as 'soldiers of Christ'.

We can also, perhaps, understand the role of the exorcist within the above scenario. Rather than the spirits being removed by God, by joining the play the exorcist strengthens the faith of the players to the point of calming the psychological mess the family finds itself in; and his authority becomes part of the production. Consider, too, the effect of a sceptical researcher investigating the outbreak. His scepticism pollutes the plot and, while he is present, no phenomena will happen. He will inevitably leave with his scepticism intact. But the moment he goes out the door. . . .

Ideas like this about the role of the sceptic have filtered into paranormal theory over the years of research as an explanation for other areas of phenomena. In particular, experiments in psychic abilities have had to take account of what has become known as the 'experimenter effect'.

Dr Gertrude Schmeidler, a researcher at the City University of New York during the 1940s and 50s, has had first-hand experience of the experimenter effect. She noticed that, of the guinea pigs taking part in her experiments, those who had an absolute faith in the phenomena being tested were more likely to succeed in producing the phenomena, while those who were outright sceptics didn't just fail, they failed dismally, as if their scepticism did produce phenomena, but of a negative nature.

In the 1950s two researchers, a Dr West from the Society for Psychical Research (generally sceptical) and G.W. Fisk, Council Member for the Society (more open to belief), carried out almost identical experiments. West's results tended to be negative, while Fisk's were positive. West, the sceptic, would today be categorized as a 'goat', while Fisk, the believer, would be known as a 'sheep'. And an American researcher, Julie Eisenbud, has argued that, no matter how many restraints you placed on laboratory experiments, the experimenter effect would manifest regardless. And not just in experiments into the paranormal.

In 1966 Robert Rosenthal published *Experimental Effects in Behavioural Research*, advising that such a problem was endemic in all research. He had done a remarkable experiment himself. Forming a number of students into two groups, he gave one group some 'genius' rats which had been trained to negotiate mazes, and the other some 'stupid' rats who had not. Research by the students confirmed that the 'genius' rats could negotiate mazes much better than the 'stupid' ones. But Rosenthal had deceived the students. Both sets of rats were the same. The positive results of the 'genius' rats were born of the expectation of success in the minds of the students.

So, with the poltergeist – as well as much of laboratory research into the paranormal – we can now begin to see how such psychological anomalies are much more than the sum total of the individual. Rather, the poltergeist phenomenon is a communal idiosyncracy. And this idea extends to the heart of scientific research.

Scientific Methodology

WHEN ARISTOTLE decided that the earth was the centre of the universe, he made a reasonable assumption based on what he could observe. The earth appeared to be stationary and the astral bodies appeared to circle it. But we now know that Aristotle was wrong. The astronomer Aristarchos of Samos had the right idea. Less than a century after Aristotle he postulated a moving earth, but by then the stationary-earth theory had become well entrenched, so he was virtually ignored. Indeed, it took two thousand years for Aristotle's idea to be banished by Copernicus's speculation and Galileo's observations.

This story has been repeated throughout history. People tend to forget that a theory is simply a theory – a foundation on which to build a picture that fits the known facts. All too often a theory is accepted as truth and any evidence that conflicts with it is ignored because it would distort the picture.

Meteorites are a perfect example.

From the beginning of history, mystics considered 'thunderbolts' to be the instruments used by the gods to strike down sinners. Because of this, science decided that these flying objects, or meteorites, were simply super-stition – stones falling from the sky contradicted the laws of nature. In 1772 the French Academy of Sciences issued a memorandum declaring that ' . . . the falling of stones from the sky is physically impossible.' At about the same time the Swiss geologist Jean Deluc said: ' . . . if I saw a meteorite fall, I would not believe my own eyes.' When a meteorite was reported as falling on a French town, Claude-Louis Berthollet, one of the 'savants' whom Napoleon took with him to Egypt, found it sad than an entire town could enter folk tales into official records.

We now know that these early scientists were wrong. But we only know that science is wrong when it is proved to be wrong. And this proof usually comes from outside the scientists' own circle. Cases in point are Gregor Mendel, founder of modern genetics, whose experiments were conducted in an Austrian monastery garden; Charles Darwin, who was an amateur naturalist; and Albert Einstein, who formulated relativity theory while a patents clerk.

Perhaps the most advanced science today is particle physics. And no other science is more reliant on theory than this. The overpowering reason for this is, as explained, that subatomic particles are so small they cannot be physically seen by the good old eyeball. In order to observe them, the particle you wish to 'see' must be bombarded with light, which is itself made up of particles. And this bombardment directly affects the particles you wish to observe. Hence you observe the result of your observation, and not the true reality of the quantum field.

Because of this, the particle physicist uses theory in the same way as an army uses scouts. Reality cannot be known until a theory suggests what the physicists should be looking for. They can theorize in this way because they assume that nature is, essentially, mathematical (whether this is true or whether mathematics is simply a human construct we define nature as being beholden to is a matter for debate).

This outlook, however, suggests two immediate problems. First of all, the mathematical stability of nature is in conflict with the widely held belief that nature is chaotic. And the second problem is that there is no guarantee that the initial theory that directs the physicist to the next stage of experimentation is correct.

So there is a real possibility that research into particle physics has gone up the wrong path. And it may continue to do so.

It appears that 'matter' is created from stable energy patterns within the quantum field. In effect, the physical reality we interact with and see is an illusion. Add this to the fact that when we look into the subatomic world we see the result of our observation, then, as I have shown, particle physics is beginning to prove a mind-over-matter (PK) ability in us all.

Because the particle physicists are finding that their theories are leading them towards a world where PK is a real possibility, they have been led to postulate a deeper level of particles as they search frantically for something 'hard' within the quantum field which could constitute 'matter' in a mechanistic sense. Theories now suggest the existence of muons, gravitons, hadrons, leprons, neutrinos, quarks, pions, kaons and a whole host more. Many of these particles, if released from the atom, would last for fractions of a microsecond only and would be not only mass-less but ghostly, having no interaction with any other part of the quantum field. Indeed, the only reason for their existence is to 'prop up' flagging mathematical calculations.

Theory is not the only tool of the particle physicist. He also has particle accelerators – huge, expensive monstrosities as big as, if not bigger than, cathedrals. These 'atom smashers' are the new shrines of science. They accelerate particles to speeds approaching the speed of light to bring them into collision with other particles and release their hidden secrets. Monitors then record the effects of the collisions. The results are compared with the theory and, usually, the theory is proved, or at least vindicated.

But is this really the case?

In the atom smasher I see the possibility of delusion. In the first instance, sheer economics dictate that only theories given wide approval by the scientific establishment get to be tested in these highly expensive machines. A consensus of opinion – a bias – is already communally present. But are the particle physicists correct in their original theory leading up to the experiment? Are they forgetting that when we observe the quantum field we only see what the observer wants to see? Are they forgetting the possibility of PK that their own theories suggest?

Is the atom smasher a particle accelerator . . . or a dream machine?

INFORMATION TALENTS

Telepathy

THE PARAPSYCHOLOGIST Stanley Krippner was one of the founders of the American Central Premonitions Unit set up in New York in 1968. Years earlier, when he was fourteen, all he wanted was an encyclopedia. However, his father – a farmer – had had a bad harvest and money was short. Stanley had no chance. Then he suddenly thought of his Uncle Max. He would buy it for him. Then he realized he couldn't. Uncle Max was dead. Seconds later the phone rang. It was a cousin, informing the family that Uncle Max had just died.

The most likely explanation for Stanley Krippner's foreknowledge of his uncle's death is that Stanley had received the information telepathically. And there are literally thousands of such cases on record. Most people can recall incidents where telepathy was a possible factor. I remember the day my wife and I were discussing girls' names for a possible future daughter. Mid-way through the conversation I went to the toilet. As I came downstairs on the way back the name 'Lucy' entered my head. I walked into the lounge and my wife said 'How about "Lucy"?'

The term 'telepathy' was coined by F.W.H. Myers in 1882 from the Greek *tele*, meaning distant, and *pathe*, or feeling. The ability is generally thought of as mind-to-mind contact without resort to the five known senses. So confident was Myers – a founder of the Society for Psychical Research – that telepathy would soon be understood, that he wrote, in the *Proceedings* of the society: 'The Society for Psychical Research was founded with the establishment of thought transference already rising within measurable distance of proof.'

He was to be disappointed. Proof was to become elusive and academic acceptance almost impossible to obtain. Even in the heyday of scientific research into phenomena such as Spiritualism, Sir William Barrett of the Royal College of Sciences in Dublin encountered problems. He was able to submit his paper 'Some Phenomena Associated with Abnormal Conditions of the Mind' to the British Association for the Advancement of Science, only because of the casting vote of the chairman, Alfred Russell Wallace, who was an enthusiastic advocate of psychical research.

The central problem to acceptance of telepathy was admirably identified by the early psychical researcher Dame Edith Lyttleton when she said: 'Telepathy does not merely bridge space, it annihilates it – space becomes an irrelevance.' And here lies the dilemma. Our scientific model of how the universe works demands that space must be crossed in line with the laws allowing such movement. Telepathy, therefore, breaks every rule of common sense within our understanding of reality. Movement of thoughts from one mind to another in an instantaneous manner is anathema to everything a scientist holds dear.

A phenomenon akin to telepathy is accepted by most primitive societies. The Australian Aborigines are a prime example. They accept mind-to-mind contact as normal. But Western understanding of the process only began with the success of mesmerism. Several practitioners, whom Mesmer called 'magnetizers', reported that patients under trance often put into effect the thoughts of the magnetizer. Later, as psychoanalysis became popular, therapists such as Sigmund Freud, Carl Jung and William James became interested in the research, especially as a similar phenomenon seemed some-how involved in the rapport between therapist and subject. Indeed, by 1924, many researchers were convinced that telepathy was an integral element of the hypnotic state.

One such researcher was L.L. Vasiliev, who led a clandestine group of Russian scientists, fearful of letting Stalin know what they were up to. He followed a Russian tradition of research that found its roots in the early-nineteenth century, when the surgeon D. Velinski had demonstrated the telepathic element in mesmerism. Vasiliev claimed to be able to hypnotize a subject from 1,700 km (1,056 miles) away, making him wake up or fall asleep on command. This ability was known as 'telehypnosis'.

The most commonly documented form of telepathic communication comes during what has been termed a 'crisis situation', usually when an individual becomes 'aware' that another – usually a friend of relative – is in danger or has died. Often such information can filter into the mind during sleep, when it surfaces as a dream. In the waking state it can manifest as a feeling of certainty or as knowledge that inexplicably pops up in conversation, the speaker unaware of why he said that someone had just died, for example, or where the information came from.

The *Census of Hallucination*, published by the Society for Psychical Research towards the end of the nineteenth century, also identified a further form of possible telepathic knowledge. Many people report 'seeing' friends or relatives at the time of their death elsewhere. Such a 'crisis apparition' appeared to Lieutenant James Larkin of the British Royal Flying Corps on 7 December 1918.

Larkin's friend Lieutenant David McConnel left Scampton in Lincolnshire, where they were both based, to fly to Tadcaster, some sixty miles away. He told McConnel that he would be back home in time for tea. However, at 3.25 p.m. McConnel was killed when his plane nose-dived in thick fog and crashed. Yet, at that moment he appeared in Larkin's doorway, in full flying kit, and offered his usual greeting of 'Hello, boy'. The two men had a short conversation before McConnel said, 'Well, cheerio,' and walked away. Later, when a colleague asked if McConnel had returned, Larkin said, 'Yes, he's back.' Only later did they find out about the accident.

The search for proof of telepathy has a long history. Yet that history can be said to have begun in earnest in 1909, when the physicist Sir Oliver Lodge published his book *The Survival of Man*. In it he documented his studies of two girls who claimed to be able to read each other's minds. However, the subject was here exposed to the first real bout of the scepticism that exists to this day. How was it that when the girls were not holding hands they had less success? They could, it was suggested, have worked out a code, using touch, to pass messages.

In the 1930s the American writer Upton Sinclair published in his book *Mental Radio* the results of experiments he and his wife had made. Sinclair would make little drawings and attempt to transmit their images to his wife. In one memorable case he had drawn a volcano with smoke coming out of it. His wife drew a beetle. This appears to be a 'miss', but both pictures involved a long, thin squiggle with an inverted 'V' coming from the bottom. In fact it was a remarkable 'hit'.

Perhaps the most impressive evidence ever gathered in the field for telepathy was collected over 68 evening sessions of mind-to-mind contact between researcher Harold Sherman and polar explorer Sir Hubert Wilkins in 1937 and 1938. Sir Hubert was in the Arctic on a rescue mission to find the crew and wreckage of a trans-polar flight piloted by Russian aviator Sigismund Levanevsky. Prior to the mission he had been approached by Sherman in the City Club of New York. After much banter, he had agreed that when he was in the Arctic he would, on three evenings a week between 11.30 p.m. and midnight Eastern Standard Time, attempt to transmit mental images of the events of that day. Sherman would attempt to pick up Sir Hubert's impressions and write them down. A third party, researcher Gardner Murphy, would take Sherman's impressions and deposit them with an attorney. At the end of the mission, Sherman's writings would be compared with Sir Hubert's log of the mission. So how did the experiment fare?

Sherman later wrote: 'The very first night I was electrified at getting the sensation that a circuit had been closed between Sir Hubert Wilkins's mind and my own.' And it appeared to be quite a circuit. Early on in the mission Sherman wrote, one night: 'Strong impression ping-pong balls – is there a table in town where people can play? Can't account for this unusual impression.' Sir Hubert later confirmed that two of his team played ping-pong in a school gymnasium that night. On a further occasion, Sherman wrote: 'You have had some rare wine offered to the crew and you tonight . . . I seem to see you all partake.' Sir Hubert confirmed it was Blueberry wine.

Perhaps Sherman's most unlikely impressions were the following:

> I had a feeling you were taking off on a flight this morning for some place that seemed like Saskatchewan. I had the feeling you've been caught in a blinding snowstorm and can probably make a forced landing at some place that sounds like Regina. I see you, Wilkins, roped in on an officers' ball that appears to have been held there this evening. I see many men and women in military attire and evening dress. You, Wilkins, are in evening dress yourself.

Certainly an unlikely possibility. After all, how many polar explorers consider evening dress essential kit? Yet, Sir Hubert confirmed:

> This morning took off on flight. Hoping to reach Saskatchewan. Was caught in heavy blizzard. Propose to turn back and make a landing in Regina. Was met at the airport by the Governor of the province who invited me to attend an officers' ball being held there this evening. My attendance at this ball was made possible by the loan to me of an evening dress suit.

Such evidence is overwhelming, yet virtually ignored by academe. We again encounter the problem of guaranteeing against cheating – highly unlikely, bearing in mind the integrity of Sir Hubert Wilkins, who, among many other achievements, was commander of the *Nautilus* submarine expedition to the Arctic in 1931. However, a further form of experiment was devised by French physiologist Charles Richet, using statistical analysis to find evidence of telepathy – a method later adapted and refined by Dr Joseph Banks Rhine.

Rhine was the principal researcher involved in devising methods of studying telepathy in a scientific way. Beginning in the 1930s and working from Duke University, he used Zener cards – packs of twenty-five cards consisting of five sets of five different symbols. The cards were turned over one at a time and the subject tried to guess which symbol was on the card. Chance dictates that you should get five right in every pack. Any substantial increase on this number over a series of tests would suggest extra-sensory perception (ESP) at work.

With several subjects Rhine achieved consistent results above chance. However, his work was never taken seriously by academe and sceptics blamed all manner of trickery for the above-chance results. With one subject, Rhine used to carry out tests in his car, thus guaranteeing there could be no safety checks against fraud. Another was accused of stealing out of his room while Rhine was turning over cards, and watching him from a window, darting back to his own room as the test ended to record his results.

One of Rhine's greatest critics was British mathematician and researcher Dr S.G. Soal. However, in the 1960s, while President of the Society for Psychical Research, Soal duplicated Rhine's above-chance results with his subject, Basil Shackleton, and medium Blanche Cooper. Soal was apparently converted. However, when his integrity was challenged, a computer expert checked out his results and pointed out many irregularities in Soal's records. Whether Soal cheated or not is unknown. But enough doubt was cast to cancel out his successes.

Statistical analysis of ESP became inconclusive, never able to cast off suspicions of trickery. And research suffered from two other problems. First of all, as with micro PK, success was only just above chance. It was so slight that it could be ignored. And, secondly, many people achieve results in other areas of life substantially above chance. Many people are naturally lucky gamblers, consistently winning. Their score above chance is far greater than statistical evidence for ESP. Hence, statistical analysis of ESP became, and still is, a lame duck.

Theories to account for ESP became equally desperate. British scientist Sir William Crookes put forward his theory in the nineteenth century that the ability rides on radio-like waves. L.L. Vasiliev built upon this in the 1920s by suggesting that mind-to-mind communication was carried within the electromagnetic spectrum. In the 1960s Dr Hilda Heine of the University of New Zealand put forward macrophages as candidates for ESP carriers. Macrophages are cells within connective tissue, tied to nerve endings. Heine suggested that they send and receive ESP below the level of everyday perception.

Such 'physical' theories for transmission and reception were fanciful in the extreme, and none have ever been taken seriously. Indeed, theories battle with each other as to whether ESP is an old, latent power which we no longer require, or a new, evolving phenomenon within our nervous system.

In terms of proof and theory, ESP remained elusive. Until, that is, researchers began to understand the effects of an altered state of consciousness upon ESP.

ESP Testing

IN 1987 the National Opinion Research Council of the University of Chicago conducted a survey into the public's awareness of ESP. They found that 67 per cent of adult Americans believed they had experienced phenomena suggestive of ESP. Indeed, should ESP exist, the figure could be much higher. For, all too often, possible ESP is shrugged off with that dismissive word, 'coincidence'. Typically, most people can recall thinking they have seen a friend in the street, only to find out they were wrong. However, turn a corner, and guess who they bump into? But is this coincidence or ESP? If the latter, it enters the statistics. If you opt for coincidence, it does not.

However, while evidence suggestive of ESP is inconclusive in normal life and statistical analysis of Zener cards, research has led to much more impressive results when tests have been incorporated with an altered state of consciousness. Indeed, mystics and yogis have been saying for centuries that paranormal powers are enhanced with meditation, trance and mind-altering drugs.

The first research into the possibility of enhancing ESP in an altered state of consciousness was carried out between 1962 and 1974 by the researchers Stanley Krippner and Montague Ullman. To their Dream Laboratory at the Maimonides Medical Centre in New York, they would bring subjects, to do nothing more than sleep. In a room away from the sleeper an experimenter would stare at an image and attempt telepathically to communicate it to the sleeper. When the sleeper achieved REM sleep he would be woken up and asked to describe his thoughts. The following morning he would be shown a number of pictures and asked to pick the one that had been communicated. In one memorable experiment, the entire audience at a pop concert were asked to concentrate upon a large image on the stage and transmit it to the sleeper.

As with statistical analysis of ESP, the Maimonides team had a number of above-chance successes, including accurate description after REM sleep, and picking the correct picture the following morning. But Maimonides failed to provide the required unchallengeable proof of ESP. However, researchers were not to be beaten. A new method of attaining a form of altered state, involving information deprivation, was devised, known as the Ganzfeld state.

Ganzfeld is German for 'a unified field'. Applied to ESP testing, it is used to create an artificial environment free of visual and auditory stimuli. This is achieved by relaxing the subject and having him lie down with half ping-pong balls over eyes and earphones over ears, through which 'white noise' is played. The effect is to remove the subject from outside stimuli while maintaining his 'awake' faculties.

The usual test is for the subject, while in this state, to speak his thoughts into a microphone over a period of thirty minutes while an experimenter, the transmitter, is staring at a target picture, chosen at random immediately before the test, attempting to communicate the picture to the subject. Descriptions offered by the subject are related to the target picture, and at the end the subject is asked to identity the target picture from a selection.

The first Ganzfeld tests were conducted in 1974 by American researcher Charles Honorton. In an early success, one subject described ' . . . a large hawk's head in front of me . . . the sense of sleek feathers.' At this time the transmitter was looking at a number of slides featuring birds. Another subject spoke of 'all these different circles' while the transmitter was concentrating on images of rare coins.

Such accurate hits inspired several other researchers to approach ESP through the Ganzfeld. Among them was British researcher Dr Carl Sargent, working from Cambridge University. Sargent achieved some striking successes:

> Keep thinking of firemen and fire station . . . Firemen definitely seen, black and white. People but not faces. I think one man at bottom in foreground, facing . . . Young face as if photographer says, 'Oi', and only he turned round.

This was the impression received during one test by the subject, Hugh Ashton. After the test, duplicates of four possible target pictures were shown to him and he was asked to identify the target picture. He had no difficulty in choosing a black and white picture of firemen training hoses with their backs to the camera. The fireman on the far left, however, was looking round at the camera.

Many similar successes were achieved by Sargent. However, other researchers, such as Dr Susan Blackmore, failed to achieve any significant results using the Ganzfeld. As can be expected, this failure soon turned into accusations of cheating against those researchers who attained results. And as with all other attempts to prove ESP, the research was discredited.

Of course, in light of mounting evidence of the communality effect, it becomes increasingly attractive to argue that the 'experimenter effect' could account for the failure of Blackmore's research. This is especially attractive when it becomes clear that Dr Blackmore is highly sceptical of the paranormal to begin with. In a real sense, the more obvious answer to her failure is the polluting effect of her own mind, imposing sceptical order upon the paranormal, prompting her many statements that she has never experienced anything suggestive of the paranormal. Very true. A sceptical researcher never has and never will. As to whether this is due to the believer cheating or the sceptic cancelling out paranormal happenings because of his or her own mind is one of the great debates of the paranormal, a debate that can only be settled by the accumulating evidence suggestive of the communality of phenomena, and the part each individual plays in the psychodrama. Indeed, the entire field of the paranormal can be said to hinge on this effect. If communality is attractive, then phenomena can be said to happen. If not, then the whole subject is bunkum. However, if you opt for the latter, then you must remember the 'uncertainty principle' at the foundation of quantum theory, and accept the argument that the particle is bunkum too. For, as regards scientific research into the paranormal, the experimenter effect is the equal of the uncertainty principle, locking proof of phenomena in a shadowy world of uncertainty.

However, having said this, let me make it plain that, as far as I'm concerned, telepathy does *not* exist. The idea of thoughts being transmitted from one mind to another is ludicrous. This is not to say that such a phenomenon does not happen, but that our understanding of it is faulty. Let me explain.

It has been noted that some subjects pick up impressions of one of the other pictures in the selection available, and not the target picture. In one amusing case the researcher monitoring the words of the subject squashed a beetle that was crawling along his sheet of paper. The subject then reported hearing the Beatles singing 'Please Please Me', which had nothing to do with the target picture. When two tests had been going on at the same time, it was not uncommon for the subjects to receive impressions from each other's tests. Sometimes the subject even recorded impressions from the target picture of the next test. Consider, for instance, the following.

In 1977 the physicists Russell Targ and Harold Puthoff published their research at the Stanford Research Institute, California, in their book, *Mind Reach*. In it they introduced the phenomenon of 'remote viewing'. They worked their tests around one target envelope from a possible nine. The envelopes were locked away in a safe prior to the test. Thirty minutes before commencement, one of the team would be situated in a room with the subject who was to receive images, whilst the other, along with a witness, would select an unopened envelope, open it and travel to the location specified. The subject would then attempt to describe the location.

Following the test, independent judges would visit the target location to assess the accuracy of the comments made by the subject.

In one series of tests the subject was Pat Price, a retired police commissioner. In the first test the target team visited the Hoover Tower on the Stanford campus. Price spoke of a tower-like structure and then actually named it. In another test the team visited the Redwood City Marina. The first words out of Price's mouth were: 'What I'm looking at is a little boat jetty or . . . dock along the bay.'

What interests me about this test is the phrase 'What I'm looking at . . .', as if it was Price's mind which had 'travelled', as opposed to getting the impression from the mind of the researcher. The reader will also recall the incorrect identification of an aluminium soap box as a cigarette case (p. 54) again as if the medium's mind had 'travelled'. Earlier I noted Upton Sinclair's success with his wife's drawing of a beetle, which was almost identical to the drawing of a volcano. The point is, if the identification had come via mind-to-mind contact, surely Sinclair would have been transmitting the thought 'volcano'. The incorrect identification of the picture suggests that, rather than mind-to-mind contact being realized, Sinclair's wife's mind had 'seen' the picture direct, hinting at clairvoyant, rather than telepathic, abilities.

The possibility of the non-existence of telepathy, or mind-to-mind contact, was first hinted at by Eleanor Sidgwick, wife of the Society for Psychical Research's first president, in 1915, when she wrote: 'It may be that the role of the so-called agent is purely passive and that it is the percipient who plays the active role in extracting a combination of ideas from the mind of the agent.'

The idea presenting itself here is that the subject receiving impressions is doing nothing of the sort. He is going out and grasping them himself. He is clairvoyant, and has a mind that can wander in search of the information required, whether from the mind of another person, or from an actual location, as in remote viewing. Indeed, J.B. Rhine adopted the term ESP to distance the phenomenon from pure telepathy, as he was often left wondering whether the information the subject received was due to telepathy or clairvoyance. He concluded that the two were essentially the same phenomenon, manifested in different ways.

The pattern which seems to be presenting itself is suggestive of telepathy and clairvoyance being one and the same. I feel it would be easier, and simpler, to discount mind-to-mind contact in the classically understood way, and rather think of mind-to-mind contact in terms of one mind acting as a 'trigger' to make the other mind bring on clairvoyant abilities.

Seeing the problem in this way should sound familiar. We are back to my memory shop – to Jung's collective unconscious. The individual mind can be seen as retrieving information from a source unknown.

As to what this source is, researcher Louisa Rhine proposed that ESP escapes through the deep unconscious and enters a storehouse of memories.

Contact is here achieved by a coming together of the objective world with the centre of the mind. Such an idea has existed within the occult since the dawn of history. Many occultists believe in the *Anima Mundi*, or Soul of the World – a treasure house of thoughts and emotions constantly enriched by the thoughts and actions of contemporary man. And more insight can be given to such ideas of a wandering mind by looking at that curious phenomenon known as dowsing.

Dowsing

URI GELLER tends to do it with his hands. Some people are said to use their noses, while one ancient manuscript describes a peculiar fellow who used to do it with a German sausage. But, traditionally, the dowser uses a forked twig.

Although usually associated with the finding of underground water, dowsers also look for oil, coal, minerals, broken pipes and archaeological sites. Oil dowsers are usually referred to as 'sniffers', for they claim to be able to smell black gold. As to the success of dowsing, some dowsers can, in 1995, charge up to £500 ($750) a day, confirming industry's belief in the phenomenon, and, during the Vietnam War, some United States Marines were trained in dowsing techniques to locate mines.

Dowsing is not a rare ability – most people are said to be able to learn to be dowsers. Indeed, the American Society of Dowsers estimate that there are 25,000 dowsers in the United States alone.

The dowser's traditional forked twig is usually of ash, hazel, willow or rowan. But anything will do – a bent wire coat hanger, a German sausage or simply the bare hands. As the dowser approaches water, or other underground substance, the twig begins to twitch, eventually jerking up and down. However, the traditional dowsing rod is, according to Sir William Barrett – another of the Society for Psychical Research's founders – a recent innovation. It only became popular in the fifteenth century.

When dowsing began is unknown, although the Bible records that Moses once found water with his staff, and ancient Egyptian art seems to portray dowsers using forked rods. Dowsing seems to have become popular in medieval Europe, principally for the finding of coal – it is mentioned in a manuscript written by a mine surveyor in 1430. By 1556, the German mineralogist Georgius Agricola's treatise on mining, *De re metallica*, discusses the process of dowsing and includes illustrations of the various stages involved in dowsing for coal.

The first known use of dowsing for finding water can be dated to the seventeenth century, when a French aristocrat, the Baroness de Beausoleil, adapted the dowsing rod for water divining. This led to France leading the world in dowsing right up to the end of the eighteenth century when the Enlightenment came along and decreed dowsing a load of mumbo jumbo.

Intellectually, dowsing has remained a taboo subject since this time. But regardless of this academic myopia, the nineteenth and twentieth centuries have seen some remarkable dowsing successes. For instance, English stone-mason John Mullins discovered he was a natural dowser in 1859. In 1882 he set up a dowsing company to find water and sink wells. He became fully employed, with hundreds of successes to his name.

L.L. Latham also advanced the success of dowsing in 1938. Adapting its practice to archaeology, he was following the course of a Tudor brick-built water culvert at Kensington Barracks, London. Having reached an awkward bend beneath some barrack blocks, he identified a buried structure. Investigation revealed the foundations of a Roman fort 5 metres (17 feet) underground.

However, dowsing was to be the object of some modern scepticism. A magician, James Randi, decided to test dowsers in Australia in July 1980. He buried ten water-pipes and ten boxes in a ploughed field. Some of the pipes contained water and one of the boxes contained various metals. Could the eleven dowsers who took part in the test find the water and metal? In fifty attempts to find water, dowsers were successful only eleven times. As for the metal, in sixty-one runs the correct box was found just four times. The test was declared a failure – especially as the dowsers had previously claimed they would have a success rate of 85 to 100 per cent.

However, such tests can never be scientific as there is no repeatable standard which can be maintained. When you test if a television is working, you judge the result in line with the fact that the television should work. Every television has a measurable performance. This does not apply to dowsers. Some dowsers are good, some are bad. Similarly, a good dowser can have an off day. Unlike a television set, a dowser does not display a definite standard of efficiency and function. Hence, tests that were devised to check out the reality of dowsing could do nothing more than test the ability of a particular dowser. The only thing Randi proved was that, on that particular day, some of the dowsers were unsuccessful. His test said nothing about the validity of dowsing in general.

To highlight this point, consider the Priddy Project – a scientifically controlled test of five dowsers in the Mendip Hills of Somerset, England. Here, the dowsers had to follow an underground cave by marking its course above ground and locate a group of cavers who were stationary somewhere in the cave. None of the dowsers was familiar with the cave, and no one but the cavers knew where they were within the cave. All five dowsers had degrees of success in plotting the caves, including a sharp bend to which the terrain above ground gave no clue. One of the dowsers – Bill Lewis – positioned his marker to indicate the location of the cavers so closely that chance was out of the question.

Such tests as the Priddy Project speak volumes for the existence of dowsing. But what, exactly, is dowsing? How does it work?

Theories to explain dowsing go back to the seventeenth century, when many priests – both Catholic and Protestant – put it down to evil forces. Even before that, Martin Luther had denounced it as a practice that broke the commandment that you should not worship false gods and graven images. To counter such attacks many dowsers baptized their rods with Christian names. However, one German Jesuit priest, Athanasius Kircher, decided to have a go. Soon convinced that dowsing worked, in 1641 he put forward the theory – still held by many today – that the dowsing rod was moved by the dowser's unconscious muscular activity.

No other ideas were put forward regarding dowsing until the nineteenth century, when the German chemist Baron Karl von Reichenbach spoke of 'Odic forces'. He put down the movement of the rod to strange radiations and vibrations within the earth itself.

This idea was furthered in 1906 by a Frenchman, the Abbé Alexis Mermet. He argued that all bodies emitted radiations. When a human body entered such a field of radiation, nervous reactions broke out within the body. A current was formed which flowed through the hands to the divining rod, which acted as an indicator to locate the source of the radiations.

Although they sound rather stupid today, these ideas did seem to be heading in the direction of dowsing being a form of sympathy with physical forces. A modern mathematician, John Taylor of London University, decided there might be mileage in this idea. Knowing that only one possible known force of a physical nature could account for the phenomenon, he decided that the answer to dowsing would lie within the electromagnetic spectrum – almost definitely in the microwave band. However, his attempts to locate this force came to nothing. Hence, it was argued by the sceptics, as no such force existed, neither did dowsing.

Of course, a full understanding of dowsing has to discount such physical theories. How could such physical forces account for Bill Lewis finding cavers? Consider, too, Jacques Aymar of France who in 1692 successfully 'dowsed' for the murderers of a wine merchant. Here, it was assumed that the murderers gave off a 'murderous matter' which was divined. Or how about Joseph Treyve, of Moulins in the Allier department of France, who dowsed a map of the area to find where wild boar were before going hunting?

It was the Abbé Mermet who popularized map dowsing. Shunning the divining rod, he opted for the pendulum – a stone or other hard object dangled from a piece of string. In his book *Principles and Practice of Radiesthesia* he documented twenty cases where he successfully located murderers, missing people, and even a cow that had fallen over a cliff.

Popularized as 'radiesthesia' by the Abbé Alex Bouly (the term meaning 'radiation perception'), dowsing reached new heights of bafflement during the 1930s with Mermet, Bouly and Father Jean Jurion using the pendulum to dowse human bodies for signs of disease and illness. Jurion went on to treat some thirty thousand patients over twenty-five years. Abilities like this seriously weaken the idea that dowsing could in some way attune the dowser to the physical forces of the earth. Body and map dowsing do, however, offer a suggestion as to where the truth behind dowsing may lie.

What becomes increasingly clear is that the divining rod or pendulum is simply an instrument to 'amplify' the mind of the dowser. It acts as a catalyst to concentrate his thoughts and allows his mind to 'connect' with the substance or person to be located, whether he is at the location or working with a map. Catalysts, after all, are used by a whole host of mystics and adepts, the most popular being the crystal ball.

I maintain that dowsing is nothing more than a variation of clairvoyance. It is, essentially, the same thing. Indeed, the nineteenth-century dowser Charles Adams, from Somerset in England, actually claimed to 'see' underground water when he had found it with his rod. In a real sense we can see the divining rod as a means of concentrating a clairvoyant ability without the need for an altered state of consciousness. The ability is simply another form of ESP, just another way of gaining information by extrasensory means – and information not confined to the species, but from the universe at large. And, by seeing the divining rod as a catalyst to be concentrated upon, we can identify its use in terms of the Ganzfeld, in that such concentration reduces the information input of the everyday world around us. Which leads me back to my idea of an 'evolved' mind – a subject we must now look at once more.

Mind Expansion

WE REPRESS traumatic experience. To many therapists, this fact is the bedrock of psychology. But although we can treat the psychologically disturbed by retrieving repressions from dreams, hypnosis or association, we are nowhere near understanding the processes involved.

Can we understand repression in terms of the repression of information? And if so, how prevalent is such a process?

When walking down a busy street our sensory systems input a vast amount of information. Most of this information is of no relevance to our conscious, so our mind acts like a sieve, allowing irrelevant information into the unconscious. For instance, we are not interested in the detail of every parked car, the contents of every shop window, the appearance of every pedestrian. If this perceived information was not repressed we would over-load our minds with the sheer weight of facts. The psychological term for this process is 'selective attention'.

Is this the same mechanism as repression of traumatic experience? The psychologist would say no. Repression of traumatic experience is known as 'motivated forgetting' – a completely different thing. But is this separation strictly true?

In a clinical sense, perhaps. But not in terms of the general functioning of the mind. The days are long gone when a doctor used to tell a patient suffering from repressed trauma to 'snap out of it'. Social conditioning now requires a diagnosis or cure to be complicated. Simple cures no longer satisfy the psychological need for complication. However, take away the consulting room and big words and place yourself in the pub, sitting with a friend who is suffering the psychological outcome of repression. When you attempt to offer help by talking of factors related to the trauma, he will say something like, 'What's that got to do with it?'

Such statements hint at repressed trauma being classed, by the sufferer, as irrelevant. In suppressing the trauma, he has invalidated it as far as consciousness is concerned. In his own way he has brought back his feeling of safety, by using the same mechanism that 'selectively' represses information not needed for survival. But why do we need this mechanism?

To understand, we must ask how much information would be retained in our conscious if it did not filter to the unconscious. We simply could not cope with the sheer weight of information if we consciously perceived everything available to be perceived. Consider being in a room full of talking people. The volume of their voices is such that we should be able to hear every word said by every individual. But luckily our attentive processes are such that we can pick up only those voices we need to hear, while relegating all others to a background drone. We hear only those voices we 'concentrate' upon. Hence, repression of general information can be said to increase our concentration.

We can now see once more the concept of close-upness in evolutionary survival terms. Man has the ability to despatch to the unconscious not only information unnecessary for survival but also information that the individual psyche decides is unnecessary.

We have already seen (pp. 114–15) how, as early man's technological skill increased, so did the amount of information his conscious was receiving. So a saturation point must have been reached when man received too much information, requiring irrelevant, non-survival information to be sieved to the unconscious.

This would have been an on-going process, requiring an ever-increasing shrinkage of the conscious as information around him increased. And, in this scenario, we repress information due to an ever-evolving mind mechanism in accordance with the survival requirements of evolution. Basically, our mind, like our body, has evolved. And in this process we have a clear hint as to what happens in the dream state, hypnosis and similar altered states of consciousness.

The mind is generally thought of as a simple model. We have a conscious mind and the unconscious. Repressed or irrelevant information is filtered from the conscious to the unconscious, where it remains in memory. In the dream state the conscious and unconscious seem to merge, with unconscious imagery filtering into the conscious, making us dream. When we think of cryptomnesia, we can see a similar process in hypnosis.

There is a similarity here to the evolved-mind scenario, in that during altered states of consciousness, a vast amount of external information is cut off from consciousness. This raises the question, does a decrease of external information result in a merging of the conscious and unconscious into a one-level mind, reverting our mind to a pre-technological and prehistoric mind state?

If we are prepared to accept this possibility, then we have a valid description of a mind, when removed from normal information input such as in the Ganzfeld state, merging into a one-level mind, releasing consciousness from its close-up imprisonment and having access to every bit of information the individual has ever inputted to his unconscious. However, when this happens, you could also say that the personal conscious as presently perceived – that part of the mind identified as the individual – ceases to exist. In a real sense, in the altered state of consciousness, you, the self, the person you are generally thought to be, is no longer there. Rather, the predominant mind within the individual has become communal.

Mass Hysteria

THE FUNDAMENTAL difference between man and other life forms is that man can plan and use artificial technology – technology may be seen as the central reason for our rise from nature. It follows from this that the mind state of other life forms is akin to that of pre-technological man.

One aspect of many of these life forms is their togetherness. A hive of bees is an example. It has been suggested that a beehive may not be a collection of individuals but an organism in its own right. The possibility was first put forward after observation of termite colonies, where termite gardeners can be seen as the organism's digestive tracts, workers as the cells of the bloodstream and the queen as the reproductive and endocrine system. The grex (p. 111) is another example, as are simple sponges, which can be scrambled cell by cell but will always recreate their form.

This togetherness in the animal world may suggest the existence of a higher form of connecting entity – something similar to a collective racial unconscious. The whole animal kingdom seems to express characteristics of instinctual behaviour, as if it is Nature that defines the rules from above the individual consciousness of the animal. Anyone who watches the flocking of geese or starlings soon becomes aware of the leaderless yet spontaneous characteristics of their actions.

This reminds us of Julian Jaynes's view (p. 115) that, in early times, man had no real consciousness of his own. Everything he did seemed to be dictated from outside the influence of the individual.

Any parent will testify to the instinctual pattern of a toddler's developing skills in crawling and walking. The child learns of its own accord, as if he or she is a product of natural instincts. Indeed, even when the child grows up, becoming adult, is man that far removed from the wider organism of his species?

Like the bee in its hive, man cannot reproduce himself. He, too, is a social creature who can quite often face insanity when isolated from his society. An individual man is useless without his society to interact with. Perhaps it is simply man's ability to repress information he doesn't like which allows him to think of himself as an individual. Indeed, there are times within human, individualistic, society when we appear to transform into a communal grouping in rather spectacular ways.

Typical were the events at a fête near the town of Kirkby-in-Ashfield in the Midlands of England in 1980. Here, three hundred children collapsed, totally without warning. They began twitching and eventually vomited en masse. Most recovered quickly and all were well by the following morning. No cause was ever found for this mysterious outbreak of illness, so it was tagged 'mass hysteria'. However, the fact that babies were also affected hints that mass hysteria is far more subtle than we at present believe.

Again, we seem to have the coming together of a group in a display of unusual behaviour, as if the behaviour is orchestrated by something higher than the individual. And this can be seen within human society more often than we normally think. What, after all, is a riot? In a riot individual common sense and personal standards of behaviour break down. A person is 'compelled' to join in, as if the decision is taken out of his or her conscious control. But, more than this, once the riot has started it becomes a co-ordinated but surprisingly leaderless animal – as if the gathering has become a single thing with a mind of its own. Once the momentum of the moment has passed the riot will fizzle out and its constituents become people once more.

The Bulgarian-born novelist and sociologist Elias Canetti gave many examples of strange crowd behaviour in his book *Crowds and Power*. He identified specific crowd forms, such as the carnival, the hunt, refugees in flight, crowds that refuse to function as society demands and those that suddenly become affluent or partake in a rare feast.

In every case, Canetti identified what he termed a 'crowd crystal' – a focal point around which individuals become an organism, and an organism that shares little of the individual characteristics of the participants. For instance, in a carnival, a usually conservative woman may display obscene behaviour in line with the wishes of the crowd. She has, we say in our Freudian way, 'ceased to be herself'. However, the process can be much more ominous than this.

On 20 March 1995 the Aum Shinrikyo cult released a deadly nerve gas, Sarin, into the Tokyo underground system, causing mass panic, hundreds of casualties and twelve fatalities. Since then there have been two more attacks and many more false alarms. In Yokohama, in July 1995, acute distress and mass panic seized commuters. There were no casualties because no gas had been released. Four months after the initial attack, Japanese commuters were still afflicted with fear, which had sporadically erupted in mass panic.

Panics like these – incidences of mass hysteria – often cause observable physical symptoms, such as the twitching and vomiting caused at Kirkby-in-Ashfield. Dizziness, fainting, headaches, shivering and constriction of the throat are also often reported.

Schools are particularly liable to such attacks. In a school in Alaska in 1989 children reported a smell like rotten eggs. Word got around that there was a strange gas permeating the classrooms. Within minutes seven hundred children were convulsed on the floor, unable to breathe properly. Similar reports have come from schools throughout the world. In Britain, schools in London, Coventry and Portsmouth had outbreaks in the mid-1990s, with children 'falling like ninepins'.

Many cases go unreported. The immediate diagnosis is usually food poisoning or problems with the central-heating system. Only when these possibilities are rejected is mass hysteria suggested as a cause. Then the authorities tend to play down the event, putting it down to the idiosyncracies of hysterical, suggestible children. Hospitals, though, are often plagued with a similar problem – the victims being not the patients but nurses and doctors.

One such incident occurred in Britain in 1975. Three hundred members of staff at the Royal Free Hospital in London suddenly collapsed with spasms and dizziness. Neither are soldiers immune. At a San Diego, California, army base in 1988 over a thousand troops succumbed to the effects of a non-existent gas. Here, a hot and humid day led a few soldiers to experience breathing difficulties. Within minutes the rumour of gas had spread and they fell.

American psychologists Michael Colligan and Michael Smith researched many cases of mass hysteria in factories. They highlighted the fact that there is always an 'index case', an individual who becomes afflicted, and whom the others seem in some way to copy. This suggests that Canetti may not have been far wrong with his crowd crystals.

An interesting pattern emerges if we look at the history of mass hysteria. It appears that hysterical symptoms presented during such outbreaks echo the fears of society in general. And this seems to have been the case through-out history. Consider, for instance, an outbreak in France in 1633.

Urbain Grandier, the parish priest of the town of Loudun, was on a visit to the local convent. He was unprepared for what followed. The nuns were suddenly 'taken over' by sexual arousal, to the point that they shouted obscenities and rolled about on the floor displaying their private parts. It was many months before the convent returned to normal. At the time, mass hysteria was unknown. The outbreak at Loudun was seen as work of the Devil, and Grandier was burnt at the stake.

Again we can see the hysteria taking the form of the fears prevalent in society. First we have diabolical possession, and second, behaviour that is totally taboo for nuns. Indeed, the whole idea of this kind of hysteria is anathema to Christianity. As to why this is so, the answer can be found in ritual practice within paganism – a religious form that Christianity spent hundreds of years suppressing.

The shaman, or witch doctor, of primitive tribes tended to be a natural hysteric. With the help of monotonous drumming, chanting and dancing, the shaman seemed to use hysterical forms to help a tribe throw away their conscious restraints. Whole tribes would readily succumb to such forms of mass hysteria, as if it was essential to the health of the tribe.

This tells us something of importance about mass hysteria. It shows not only that can it be induced at will but that it provides vital therapy for our wellbeing. Indeed, this pagan influence is still very much with us. Most obviously, mass hysteria is often present at pop concerts, where the modern cultural shaman – the pop star – whips up frenzy in thousands of fans. Consider, also, the comedian, who can reduce an audience to hysterical, infectious, laughter.

In order to impose social order and standards Christianity condemned such outbreaks, ascribing them to heretical lack of control or mass diabolical possession. As the Middle Ages came to a close amid war and famine, the Christian authorities were severely tested by a form of dancing hysteria – St Vitus's dance – which broke out throughout Europe. Yet both the birth of Christianity and its modern expression involve episodes of mass hysteria.

If the Christian Church has an inaugural event, then it is clearly the time when the Holy Spirit descended and possessed the disciples. This happened shortly after the death of Jesus, when his disciples, worried, alone and afraid, suddenly became imbued with hysterical behaviour, even to the point of 'speaking in tongues'. So uncharacteristic was this behaviour that Peter had to explain to passers-by that they couldn't possibly be drunk at that time of day.

Early seventeenth-century Swiss priest Johan Gassner was the first to realize that mass hysteria could help to shrug off diabolical possession. In an early form of exorcism he used to induce mass hysteria as a form of healing. John Wesley, the eighteenth-century English evangelist and founder of Methodism, at his revivalist meetings used to induce mass hysteria under the pretence that the act brought out the Holy Spirit in those present. Today the Charismatic movement involves producing mass hysteria as a normal event in meetings.

It appears that through mass hysteria man ceases to be an individual and becomes part of a wider organism expressed through his society. In other words, it is an expression of our communality. As such, it is vital to an understanding of the paranormal.

The first attempt to understand mass hysteria can be traced back to the *Hippocratic Collection*, written in the third century BC. Up until this time it was thought to be a process initiated by the gods, but here we find it being diagnosed as an illness. However, for further understanding – other than as diabolical possession – we have to wait until 1896, and Gustave Le Bon's book *The Crowd*. Le Bon argued that people could be 'carried away' if gathered together in large enough numbers. Then their relative anonymity suppressed individuality, allowing them to act out of character as if possessed by some sort of social hypnotism. It was as if the crowd had been overtaken by a form of contagion.

These theories of psychic contagion suggest that, in expressing mass hysteria, we are clinging to a pre-technological and prehistoric collective human instinct. Such an instinct controls other life forms. Only we have broken the hold of this collective control, reverting to our primeval state only at times of great excitation.

Some biologists have suggested that this instinct is born from subliminal communication, possibly beginning with the subtle and co-ordinated action of cells. Other researchers explain it in terms of pheromones. A pheromone is a scent molecule released in small quantities by animals, and is known to affect the behaviour of other animals. For instance, pheromonal influence is blamed when a dog barks at night, aware that a nearby bitch is on heat. Eugene Marais independently came to the conclusion that scent, used as a form of instinctual communication, could be at the root of ant interaction. But it is hard to believe that pheromones account for mass hysteria. Although humans have body odour, it is arguable whether we give off pheromones at all.

So how should we understand the processes that lead to mass hysteria? One factor that seems to be present in cases of mass hysteria, whether spontaneous or controlled, is the excitation. And it is this we must now go on to consider.

Emotion as Trigger

THE POPULATION of the Albanian enclave of Kosovo tend to live their life in fear. Often discriminated against, their central fear is of the neighbouring Serbs in former Yugoslavia. Recently, a class in a school in Kosovo began to display odd symptoms. When no cause was found a rumour circulated that the Serbs were carrying out a gas attack. Within a couple of hours thousands of local Albanians collapsed. Of the smaller, integrated Serbian population, only one person was affected.

Unless we accept that pheromones have ethnic qualities, they could not have been responsible for the outbreak of mass hysteria in Kosovo. Rather, as in most cases, the uppermost factor was extreme emotion, leading to spontaneous psychic contagion. And what is interesting about such spontaneous human behaviour is the way it echoes the mentality involved in outbreaks of paranormal activity.

Psychic events tend to manifest in altered states of consciousness. But much more is going on that this simple statement implies. Clearly an individual can enter an immediate altered state during hypnosis. However, in the dream state there is another element prevalent. If the dreamer is happy and contented during sleep he is more likely to have a pleasant dream but should he be suffering from fear or insecurity he is more likely to have a nightmare.

Happiness, fear and insecurity are, of course, emotional states. And in many cases we have seen the subjects had been experiencing strong emotion at the time, most clearly seen in the cauldron of emotions expressed in poltergeist activity. And supernatural phenomena manifest best between emotionally involved people, such as husband and wife or mother and child. Arguably, then, emotion is the means through which an altered state could be achievable.

The American psychologist Abraham Maslow invented the term 'peak experience' to describe a sudden feeling of extreme pleasure, such as that experienced by a child on Christmas morning. Colin Wilson has suggested it can be thought of as a form of 'holiday consciousness'. The feeling makes us totally happy, and suddenly all the problems of the world leave us and we feel as if we could walk on air. So potent is the peak experience that Maslow noted that when his students talked about the experience they could summon it at will.

The repeatable peak experience is, it seems to me, the opposite of depression. With the peak experience we have been imbued with optimism; in depression pessimism is the driving emotion. There are, however, similarities. At both ends of this emotional spectrum we find that concentration on normal life becomes difficult, if not impossible. We don't eat; we act stupidly; we listen to no one; we can even become accident prone. And these things happen regardless of whether it is the peak experience or depression. It is as if close-upness has receded and our unconscious emotional traits have been dredged up. And a similar thing happens in lesser emotional states, too.

For instance, emotion tends to suppress logic. The angry man sees only the focal point of his anger; the man in love sees only the object of his affection. And, as logic seems to be a conscious ability, its suppression suggests interaction with the unconscious. But, most important of all, directing all your conscious energy on to one thing reduces your perception of information around you. And, as shown with the information-depriving Ganzfeld and catalyst objects such as the divining rod and crystal ball, when you cut yourself off from general information input, your mind could well revert to its pre-technological state – to the altered state of consciousness.

The emotional state can be seen as the volume control of the paranormal. Through extreme emotion, whether negative or positive, we can do ourselves what the hypnotist does with his ticking watch – take ourselves into the inner mind. So we bring the collective mind of man into the collective state of the beehive; what the naturalist William Wheeler would call 'the spirit of the hive'.

We must now go in search of this 'spirit'. And to do so we begin with the greatest expression of the wandering, communal, information-gathering mind – the out-of-body experience.

Astral Travel

ON 8 JULY 1918, while serving with an American ambulance unit in Italy, Ernest Hemingway was injured by shrapnel from a mortar shell. Describing the experience that followed to Guy Hickok of the *Brooklyn Daily Eagle*, he said: 'I felt my soul or something coming right out of my body, like you'd pull a silk handkerchief out of a pocket by one corner. It flew around and then came back and went in again, and I wasn't dead anymore.'

On that fateful day, Hemingway had an out-of-the-body experience, or OBE. And he is not alone. In 1952, sociologist Hornell Hart asked 155 of his students at Duke University if they had ever experienced an OBE. Thirty per cent said they had. In 1966 researcher Celia Green surveyed 115 students at Southampton University. Nineteen per cent had had an OBE. One year later, out of 350 students at Oxford 34 per cent reported OBEs.

Many OBEs occur close to death or after injury. They often involve para-normal sensing of the environment. Cardiologist Dr Michael Rawlings recalls one of his female patients:

> About the second day after recovery from her coma, I asked her if she remembered anything about it. She said, 'Oh, I remember you working on me. You took off your plaid brown coat and threw it on the floor, and then you loosened your tie. I also remember that your tie had white and brown stripes on it. The nurse who came to help you looked so worried. I tried to tell her I was alright. You told her to get an Ambubag and also an intracath to start an IV. Then the two men came in with a stretcher . . . '
>
> Recall with me – she was in deep coma at that particular time, and remained in a coma for another four days! At the time I took off my brown plaid coat, only she and I were in the room. And she was clinically dead.

Not all OBEs occur at such life-threatening times. Indeed, they commonly occur when the subject is simply relaxed or tired. As a student, para-psychologist D. Scott Rogo experienced an OBE. As he recalled in his book, *Mind Beyond the Body*, he had lain down for an afternoon nap one hot, sunny day in August, 1965, when:

> I flipped over onto my side, realising at the same moment that my whole body was pulsating and that I was almost paralysed . . . An instant later I found myself floating in the air and, in another instant, I was standing at the foot of the bed staring at myself. I made an abrupt about-face . . . and tried to walk to the door to my room, which led to a hallway. I felt as though I were gliding through jelly as I moved, and I lost balance for a moment and almost fell over. Everything was blurred by a cloudy hue that enveloped a whitish form, which I perceived as my body. A moment later I found myself awakening on my bed. But I also realised that I had never been asleep.

Rogo describes the experience perfectly. The OBE is said to be a detachment of the soul, or astral body, from the physical body. The astral body wanders through the physical world. Occultists would argue that, in fact, the astral body exists in an astral plane, which, while encompassing the physical world, extends to other dimensions.

The astral body itself is thought of as a double of the physical – it even wears its clothes – but it has a translucence which makes it seem like an apparition. It can pass through walls and travel at incredible speed.

The process of leaving the body is astonishingly similar in many varied cases. Travellers report leaving their body through the head or solar plexus, or simply rising from their body and floating away. Often a silver cord is perceived attaching the astral body to the physical. Many believe that if the cord becomes detached or cut the soul is unable to return to the body, resulting in death. The idea that you should not wake a sleepwalker seems to be allied to the silver-cord idea.

Many believers argue that the OBE is so common that we all wander in the astral plane when we sleep, our dreams being garbled recollections of our travels. Even espionage has not been free of the OBE. Several theorists have suggested the possibility of secret agents inducing OBEs and invisibly infiltrating secret complexes. One researcher dubbed such an ability ESPionage.

Astral travel is prevalent in tribal cultures. During the 1970s Dr Dean Sheils of the University of Wisconsin identified the phenomenon in 95 per cent of the 70 non-Western cultures he surveyed. Shamans from primitive cultures claim to achieve the OBE at will by attaining an altered state of consciousness. Indeed, the phenomenon often occurs during yoga.

Drawings from ancient Egypt suggest OBEs, the astral plane being entered through ten gates and seven doors. The astral body was known as the *ka*.

Ancient Indian writings speak of eight supernatural powers or siddhis, with the sixth siddhi being the ability to fly through the sky. In the Tibetan Book of the Dead we come across the 'bardo-body', a translucent duplicate body which is taken over by the dead.

Even the classical world had its astral travellers. Plato theorized about OBEs, while Socrates, Pliny, Plotinus and Plutarch are all claimed to have been astral travellers.

In his second letter to the Corinthians, St Paul reports:

> I knew a man in Christ above fourteen years ago, (whether in the body I cannot tell; or whether out of the body, I cannot tell: God knoweth) such an one caught up to the third heaven. And I knew such a man . . . how that he was caught up into Paradise, and heard unspeakable words, which it is not lawful for a man to utter.

Here we have not only a description of an astral traveller, but a reference to paranormal information gleaned while out of the body.

Over the last one hundred years or so, several astral travellers have achieved a high degree of fame. At the turn of the century Marcel Forhan, later known as Yram, achieved astral travel. Believing that everyone could do it, he documented his adventures in his book *Practical Astral Travel*. He met his wife while travelling astrally. When married, they travelled together, even, he claimed, achieving astral sex.

In 1920 an account of astral travel appeared in the *English Occult Review*; it was later published in the book *Astral Travel* in which Oliver Fox introduced a British audience to the phenomenon. He induced astral travel through dreaming between 1902 and 1938, and pioneered the ability to remain mentally awake while physically asleep.

Perhaps the most famous astral traveller from the early-twentieth century was the American Sylvan Muldoon. He learnt how to travel astrally at the age of twelve, and did so from 1915 to 1950. He was a sickly individual who was bedridden for much of his life, but his 'double' regularly roamed the earth. To him, our experiences of falling and flying in the dream state are remembrances of astral travel. His early research on the subject of the OBE was co-written with Hereward Carrington in the book *The Projection of the Astral Body*.

Perhaps the most enigmatic figure in the history of astral travel was Virginia businessman Robert Monroe. In his book *Journeys Out of the Body* he tells how he first achieved astral travel while asleep in 1958. By 1962 he was conducting full-scale research into the phenomenon. He noted that the experience could be pleasant or unpleasant, depending on what was encountered. As well as coming across fellow humans, he claimed to have met vicious sub-human entities which attacked him and, on some occasions, non-human intelligences. At times, he claimed, he had difficulty re-entering his body, once even getting it wrong and entering a corpse by mistake. Of course, most people will take such writings with a pinch of salt, but Monroe is vital to the subject as he took part in the first scientific investigation of the phenomenon.

In 1965 he teamed up with psychologist Dr Charles Tart at the University of California. He was placed in a laboratory-cum-bedroom amid a whole plethora of monitors, registering everything from brain waves to heartbeat. The intention was for him to achieve an OBE, travel to another room and read a five-digit target number. The first seven sessions failed to achieve astral travel, but on the eighth Monroe claimed to have had two brief OBEs. Did he read the number? No. He failed. But, interestingly, he did describe the room and occupants; even the fact, later confirmed, that a female technician was not in the room but talking to someone in the corridor.

Of course, the Monroe–Tart experiment was inconclusive, but it did set a precedent for scientifically controlled tests for OBEs, two of which occurred between 1972 and 1973.

The first was headed by Dr Karlis Osis, director of research of the American Society for Psychical Research, at the society's headquarters in Manhattan. The idea was for various test subjects to lie down with monitors attached to them. On a platform some ten feet above them would be placed various objects, which would be changed for every session. The idea was for the subject to achieve an OBE and identify the objects above him, yet out of sight.

One such subject was the New York artist Ingo Swann. After each OBE he claimed to attain he described and sketched what he saw. Although he had difficulty in identifying numbers or letters, he had some remarkable hits, giving strong evidence for OBEs.

Meanwhile, in 1973, Dr Robert Morris, then of the Psychical Research Foundation in Durham, North Carolina, teamed up with astral traveller Stuart 'Blue' Harary. Harary was first asked to 'travel' out of the PRF building and into another, where he would find a number of target pictures and letters. Again the findings were inconclusive, but Harary was successful in correct identification on a number of occasions. Later, using the same route for 'travel', he was asked to identify the positions of certain persons and animals in the target building. At first he proved very successful, but his abilities seemed to decline as he got bored.

Morris then asked Harary to attempt to make his presence known to a number of animals. One was a kitten called Spirit, which was placed in a cage whose floor was marked out into 24 10-inch squares so that Spirit's activity could be measured. Harary was half a mile (almost a kilometre) from the cage. Several times he claimed to have travelled astrally to the cage and at those times Spirit's behaviour markedly changed.

None of this proves anything in a scientific sense. Indeed, many researchers, while admitting that consciousness is somehow changed during an OBE, question whether the mind ever does actually leave the body. Principal among such researchers is psychologist Dr Susan Blackmore, who, in her book *Beyond the Body* propounds her theory that OBEs are creations of the individual's mind – a world of thought and imagination born of the desire to be free of the limitations of bodily existence.

This theory, of course, precludes the possibility of paranormal information gathering. Or could it? While I broadly agree with Dr Blackmore that nothing travels out of the body, could the world at large travel into the individual's mind?

In a sense, much of what we know about the world comes to us through paranormal means. While science maintains that experience can only come to us via the senses of sight, hearing, touch, feeling and smelling, this is not exactly the case. Sensory experience is a partnership between the senses and the analysis of those experiences by the conscious mind. However, as we have seen, much of the experienced information that arrives in the mind involves unconscious analysis rather than conscious, with the conscious mind sieving information that is not required out of perceived consciousness.

This survival mechanism is vital to aid our concentration, and it could be argued that such unconscious input is paranormal. In cryptomnesia the text of a book can be retained in unconscious memory by simply flicking through the pages. Bearing this ability in mind, we can, perhaps, build a new model of our mental processes.

At present we view the unconscious memory store as nothing more than a repository for unwanted thoughts and memories, as though it were a filing cabinet in which information lies dormant until required. I propose a different view of the unconscious mind.

Earlier I referred to the belief that the astral body travels within the astral plane, which, as well as other dimensions, includes the earth plane. What does this idea suggest? Could it be that in the OBE the mind does not travel 'outside' in the world at large, but rather, inhabits a reflection of the outside world?

Bearing this in mind, let me offer my own view of the unconscious. Could it be that the unconscious is, in reality, an interactive inner fantasy world, created by our total conscious and unconscious sensory input, and experienced, with the OBE, as a sensory representation; a world which builds, from our memories and current sense perceptions, a cryptomnesic map of the reality outside? In other words, could the unconscious be an inner model, an inner microcosm of existence in which you can participate?

Near-death Experience

'I SAW MYSELF lying on the bed. I saw a young nurse. She was preparing me for the mortuary. I remember thinking at the time how young she was to do such a thing as getting me ready and even shaving me. . . . '

'That was the most beautiful instant in the whole world when I came out of my body. . . . '

'Someone said, "Leave him, he's dead." I shouted from about fifteen feet above ground, "No, I'm not." . . . '

'They had surgical gowns on . . . I could see them operating on my back. . . . '

'From where I was looking, I could look down on this enormous fluo-rescent light . . . and it was so dirty on top of that light. . . . '

'I could see anywhere I wanted to. I could see out in the parking lot, but I was still in the corridor. . . . '

These quotations are taken from accounts of OBEs associated with the near-death experience collected by the researcher Ian Wilson for his book *The After Death Experience*.

We know of this phenomenon for two main reasons. First, advanced forms of resuscitation provided by modern medical technology increasingly allow people to cheat death and so to come back from the brink of death to tell their amazing tales. And, secondly, Dr Elizabeth Kubler-Ross, and her pioneering research on death in the early 1970s, brought the phenomenon to public attention.

The term 'near-death experience' – or NDE – was coined by Raymond Moody, and until the publication of his book *Life after Life* in 1975 few people would talk of their strange experiences, usually thinking they would be thought mad or wouldn't be believed. However, by 1982 a Gallup poll suggested that as many as eight million people could have had an NDE in America alone.

By the late 1970s a small number of doctors had begun to ask their patients if they had had an NDE. Other than Moody, one of the principal doctors involved was Kenneth Ring, who went on to found the International Association for Near Death Studies, or IANDS. Doctors usually became interested in the phenomenon after being told the most unlikely things by some of their patients. And, as accounts began to pour out, doctors were impressed by the fact that most experiencers were normal, level-headed individuals. This was clearly not an experience confined to the usual fantasy-prone personality.

The NDE usually occurs at the point of clinical death, either at the scene of an accident or in hospital. Many people have observed operations carried out on them, and have later described the process in such detail that no explanation is credible other than the fact that some form of sensory system had observed the operation.

At the point of entering the NDE, although sensing continues, as if through a form of clairvoyance, all pain goes. (That drugs, medically administered, have caused hallucination can be ruled out. Many people have had NDEs at the scene of their accident, before the arrival of the emergency services.)

Some experiencers simply return to consciousness after an OBE and become alive once more. But many have even more remarkable experiences:

'Next I was hurtling down this dark tunnel at high speed, not touching the sides. It made a sort of swishing sound. At the end of this tunnel was this yellow-white light. . . . '

'I felt I was floating through a tunnel . . . When I say tunnel the only thing I can think of is – you know, those sewer-pipes. . . . '

'At the end of the tunnel was a glowing light. It looked like an orange. . . . '

What goes down the tunnel? What perceives the experience?

'It seemed like I was up there in space and just my mind was active. No body feeling, just like my brain was up in space. I had nothing but my mind. Weightless, I had nothing.'

The light is often seen as an inquisitor, deciding if death should occur. Should the experiencer pass through the light, the experience becomes personal. People talk of all sorts of experiences – being in another world, meeting dead relatives and friends, conversing with beings of higher intelligence. They may be associated with the Christian Heaven, but it happens to atheists and those who are from cultures that do not believe in the same form of life after death. Exceptionally, as noted by Michael Rawlings, a small percentage of experiencers suffer horrors, typically associated with Hell. Panic and desolation are often reported during such bad experiences. However, it has also been noted that many such negative NDEs are associated with attempted suicides.

The bad NDE aside, most experiencers remember a reluctance to return to life, but, once they come to terms with the experience, their future lives can often be fulfilling. No longer afraid of death, they acquire a new-found spirituality which allows them to be 'nicer' people than they were previously.

Several theories have been offered to account for the NDE in purely physiological terms. One popular view attributes them to the interaction of endorphins. Endorphins are pain-relieving substances within the body with a similar chemical construction to morphine. As well as relieving pain, they are also mood enhancers, helping in the relief of stress. At times of crisis, such as approaching death, the body is flooded with endorphins, leading researchers to believe that their pain-suppressing qualities and mood-enhancing elements could trigger extreme pleasure within the individual, thus causing the NDE. The question of how such interaction could cause the negative NDE is usually ignored.

Oxygen starvation is also suggested as a cause of the NDE. This view has recently been reinforced by research at the University Clinic Rudolf Vichow in Berlin. Here Dr Thomas Lempert has induced fainting for periods of up to twenty-two seconds in forty-two young, healthy students. During their prolonged faints most hallucinated – some had visions of strange landscapes, 47 per cent reported entering another world, 16 per cent had OBEs. As reported in the *Lancet* in September 1994, one student actually said: 'I thought that if I had to die this very moment I would willingly agree.'

This strongly suggests that it is not necessary to be near death to have an NDE. But, if this is so, how do we account for the amazing similarity of the experience throughout the world?

This goes to the heart of the NDE. For, while oxygen deprivation and endorphin interaction could account for certain elements of the NDE, they fail to explain why the experience appears to affect people in almost exactly the same way, including the hallucination of Heaven (or, rarely, Hell). A further argument against physiological theories is that experiencers never experience things to do with sex, possessions or money. Materialist and personal factors just do not enter into the experience, and, as many Westerners would consider an abundance of sex and money as the true Heaven, their failure to exist in the NDE suggests strongly that something more than simple physiology is going on.

New York psychiatrist Dr Jan Ehrenwald argued that such experiences ' . . . are expressions of man's perennial quest for immortality; they are faltering attempts to assert the reality and autonomous existence of the "soul" – a deliberate challenge to the threat of extinction.'

This, the 'wishful thinking' view, is fine if we are talking about Christians or believers in other religions, but it fails to account for such experiences in confirmed atheists, who believe in neither immortality nor the soul. It has been dismissed by Kenneth Ring in the words: 'The wishful thinking explanation is . . . just wishful thinking.'

Some scientists have grasped at the absurd in order to deny the possibilities of life after death suggested by the NDE. Cosmologist Carl Sagan even suggested that going down a tunnel, reaching a bright light and then going on to experience a strange world is simply a remembrance of a person's most traumatic experience – birth.

Yet could it be that cosmologists and physicists have provided an answer to the NDE, if they only realized it? For instance, the recent research in Berlin, which suggested that the NDE is a product of loss of consciousness, could well be correct. But then again, what is death if not the absolute removal of consciousness?

We tend to look at what happens to consciousness once life has been extinguished in terms of religion and survival of the soul. But could 'after death' be better understood in terms of consciousness going elsewhere in the universe at large?

The Quantum Mind

THERE IS an underlying pattern to scientific advancement. In the early days of scientific methodology, we thought that the earth and the universe obeyed different laws. Newton destroyed that notion when he discovered gravity. All existence appears to obey a single set of rules. Man was also seen as a life form separate from other animals. Darwin undermined that view with his theory of evolution, which demonstrated that all animals derived from the same organisms. Magnetism and electricity were seen as separate forces. Maxwell allied them with the electromagnetic field. Light was later shown to be part of this field.

Chemistry and physics are seen as separate principles. But both came together in the understanding of the atom. Light and gravity were seen as separate forces. Einstein incorporated them in his theories of relativity, and went on to show that space and time were also inseparable. Space exists only when there is time for it to exist within. Particle physics and astrophysics are now separate sciences, yet theories on black holes have shown that the large elements of the universe are better understood through particle physics. Today's Holy Grail of science is the Grand Unified Theory, to be achieved by a marriage of the quantum world and the universe at large.

Science follows many paths, but they all seem to be converging on the same point. Animate and inanimate; macro and micro; all the same creation?

But what of the mind? What of the scientific discipline of psychology? This is part of the creation of existence. So will this eventually converge with the material sciences? It already has. With theories suggesting consciousness to be the main factor in our observation of the universe, the mind and material sciences are beginning to knit together as one.

One speculative hypothesis of theoretical physics points out that, since the quantum field can only be seen to exist when it is observed by an intelligence capable of appreciating it, then intelligence, or consciousness, would have had to exist 'in the beginning' for the universe to come into existence. Basically, without the observer, there can be nothing to observe. So did intelligence – did consciousness – exist in the beginning?

Listen to these sayings:

'The stuff of the world is mind stuff.'

'The more we come to understand the universe, the less it looks like a great machine, and the more it looks like a great thought.'

These mystical words were spoken, not by mystics, but by the modern British astronomers Sir Arthur Eddington and Sir James Jeans. Indeed, today the greatest debate going on in theoretical physics concerns the nature of a possible intelligence at large in the universe, a debate to which our knowledge of the OBE and NDE might usefully contribute.

The American physicist John Wheeler suggested that within the foam-like existence of the quantum field there could be a vast number of 'wormholes' – tiny tubes several centimetres in length, yet with a diameter 100 billion billion times smaller than an electron. They would exist everywhere, connecting every part of the universe to every other part. It has been suggested that through wormholes we may one day achieve instantaneous communication throughout the universe.

According to more recent theories which suggest the existence of hollow, string-like constructions called 'super-strings', the particles we perceive in the quantum field are simply the ends of these super-strings. Each string forms a total connection to all other ends, or particles, the actual string existing within no less than seven dimensions presently hidden from us, and outside nature as we know it.

What I am about to suggest is tenuous, vacuous, speculative – call it what you will. But I remind the reader of the NDE, where the individual, suffering the greatest emotional trauma of all – imminent death – sees himself leave the physical domain of bodily existence and travel down a tunnel. What better description can you have for a wormhole, or super-string, than a tunnel?

Which brings me to a simple hypothesis. The physicist, in discovering the quantum field, in arguing that the mind of man is inseparable from it, has discovered mind. The trip down the tunnel is the return of the energy of consciousness to the universe at large – to dimensions so far shrouded from our understanding.

Indeed, bearing in mind the converging paths of science highlighted earlier, I am making nothing more than a logical deduction based upon the trends in science itself. The quantum field, and mind, are, I suggest, one and the same thing. And in looking at the problem in this way, we can argue that any irregularity which exists within the quantum field could also be applied to the mind (and let us not forget the possibilities of quantum interaction inherent in Roger Penrose's theory of microtubules affecting consciousness).

For instance, there is an enigma of the quantum field in which a particle can directly, and spontaneously, affect another particle. Distance is cancelled out, with an event in one location affecting an event in another. Quantum theory provides a fundamental, non-local connection. This process is uncanny in its exact description of the spontaneity of ESP.

One answer to this enigma – suggested by physicist David Bohm – is that the universe folds in upon itself to such an extent that every particle contains all the information of the whole. The part and the whole are inseparable. They – the particle and the universe – are one and the same. This idea can be seen in action with the hologram, where the destruction of part of the source image for the hologram does not affect the completeness of the hologram itself. Indeed, in super-string theory, the unrecognized seven dimensions exist in a similarly enfolded state as Bohm's 'holographic' universe. The universe simply folds itself 'out of spacetime'.

If such theories are correct, and the mind and quantum field are one and the same, then each individual would logically have access to the information, not only of his species, but of the entire universal construction. Indeed, some people do appear to have their mind filled with the 'wholeness' experience of universal knowledge. Such an invasion of information is known as the mystical experience, where facts invade the mind to such an extent that concentration on any one bit of information is impossible. So could it be that such experiences do nothing more than unlock the total memory of the particle, through which all universal knowledge appears to be attainable?

What better description could there be for this than the *Anima Mundi* – a treasure house of thoughts and emotions, constantly enriched by the thoughts and actions of contemporary man? What better vehicle could there be to allow this connection than a deeper mind level than the personal unconscious, as suggested in Jung's collective racial unconscious?

With my suggested evolved mind-state we can even see why we no longer access this information store in normal consciousness. It has been suppressed by our personal mind, allowing close-upness in order for us to concentrate. Only in the altered state, where we decrease close-upness, does the invasion filter in. And the evolved mind-state also suggests that ancient man would have had a closer understanding of the connectedness of this total mind level. Can we now understand that 'there is one common flow, one common breathing, all things are in sympathy,' as Hippocrates said in the fifth century BC? Or how about that famous dictum said to have been first spoken by the mystic, Hermes Trismegistos: 'As above, so below'?

Remembering cryptomnesia, what would happen if the one-level, pre-historic mind I have suggested also connected with a level akin to the collective racial unconscious, or down to the universal 'software' indicated above? Could it provide a bee-line to absolute knowledge?

Earlier I put forward my belief that the unconscious mind provides a mental map – an inner world to reflect the world 'outside'. This is the world of the out-of-body experience. It is, within my hypothesis, a microcosm of the macro world; the 'part' of the whole. And wouldn't such a 'map' answer the enigma of ESP, including dowsing and psychometry? Wouldn't it, in a phrase, be my suggested memory shop?

Perhaps all we need to account for my suggested retrieval of information is cryptomnesia, with a reflection of all that has gone before becoming immediately, and spontaneously, within our own unconscious. Or should I say quantum cryptomnesia?

But the unconscious map could be seen in another way too. For instance, we must remember the idea of the part and the whole being one and the same. Hence, could a descent into the deeper mind allow us to interact with reality itself as in PK? Could it be that going into the deep mind to manifest the OBE, we are also creeping out of the 'back door', interacting in the world at large in a physical way?

Of course, there can be no proof of any of this. I am simply putting forward a philosophical hypothesis, some would even say a belief system – although I would counter that by stating that all I've actually done is take valid scientific theory and extend it out of its exact frame of reference, which is something scientists do all the time. But the point of supreme importance in such speculation is that the history of culture has shown that the prevalent world view has always been dependent on philosophical hypotheses like my own.

For instance, beliefs in the existence of a God-force have always been above logical deduction. They are simply a form of making sense of the universe. Science would argue that such speculations do not occur today. But is this the case?

Take evolution theory. Although we are beginning to understand our inheritance through genetics and fossil finds, we have only accumulated a hundredth of the evidence that would be required to prove evolution.

Take Big Bang Theory. Although evidence points in the direction of a temporal beginning to the universe, no theory can explain the fundamental question of how the universe was created out of nothing. The scientific answer to this problem is that, prior to the Big Bang, nature would not exist. As science is a process of understanding nature, such speculation is not relevant.

Take the particle. No one has ever seen it. No one can ever see it. Even monitoring it can only be explained in terms of us 'changing' its existence. A particle is shrouded in uncertainty and probability, and can never be understood, viewed, measured or defined by science.

Take mathematics. We know that $1 + 1 = 2$. But there is no absolute truth to that calculation. We only assume that nature is answerable to numbers. Indeed, when the British mathematicians Bertrand Russell and Alfred North

Whitehead attempted to prove the correctness of mathematics, they had to admit that no absolute proof of its reality can ever exist.

We talk of science being logical analysis. To a certain extent this is true. From the point of conception of a theory, logic is pursued ruthlessly. But in the case of evolution, Big Bang Theory, the particle and mathematics – as well as most other world views throughout history – the theory itself is based upon an axiom, or self-evident truth. At the fundamental roots of all knowledge ever devised by man there has been the axiom, which cannot be rationalized by logic. As to why the axiom exists, it is required to allow humanity to make sense of the world and the things we experience within the world. The axiom is simply an intellectual expression of what a particular culture defines the state of knowledge to be.

My speculation becomes, then, just a new, redefined axiom. And in providing it, I am on as secure ground as any scientific theory of the past and present. Within the axiom is understanding in terms of the present theorizing in science itself. And this is the main indicator of the possible success of an axiomatic theory.

A belief, such as that concerning God, is a massive leap into the darkness of knowledge. An axiom is a small step into the unknown, but takes with it the existing baggage of prevalent theory. I take such baggage with me. But, also, the axiom is based on the feelings, emotions and requirements of the existing culture. When we look at the mess our society is in today, it is logical to assume that our present world view is redundant. The intellectual baggage of academe filters down to society. The present ideals of materialism, individuality, a cold and chaotic universe, and the prominence of the self have filtered down and turned our society into a cold, materialistic and egoistic culture.

Perhaps we require an axiomatic shift today in order to understand, not just the paranormal, but the importance of our communality. Who knows, it may lead to a safer, more peaceful world.

TIME ANOMALY

Sceptics

IT IS time to sit back and rationalize the ideas developing in this book. In all cultures, and throughout history, there has been a consistent group of mysteries, known collectively as the paranormal, which have remained aloof from scientific understanding. They have usually been classed as supernatural happenings and the activities of other-worldly forces have been invoked to explain them.

Research has hardly moved away from this position for two central reasons. First of all, people find a need to believe in other-worldly forces. Normal life is a bore; with mysteries to titillate the imagination boredom is nudged forward towards excitement. A believer doesn't really want the illusion shattered by being told that such mysteries could eventually come within a logical framework.

And then, second, we have the scientist. He shuns the paranormal – and for two basic reasons. Uppermost in his arsenal for understanding the natural world is the repeatable experiment. 'Facts' must be hard, undeniable things and must be collated within the arena of a theory, or world view. When they are knitted together, truth becomes apparent. Unfortunately, the paranormal seems to provide nothing in the form of fact or repeatable experiment.

However, to a certain extent, this is equally true of evolution theory, the Big Bang hypothesis and quantum theory. So why are these studies considered hard science while the paranormal is not? The principal reason can be found in the history of science. Science has been the process of imposing rationality over belief. Throughout its history, it has slowly eroded religious, supernatural systems by hard theory and experiment. Hence, anything smelling in the slightest of the supernatural is blasphemous and must be stamped out.

I have tried to show how an understanding of the paranormal need not involve the slightest hint of the supernatural. Rather, our advancing under-standing of the psychological idiosyncrasies of man is pulling back the veil of the paranormal. Cryptomnesia, multiple personality, split-brain research, dreaming, hallucination, hysteria and hypnosis are all telling us that the mind is much more 'paranormal' than we at first thought. Indeed, a new understanding of the altered state of consciousness and the memory shop are all that stand in the way of explaining the vast majority of paranormal happenings.

The altered state of consciousness can be understood in terms of an evolved human consciousness. With the exception of *Homo sapiens*, life forms on planet earth have a one-level mind. There is no conscious or unconscious state. There is simply a mind through which instinctual controls operate, locking an individual life form into its species.

Man has a conscious and an unconscious mind. This is an evolutionary mechanism which enabled man to survive once he had begun to create his own information outside his instinctual drives. Once man had begun to devise technology he required a mind that allowed concentration. And, to concentrate, he needed a repository for unwanted information. However, as this mind-model is not essential for life it is a temporary mechanism. At times when information is cut off from sensory input, the human mind reverts to its pre-technological state, with primeval instinctuality being unlocked from its unconscious prison. It is within this primeval instinctuality that paranormal events happen.

As for the source of such paranormal happenings, the mind and quantum field are one and the same thing. The deep abilities of the quantum mind are kept out of normal consciousness by our personal conscious mind. For normal life, such abilities need not be perceived. Only in the altered state of consciousness, when the information processing of the outside world dissipates, does the paranormal mind filter into consciousness.

While this theory may be scientifically untenable it is philosophically credible. Only our world view disallows it. And in opposing the prevalent world view we face the central prejudice regarding the paranormal. For the theory degrades the prevalence of the self. It eats away at our egoistic view that man is an autonomous individual. But we only appear to be individuals because we have evolved a personal conscious. Underneath it the idiosyncrasies of species controls exist. Below the personal mind we have an inherent communality.

In defence of the self a whole host of people have risen from obscurity to champion science and put down the paranormal. Heading this sceptical approach to the paranormal is the Committee for the Scientific Investigation of Claims of the Paranormal, or CSICOP. Founded in 1976 under the co-chairmanship of Paul Kurtz and Marcello Truzzi, CSICOP has the stated intention to ' . . . investigate *carefully* the extraordinary claims of true believers and charlatans of the paranormal world'.

Scepticism is a valid approach to the paranormal. I am sceptical of areas of it myself. But scepticism must never be allowed totally to suppress wonder or open-mindedness. Logical analysis of the paranormal is possible, but not in terms acceptable to CSICOP. But what, above all else, fuels CSICOP's hatred of all things paranormal? As a 1985 fund-raising document made clear: 'Belief in the paranormal is still growing, and the dangers to our society are real. . . . '

This encapsulates the reason for CSICOP's hatred and need to put down the paranormal – fear. The committee is composed predominantly of scientists who uphold our individuality. They fear anything that degrades this sacred cow. They are convinced that a return to the paranormal as acceptable within society would be a return to religious intolerance and superstition, and the self would again be submissive to a God-force. There are sensible objections to the paranormal, but this is not one.

The principal sceptical objection is that those who claim psychic abilities tend to be charlatans. Quite so. Most of them are. Some of that majority are total charlatans without a single degree of paranormal power. They should be weeded out and exposed whenever they surface. But other charlatans *could* have paranormal abilities. It is not that their powers do not exist but that their attitude to life makes them charlatans. We can now, perhaps, see why. In connecting with the deep unconscious they lose their ability to concentrate to the degree that orderly behaviour demands. They are charlatans only in terms of their interactions within society. And understanding this mentality would allow society to identify such people, tolerate them, but not allow them the power that they can exert over others at present. Basically, an understanding of charlatans would degrade the power of the cults which seem to be causing so many problems in the world today.

The charlatan also seems to surface in many one-off paranormal events. The medium cheats at seances; in poltergeist activity a child plays pranks. However, this need not mean that the whole event is trickery. In multiple personality, fragmentation of the mentally unstable mind allows 'mischievous' personalities to rise to take over the host. These personalities have been shown to indulge in any form of trickery they can. Such trickery should not, any more, result in automatic claims of fraud – given an understanding of the human mind it is completely explicable.

The elusiveness of paranormal events is often seen as a valid reason to discount the phenomenon. This argument no longer holds up to logical scrutiny. Paranormal happenings are expressions of our communality. The event is dependent upon all those involved in it. As soon as a sceptic becomes involved, his mind will cancel out any paranormal happening. A sceptic will never be able to witness such an event because his own mind will not allow it. Of course, the sceptic can throw out the experimenter effect as a cosy theory to hide the fact that paranormal events do not happen. But if he does so, then, to safeguard himself from claims of hypocrisy, he must also throw out our entire understanding of quantum physics, which includes its own version of the experimenter effect, not to mention the uncertainty principle, which tells us that, although the particle must exist, we can never prove it.

However, let us not waste too much time on minor objections to the paranormal. Let's approach the central objection that so far has withstood the sands of time. If telepathy exists why did we bother to learn to speak? Surely mind-to-mind contact would be far better than having laboriously to learn physical communication, causing linguistic barriers to our togetherness in the process. If we could communicate in this subliminal way, speech would never have evolved.

Quite true. We didn't learn to speak until our more subliminal forms of communication waned. As our technological mind advanced, locking our communality within the deep unconscious, our personal conscious interfered with our previous mode of communication. As our personal mind evolved, our general paranormal powers decreased, leaving us unable to communicate subliminally, and needing a new mode of communication.

Once man had begun to forge his individuality outside his instinctual drives, he needed neither paranormal powers nor speech to communicate in order to survive. To this day human beings can survive as a society within nature without speech. Fear, hunger, leadership qualities, surrender, happiness and the need for procreation can all be communicated by body language without the need for speech. Formulated speech is only required to allow abstract communication, in order that men may use technology and organize themselves into an hierarchical culture. Speech has no survival value whatsoever in the natural world. It is simply a mode of communication we have devised to allow the organization of society within an egoistic framework and technological and artistic endeavour.

Once the supernatural is removed from paranormal activity, all credible arguments against it melt away. There no longer exists a single objection to the paranormal. The whole field can be understood in terms of logic and reason, and within an acceptable scientific and philosophical framework. Those who say the latter is untrue have failed to understand the subtleties of scientific theory, and the way our culture decrees what our acceptable knowledge will be.

However, there appears to be one exception to this scenario. The supposed ability to foretell the future.

The Creative Unconscious

WALTER MITTY, in American humorist James Thurber's short story, is a man who lives his life in a sequence of daydreams in which he imagines himself as a hero. He spies a normal man walking down the street and, suddenly, the man is a killer and Walter is there, snatching the beautiful intended victim from death. Such a daydreamer appears to have no place in normal society and he becomes the victim of ridicule. But who's the bigger fool – the daydreamer or the mocker?

Instead of scoffing at him, shouldn't we see in the Walter Mitty individual the seed of creativity? Shouldn't we nurture his talent, rather than scorn it? What was Sir Isaac Newton doing one day in a garden if not daydreaming? Was Archimedes playing with his rubber duck in the bath, or descending into a fantasy world?

Seen like this, it could be argued that daydreaming is vital to human advancement. It is therefore essential to understand what is going on in the daydream.

I can testify that while daydreaming you can cut yourself off from normal life. If you daydream when you're out for a stroll you continue to walk and react to reality, but you seem to go on automatic pilot.

I remember walking down a country lane in the early 1980s. Suddenly two jet fighters, a Jaguar and a Phantom, flew overhead. I thought to myself, 'What if they crash?' A second later my mind's eye played out the event and I 'saw' the plane crash in a nearby field. That night, on television, I saw a report of a Jaguar and a Phantom fighter crashing in a field some seventy miles away.

I first became fascinated with visualizations like this the night before my eldest son's christening. There was to be a big party following the christening and so there were a lot of drinks in the house bought for the occasion.

That night, in bed, I awoke to hear someone coming up the stairs. My wife was in bed and there was no one else in the house other than my four-month-old son. The footsteps stopped outside the closed bedroom door. Then I 'saw' the handle being depressed and the door slowly open.

My immediate impression was that we had a burglar and he was after the drinks, so I jumped out of bed and raced through the door – to find there was no one there. (I cannot remember whether, as I raced through the door, it was open or not.)

Over the years I've carried out various experiments in visualization. I've always had a vivid imagination, so I'm an ideal guinea pig for such exercises. Lying in bed, near sleep, I occasionally concentrate on a point just in front of my eyes. My eyes are closed and I imagine that my closed eyelids are tiny screens. I then look for images on these screens.

It doesn't always work, but occasionally faint images of faces and scenes appear. The faces are constantly changing and I seem to have no conscious control over which faces appear. Most of them are unknown to me, but occasionally I recognize them. I've seen friends and even dead relatives on this screen and some of the images have gone on to feature in my fiction writing. These visualizations are obviously waking dreams from my unconscious, hence my lack of conscious control over them – the unconscious is a rogue who refuses to be tamed by conscious thought.

A story tends to come to me. I wouldn't be so melodramatic as to say they come in flashes, but rather a filtering-in into consciousness. But the above suggests that unconsciously the creative process is going on relentlessly within the mind, giving, through the above recounted visualizations, a creative necessity to daydreaming. Visualizations like these perhaps provide further insight into ghosts. They could also have implications for the possibility of foreseeing the future.

Most of us take it for granted that time is made up of units which advance in a specific direction – forwards. But time is far more complicated than this. Take an example. Gold doesn't degrade through the ravages of time. In terms of both consciousness and physical anomalies it is unaffected by time. Time cannot enter into its universe. Man, however, is different. He perceives time and he ages within time. Hence, time is essential to his universe.

We fill time with human events. We remember specific times in terms of what we were doing then. And anything we do requires thought – in planning the event we think about how it will go and about its hoped-for outcome. In other words, we creatively ponder the future before the future happens.

However, time anomaly does not only involve glimpses into the future. One of the most puzzling of time anomalies usually looks into the past. And in time slip, the experiencer not only looks into the past but visualizes, and sometimes interacts with, it. Indeed, it could be classed as the ultimate daydream.

Time Slips

A N EPISODE of British history: on 20 May 685 King Ecgfrith of Northumbria, an Anglo-Saxon kingdom of northern England, attempted an invasion of Scotland. At the following Battle of Nechanesmere the Picts, the inhabitants of southern Scotland, routed the Northumbrians, killing most of them. The few survivors fled into the surrounding country-side.

On 2 January 1950 a middle-aged lady called Mrs Smith had a not-too-serious car accident close to Nechanesmere. Although it was rapidly becoming dark, she decided to walk for help. Soon she saw a large number of torches moving at the side of the road. She then saw that they were carried by figures who were turning over bodies littered over a field. From the accounts she gave later it appeared that she had witnessed the Picts searching for survivors of the seventh-century battle.

This is a classic case of time slip, sometimes called retrocognition. Whether in vision or hallucination, the viewer's surroundings suddenly change to the scene of the past. Often the hallucination is only fleeting, but sometimes the experience can last for up to half an hour, and in rare cases has even involved interaction by the viewer with people from the past.

Colin Wilson offered an intriguing English case in his book *Mysteries*. In the 1970s Mrs Jane O'Neill visited the church at Fotheringay in Northamptonshire. She spent some time admiring the picture of the crucifixion behind the altar. Later she spoke about the picture to a friend – who was mystified, for there was no picture in the church.

A year later they revisited Fotheringay church and, sure enough, no picture could be seen. Mrs O'Neill wrote to time-slip expert Joan Forman, who discovered that the viewer had witnessed the church as it had been prior to 1553.

Mrs O'Neill had somehow 'connected' with the past. Indeed, this vision was just one of a whole host which she experienced after the shock of being the first on the scene of a serious accident. Somehow the shock had released her abilities. However, not all viewers have an acknowledged history of such visions.

Joan Forman has collected accounts of time slips, many of which are recounted in her book, *The Mask of Time*. Typical is the case of Louisa Hand, who, as a child, visited her grandmother's cottage one day to find that all the furniture was different, as if from another time. Thinking she had entered the wrong cottage, she went outside before going back in again. Still the furniture was different. Only upon entering the cottage for a third time did the interior appear as she expected.

Consider too the case of teacher Anne May, also recounted in *The Mask of Time*. Visiting a monolith at Clava Cairns near Inverness in Scotland, she saw a group of men dressed in shaggy tunics and cross-gartered trousers. They were dragging one of the monoliths. When a group of tourists arrived on the scene, the apparition disappeared.

Forman feels that such experiences are somehow tied in with a human electromagnetic field. I believe them to be creative daydreams. Consider, for instance, the most famous time slip of all.

In 1901 two English spinsters, Charlotte Moberley and Eleanor Jourdain, visited the Palace of Versailles, just outside Paris. Looking for the Petit Trianon, Marie Antoinette's mini-palace, they took a rather long route through the gardens. They met two men, whom they took to be gardeners. Then they saw two more men and a fair-haired woman in old-fashioned dress. Some time later they compared experiences and did some research. The costumes of the people they had seen, they discovered, matched those of pre-Revolutionary France – and the woman looked like Marie Antoinette.

The experience of the ladies at Versailles has many characteristics of a dream, so could we simply be talking about daydreams? For instance, if you go into a house which you believe is haunted, you will jump at every flitting shadow you see. Use imagination to titillate your unconscious and a trigger fires in the mind, creating the vision.

The modern English historian Arnold Toynbee visited many historic sites the world over and often wrote about his visualizations of history repeating before his eyes. I'm not surprised. He was a deep-thinking historian, his mind full of triggers, or information input, capable of bringing about what I would call cryptomnesic hallucination. But could such a predisposition in the minds of Charlotte Moberley and Eleanor Jourdain have provided a trigger for their vision?

First of all, both were respected academics. But, more than this, Eleanor Jourdain specialized in modern history and had a keen interest in French literature. Hence, her mind was predisposed to approach ecstacy when she visited the most romantic location of French history and folklore.

I feel it would be better to drop the idea of time slips being actual visits to the past. Rather, accepting the creative urges constantly going on in the unconscious, and their ability to spark creative visions, could be a far more productive avenue of research. I am intrigued by Anne May's cross-gartered monolith builders. As she described them, they remind me of old history textbook portraits, as if the hallucination was conjured up from the mind, triggered by the emotions felt in that particular location. And Anne May was a teacher, who would have certainly come across such portraits.

Time slips can be explained quite easily in terms of daydreaming theory. But what would an observer have seen if he had been walking behind Charlotte Moberley and Eleanor Jourdain in the gardens that day? The chances are that he would have seen nothing but two ladies casually walking along and would have been totally unaware of the drama going on around him within their perception. And this 'normalness' to the outside observer gives us a vital clue to what is going on.

The Instinctual Self

WE HAVE all experienced reading a book only to find the mind has wandered and we are no longer registering the words we are reading. When this daydreaming is over, we have to go back to the point at which we began fantasizing to re-read the words we didn't take in. But what has happened here? How could we continue to read the words when our mind was on other things? It is as if we have become two different people.

Colin Wilson would say that our 'robot' has taken over the reading for us, allowing our mind to go on to other things. Wilson's robot is vital to our survival. It is the robot who carries out our autonomic functions, such as breathing and digestion – the things we seem to do without mental effort. I'm sitting here typing, Wilson argued, but my mind is not working out which key I should depress next. My mind is thinking ahead to the next words I am to type, transferring my mental processes to paper. When I was learning to type, my mind was concentrating on the next key, but now, the robot takes over and releases me to think about other things. Wilson has even joked that he has caught the robot making love to his wife.

One way of looking at the robot is to say that the logical left brain is an automaton. In learning to type you are creating a new ability, so the right, emotional side of the brain takes note and digests the ability, eventually saying, 'I'm bored,' and handing over the function to the left brain.

So what is the right brain doing while the left brain is boringly going about life? It is fantasizing, or daydreaming. It is a separate entity, interacting with the deep, cryptomnesic unconscious and descending to a world of its own, with its fantasies bubbling up at times to consciousness, making us daydream.

There is great mileage in Wilson's robot. It immediately gives an indication of the mind being more than a single entity. The robot shows that unconscious abilities can keep the machine of the human body operational without recourse, in normal circumstances, to the conscious mind. The fact that the robot can also take over the control of learnt skills, such as typing, or even riding a bike, is also indicative that the conscious mind can hand down abilities to the robot, as if the skill learnt has become unnecessary as far as conscious control is concerned, so it can be sieved down to the unconscious. It becomes 'second nature' to us.

This ability is similar to our repression of information not needed for survival, which I explain as an ability to allow us to concentrate and cut down on conscious information, allowing us to live a normal life.

We also noted earlier that the robot can take control of our autonomic functions, which are essential to our survival. This is logical. If we had to think through the process of digestion every time we ate, or consciously control every breath we took, we would be unable to concentrate on anything else. Hence, we could say that our close-upness has relegated the robot to the unconscious.

I explained earlier that an earthworm, if cut in half, can re-create its whole. The earthworm is a rudimentary creature, which probably has little in the way of close-upness; it must be aware of its basic autonomic functions. We can therefore argue that when we were evolutionarily more rudimentary creatures, then we also consciously controlled our bodies, the ability being sieved to the unconscious as we became more evolutionarily complex.

This idea is borne out by the growing phenomenon of biofeedback, where people have learnt how to directly affect autonomic function. Such abilities show that autonomic functions can be tampered with by conscious thought. Therefore, such abilities must be controlled by mind. But how?

A baby acts instinctually, like other animals. As it grows its vital learning processes are also indicative of instinctual conditioning. Is there much difference between these early learning processes and the learning process I used when learning to type? For instance, it could be said that I now type 'instinctually'.

I have also shown that instinctual behaviour is more akin to species conditioning than to individual ability, explaining how the members of an animal species seem to conform to nature's laws, as if compelled to do so by a higher, overall entity. We, of course, were once natural animals, the only reason why we are not so today being our close-upness. Hence, we could argue that our conscious has driven out instinct into the deep unconscious. However, is this really the case?

Carl Jung developed his theory of a collective racial unconscious after noticing the existence of archetypes, which are symbolic, racial representations. They could, of course, also be seen as racial controls, conditioning memories of our species past. But there is little difference between this notion and instinctual controls. Could it be that we are still influenced by instinctual drives as seen in the animal kingdom, but because of human consciousness, we represent such controls as archetypes?

Sigmund Freud revolutionized our understanding of the mind when he devised the practice of psychoanalysis. He saw the mind as being a conglomeration of various parts. He recognized four main elements of the mind. First of all we have the Ego, which is the conscious part of the mind. The Ego is essentially the personality, the part of the mind we call the self. But as well as the Ego, Freud noted three unconscious elements. The most primitive part of the mind he called the Id. This is the root of our most instinctual drives. Next he noted the Superego. This oversees the Ego, and houses standards imposed by parents and other authoritative figures. And finally he identified Libido – the centre of extreme instinctual drives such as our thirst for sex.

Freud's basic identification of these parts of the mind has become unfashionable in modern psychotherapy – again, they attack the primacy of the self – but perhaps we should step back and consider just what he is saying, especially in the light of my theory of there being a wider mind which, to a great extent, controls us through archetypal representations of instinct.

We have the Ego, which is the self – the part of the person which is conscious. But the Ego can be influenced by three distinct sections of the instinctual unconscious. First of all we have the primitive Id. This is the source of our most primeval instincts, the laws of the jungle, as it were, where animal instinctual behaviour is rooted. But as I've shown, in lower animal forms it is likely that autonomic functions are open to conscious control. We could therefore speculatively identify the Id, or something similar to it, as the standard Wilsonian robot.

Next we have the Superego, where we could say that human standards and learning processes are imposed. In fact, this could be identified as the conscience – the judge of our behaviour, telling us, unconsciously, when we are doing wrong. And, finally, we have the Libido, the centre of extreme instinctual behaviour such as sex. How close this sounds to the seat of our emotions.

Looking at the mind in such basic Freudian ways can be most instructive. It tells us that instinctual influences are forever bubbling up into the Ego, as if the Ego is continually bombarded by racial and instinctual idiosyncracies. It is almost as if the self is not the self at all, but the sensor of species characteristics; as if the thing we call an individual is not an individual at all, but a part of a wider controlling organism. Indeed, I've already noted that emotional influences are not personal, but the possible products of species conditioning.

Carl Jung, in his interpretation of the mind, identified individuals as either extrovert or introvert – i.e. outgoing towards society or inward-looking upon themselves. To Jung, a balance of these traits led to the healthy individual. But this is rarely the case. In good company I am extremely extroverted, often being the life and soul of the party, but because I'm a writer, I must also have the ability to look inwards. Hence, I could be identified as both extrovert and introvert, but not in a balanced form.

My wife can also be the life and soul of the party, yet she enjoys, even craves for, times of solitude. I've known many people who seem to be extremely introverted, but, if you get them talking on a subject they particularly identify with, they can speak with such authority and compulsion they immediately become extroverted.

Such observations have led me to the conclusion that we are all a mixture of extremes of extrovert and introvert. There can be no such classification of the total self. Indeed, I've even noted that some people use extrovertedness to mask their inner introvertedness. The classic case of this is when a man chats up a woman with the use of clichés, seeming to be extrovert to impress, but in reality wanting to crawl into his shell because of his shyness and fundamental introvertedness.

All this suggests that the Ego is a point at which various personality idiosyncracies can manifest in order to allow the person to relate to certain circumstances. In its extreme form we can identify the manic depressive, who seems to sway between personality characteristics at an alarming rate. And the sharp reader will by now have identified, in the above, the concept of multiple personality.

Could multiple personality be no more than an extreme form of normal behaviour, with the sufferer displaying personality fragmentation born of instinctual influences rising from the instinctual species mind?

We can say that, like the honey bee, we are part of a greater organism. And that organism can take over the individual at various times to intensify the mood the individual is presently in, while still retaining more autonomic control from deeper instinctual mechanisms. Which, going back to the phenomenon which prompted this theorizing, tells us that we can unconsciously carry on doing normal activities – such as reading a book, or mechanically walking round the gardens of Versailles – while our fantasizing mind is on other things. We can exist in fantasy and reality at the same time.

Psychic Volume Control

TIME SLIPS – especially those involving two or more individuals – prompt an interesting speculation upon the nature of reality. We can see the possibility that Eleanor Jourdain created at Versailles an alternative, communal reality similar to a poltergeist psychodrama, passing on her emotions of the beauty of the scene, invoking the higher, collective mind and allowing her, and her companion, to walk within an alternate world. The inner, cryptomnesic map within her had come out of the back door and influenced the world at large within the perceptions of both women.

This could prompt the question: how many people would it need to interact together in this way before the alternative reality becomes no longer alternative but reality itself? For, in a real sense, if you accept the mechanism through which the time slip manifested itself at Versailles, then we could philosophize upon the possibility that what we term normal reality is nothing more than a communal time-slip phenomenon within which we all live, and constantly interact. In other words, as some philosophers have thought for centuries, the universe may not be a solid, machine-like reality, but a huge cosmic illusion, in which we play a vital part.

Soon we will go in search of evidence for our supposed ability to foretell the future. But, before doing so, perhaps it would be instructive to look at the whole field of the paranormal in terms of this cosmic-illusion hypothesis. And to do so I will use the analogy of a volume control.

All forms of the phenomena so far highlighted can be seen in terms of clairaudient and clairvoyant manifestation from the deep, communal unconscious. In the Ganzfeld state we seem briefly to manifest telepathic abilities. Such abilities are also manifested between emotionally involved people. Could it be that this manifestation is so brief because the altered state needed to achieve it is slight? Indeed, as the altered state becomes deeper, so the intensity of the manifestation increases, to the point that actual personalities can manifest, as in cases of past-life regression. Similarly, a deepening emotional state can also be seen as the prompter for cases of classic reincarnation, where a disturbed individual actually becomes someone else.

This idea of greater possession by outside information increasing with the depth of the altered state achieved fits my volume-control analogy. Basically, that part of the mind which is essentially personal can tap deeper and deeper into the memory shop. And the same analogy can work with hallucination.

In the dream state we delve only slightly into the unconscious, receiving mental imagery which exists solely in the personal mind. It is almost inconsequential, and unable to impinge on the reality of the outside illusion. Should the impression be intensified and we wake up, then visualization is achievable, suggesting the existence of ghosts or other archetypal entities. Mild time slips can also be seen in this context.

Should the descent be deeper, such as in extreme emotion or ecstasy, the volume of manifestation can begin to impinge more on the outside illusion. Here we can infect a group of people sharing our communality. And here we have the more extreme time slip which, although impinging upon reality, only does so within the reality of the group. But what would happen if the intensity of the reaction upon the outside illusion increased further?

Just as interference can distort a television picture, we would begin to distort reality. And this is where the poltergeist and psychokinesis come in.

Finally, at the point where the altered state is approaching death, we go out of the picture altogether. We go outside of the universal illusion and into the tunnel of the near-death experience. In other words, we have gone out of existence.

I will leave it up to the reader to decide whether, if we actually died, we would still exist in some form when out of the illusion. If you decide yes, then maybe there is a form of life after death after all. Maybe we do go to Heaven, but a Heaven ruled by the mathematics of universal energies. All I will say on the subject is that such theorizing is outside what we term the natural world, so any thought upon the subject would constitute belief – that massive leap into the darkness of knowledge – and has no place in this book.

And thus we have a rationalization of all the phenomena so far highlighted within a logical, if philosophical, system. No supernatural influences are involved. It is fully conceptualized in terms of existing ideas already gleaned by human intellect, as opposed to superstition. Perhaps we should simply remember that human intellect can be a far more fascinating thing than we realize.

Precognition

S AM CLEMENS, who eventually found fame as the writer Mark Twain, used to work as an apprentice pilot on the Mississippi steamboat *Pennsylvania* along with his younger brother, Henry. One night, while on leave, he had a vivid dream. In it, Henry was lying in a metal coffin resting on two chairs. On his chest was a bouquet of flowers.

Returning to duty, Sam had an argument with the chief pilot and was transferred to another boat. Shortly after this the *Pennsylvania* blew up outside Memphis, claiming 150 lives. Henry was alive but injured. For six days Sam nursed him before he died. Exhausted, Sam fell asleep. When he awoke Henry was gone. Sam found him exactly as in his dream, except, that is, for the flowers. However, as Sam watched, an elderly lady approached and put a bouquet on his chest.

Sam Clemens is generally thought to have had a precognitive experience. And they are quite common. Indeed, very similar to Sam Clemens's was the precognitive dream of Abraham Lincoln, who, six weeks before his assassination, had a dream in which he was the observer of his own lying-in-state in a coffin in the White House.

Precognition is generally thought of as the perception of a future event. Some 60 to 70 per cent of precognitions happen during dreams. More rarely, they can occur as auditory hallucinations, waking visions or a strong feeling of knowledge concerning the future. Often, the intuitive mind invasion is more subtle, giving the percipient a feeling of impending doom concerning a future event. When this occurs we tend to call the invasion a premonition, although the margins between premonition and precognition are so blurred that to separate them can cause unnecessary complication.

Most precognitive experiences happen within two days of the perceived event, and the majority within twenty-four hours. Some frequently written-about experiences occurred months before the event, though these are very rare indeed, their sometimes fanatical reporting in journals and books tending to distort their frequency.

Again, the most often-recorded precognitive experiences concern spectacular and major accidents, whereas in reality 80 per cent of precognitions concern a spouse, relative or friend. It is also believed that over 80 per cent of experiences concern tragedies such as death, accident or illness. But this is not necessarily the case.

Margot Grey's book *Return from Death* noted that many of the life-changing characteristics of the near-death experience could be seen as precognitive. During the experience many travellers had both personal and global visions of the future. The deaths of loved ones were predicted, and catastrophic global disasters. Interestingly the book, which was published in 1985, predicted earthquakes, volcanic eruptions and tidal waves for 1988. Unprecedented tidal flooding did occur throughout the world in this year and Armenia suffered a massive earthquake. However, whether such visions were precognitive is open to interpretation. For instance, the research was undertaken as the greenhouse effect and the stripping of the ozone layer were coming to popular notice. So are we dealing with a vision of the future or a fear of the future?

Consider, for instance, two famous precognitive experiences.

In 1914, Joseph de Lanyi, a Balkan bishop, had a nightmare in which he saw the Archduke Franz Ferdinand shot and killed in a car in Sarajevo. A letter also appeared in his dream, which read: 'Your Eminence . . . my wife and I have been victims of a political crime at Sarajevo. We commend ourselves to your prayers. Sarajevo, 28 June 1914, 4 a.m.' The following day, Archduke Franz Ferdinand was assassinated at Sarajevo, triggering World War 1.

Earlier, in February 1914, Sir Arthur Conan Doyle saw prophetic meaning in a message he received from an Australian medium: 'Now, although there is not at present a whisper of a great European war at hand, yet I want to warn you that before this year, 1914, has run its course, Europe will be deluged in blood.'

Of course, neither of these events was precognitive. The two combatant blocs of the Triple Entente and Triple Alliance had been set up before the turn of the century. From 1906 onwards every crisis brought the two sides closer to war. Rumours of a German Fifth Column had, by 1914, reached epidemic proportions, and a massive naval arms race ensued between Britain and Germany. And many guessed that the ongoing Balkan crisis would finally lead to war.

As for the assassination of Archduke Franz Ferdinand, it was sheer folly for him to have made the visit to Sarajevo. Indeed, he was warned not to do so, as terrorist organizations such as The Black Hand Gang were active in the area. As a bishop in the Balkans, Joseph de Lanyi would have been very aware of this fact. A nightmare like the one the bishop had can be understood as nothing more than a product of his unconscious fear of the visit. In this case, the dream just happened to come true.

Many ancient precognitive dreams can be seen as falling into the same category, but in their case the causes were not so much fear, but hopes for a successful outcome.

In the book of Daniel we hear of the Babylonian king Nebuchadnezzar waking up convinced he had had a dream, but unable to recall it. Told of this, and believing the dream to be divine in origin, Daniel prayed to God for understanding. That night he had a dream, which the king recognized as his own. The dream was interpreted favourably regarding the king's future, resulting in Daniel being elevated to high office.

In 332 BC Alexander the Great was beseiging the city of Tyre. One night he had a dream in which a satyr danced on a shield. His dream interpreter suggested that the satyr was symbolic of the words *sa Tyros*, meaning 'Tyre is yours.' Consequently Tyre fell to Alexander. But was this dream precognitive, or did it simply express Alexander's hopes of a successful campaign?

Obviously, if precognitive experiences are valid, then their monitoring could well provide early warning of disaster. It was with this intention in mind that the British Premonitions Bureau was set up in 1967, followed by the Central Premonitions Bureau a year later in New York. Sadly, neither organization proved successful in forewarning us of a single disaster. Whether this was due to the non-existence of precognitive events or to the fact that both organizations were starved of cash is open to debate. But, interestingly, the more spectacular the claim of a precognitive event, the easier it is to find a logical reason for it.

Take the case of Cincinnati office manager, David Booth. For ten consecutive nights in 1979 he had a nightmare in which an American Airlines aircraft swerved sharply off a runway, rolled over and crashed in a mass of flame. So worried was he about the dream that he phoned the Cincinnati branch of the Federal Aviation Authority, the office of American Airlines and a psychiatrist at the University of Cincinnati. On 26 May 1979 an American Airlines DC 10 crashed on take-off from Chicago's O'Hare Airport, killing 273 people. Booth's phone calls had been made three days before the crash.

This dream was not necessarily precognitive. There is a logical explanation. As dream psychologist, Dr Keith Hearne of Hull University, has pointed out, some four hundred thousand people in the United Kingdom alone have nightmares – often recurrent – on any given night. In the United States the number would be far greater, possibly as high as two million nightmares per night. By the sheer law of averages many of these will involve elements of future disasters. Add the fact that people often have an un-conscious, irrational fear of flying, plus the reality that the air-traffic con-trollers in America were becoming militant at the time (a few years later

President Reagan sacked the lot of them), and it would have been unusual if at least one person did not have a recurrent series of nightmares which echoed a crash like the one in Chicago.

A similar scenario can account for the bunkum written concerning the sinking of the *Titanic*, which went down with over a thousand lives on 14 April 1912 after hitting an iceberg in the Atlantic. In 1898 Morgan Robertson published his novel, *Futility*, in which a ship similar to the future *Titanic* sank after hitting an iceberg. As with the *Titanic*, most passengers were lost because of a lack of lifeboats. A similar concern was aired concerning lifeboats in a piece in a London newspaper a few years prior to the tragedy by journalist W.T. Stead. The piece included the words: 'This is exactly what might take place, and what will take place, if liners are sent to sea short of boats'. It is an ironic twist of fate that Stead was on the *Titanic* and perished when it sank.

Further mileage is wrenched out of the tragedy by the fact that the *Titanic* sailed with just over half its capacity of passengers, many of whom had cancelled prior to the sailing. Even many members of the crew refused to turn up for sailing. Yet, with all this speculation, there is not a single authentic precognitive event connected with the *Titanic*.

If you are a reader of adventure novels you will be well aware that for years prior to the completion of some new technological wonder, adventure novelists wring every combination of political intrigue or technological breakdown out of the wonder in order to achieve their story. To add realism, they usually research their subject to find out prevalent fears. Hence, as great liners began to plough the Atlantic, bringing a new luxury and freedom to travel, it was obvious that someone would write a novel about a liner sinking in the Atlantic, including the very real, and often aired, fears of icebergs and the shortage of lifeboats. Rather than being precognitive, *Futility* was simply a well-researched novel. It just happened that for once, and arguably in line with the laws of chance, a liner did hit an iceberg and have a lack of lifeboats, confirming the fears that had been about for years.

Stead's newspaper piece similarly reflected the fears of those in the know. And, let's face it, if it was *that* precognitive, would Stead have gone on the voyage? As for the many cancellations, great superstition has always accompanied sea travel. And when a ship is hyped up as being 'unsinkable' superstition will go into overdrive.

If I seem particularly dismissive of these *Titanic* stories, it is for a very good reason. Many writers, eager to prove the existence of precognitive experiences, go to extremes in their thirst for spectacular cases. But these pollute sensible inquiry, and it is important to clear them out of the way in order to proceed in a sensible fashion. For many cases of precognition are not so easily dismissed.

In 1979, Spanish hotel manager Jamie Castell had a dream that he would never see his child, which was to be born in three months time. So convinced was he of this fact that he took out a large insurance policy, payable on his death. Several weeks later a speeding car swerved, lost control, turned over and landed right on top of Jamie's car, killing both drivers instantly.

In 1948 the Soviet psychic Wolf Messing travelled to Ashkhabad to give a number of performances. As he walked through the city he was overtaken by a terrible fear of disaster and a need to escape the area. So strong were his fears that he cancelled his performances and left the city. Three days later there was a massive earthquake in which 50,000 people perished.

There are literally thousands of experiences like these. None of them fall into logically explainable categories regarding reality as we know it. Cleared of the chaff, the subject of precognition is still intriguing, because it suggests that somehow time can be distorted and we can peer, tentatively, into the future.

Theories of Time

W E SPEAK in past, present and future tense; we divide and plan our
activity into seconds, minutes, hours, days, weeks, months and years;
we are slaves to that irritating mechanism we strap to our wrist, imprisoning
us in a rush of activity and order. Time, it appears, is a real property of
a mechanistic universe. Yet, as soon as you attempt to pin down an understanding of time, a definite fact dissolves into an ethereal fuzz.

To the ancient Greeks time was immutable. It existed and was unchanging
throughout the universe. The philosopher Immanuel Kant thought likewise.
Time was a fundamental property of the universe, separate from ourselves or
any other part of the universe. Everything existed within its scope and it had
been with us from the beginning. According to this concept of 'scientific'
time, time would exist whether we were here to experience it or not.

Not all philosophers were happy with this mechanical view of time. To
the French humanist Henri Bergson the experience of time was a purely
subjective experience. Time, to him, was a process by which we place order
upon the universe. A new-born baby would not experience time. It was a
property that had to be learnt. The English author J.B. Priestley furthered
this idea, arguing that in being taught to appreciate time we are imprisoned
by it. But it only imprisons us because we believe that it does. Time is
subjective; it exists only because we choose to experience it.

Subjective time took a severe beating with the relativity theories of Albert
Einstein. Yet scientific time didn't come out of such theorizing unbattered
either.

Einstein showed that nothing in the universe was at rest. Since everything
moved it was impossible for there to be a static point of reference from
which to measure another point. Everything was relative to everything else.
However, he also noted that light had a definite speed – 186,000 miles
per second. No matter where you were in the universe, no matter how fast

or slow you were moving, light would still be perceived as travelling at its constant speed.

How was this possible? Surely light would appear to be going slower or faster, dependent upon the speed of the observer? Not at all, said Einstein. Light can only travel at its constant speed. Hence, time must slow down or speed up for the observer, relative to the constant speed of light. The universe was a four-dimensional amalgam of space and time. The two were inseparable, a concept he named the space-time continuum. Space-time could stretch, bend or distort like a sheet of rubber, dependent upon the situation of the observer. Large masses, such as a sun or planet, exerted forces upon space-time to bend it, thereby affecting both space and time.

A useful analogy to explain relativity is the case of the twins. One, an astronaut, travels to Alpha Centauri and back at half the speed of light; the other remains on earth. For the astronaut time slows down to allow him to observe the constant speed of light. Hence, when he returns to earth he has experienced a shorter period of time than his brother. He has aged less than his brother and is substantially younger.

Relativity had specific implications for the concept of nowness. Now is a point in time experienced at the present. However, as light takes time to travel, and what we see is dependent upon light, by the time we observe the information of the present it has become the past. For instance, light takes 4.3 years to travel from Alpha Centauri. Hence, when we look at this star, we do not see it in the present, but how it was 4.3 years ago. If Alpha Centauri disappeared, we would still see it for 4.3 years after its disappearance.

Time has a single direction. It goes forward by virtue of a logical process of events. It cannot go backwards; neither can it jump forwards ahead of a process of events. This is 'the arrow of time'. So relativity makes predicting the future impossible. But there have been several theories proposed by physicists that seem to break this logical process of events.

Paul Davies, Professor of Mathematical Physics at the University of Adelaide, has argued that there could be an infinite number of other universes indistinguishable from our own. If a time traveller could cross from our universe to another he would seem to re-enter the same universe but possibly at a different point in time. Then perception of an alternative universe could provide information about the future.

Cosmologist Thomas Gold theorized that the present direction of time is a product of the way the universe is expanding. When the universe begins to contract time will go backwards. To take this idea a stage further, if we are deceived in thinking that the universe is presently expanding and in reality it is contracting, then time could already be running backwards. In which case precognition is a perception of when time ran forwards.

But some theories of precognition discount the properties of time altogether and postulate a form of super-psychokinetic influence at work. A person dreams of a future event, and his absolute belief that it will come true causes PK to be manifested and the event does come true. Jamie Castell's belief that he was going to die caused PK effects upon the car that crashed into his.

Psychiatrist John Barker offered a perhaps more plausible theory in his book *Scared to Death*, where he argued the potency of the self-fulfilling prophecy. Should a fortune-teller tell you of a coming event, such as your imminent death, your mind might make it a reality – you have been scared to death.

Other theories concerning precognition do take into account the peculiarities of time. There is, for example, the bow-wave effect. When a boat ploughs through water it leaves a wake, ripples that fan out from the bow and become weaker the further they travel from the boat. In the same way a future event leaves a wake causing ripples that reach back into the past, eventually becoming so weak that they cannot be detected. The more momentous the event, the stronger the ripples. Hence, major disasters would be felt more strongly than personal tragedies.

Then there is the block-universe hypothesis. Here the four known dimensions, including time, are like immovable statues, forever in the same state. The universe is completely static. Fluctuations and movements within it are caused not by physical interaction but by the movement of consciousness through it. Consciousness is a beam of light lighting up segment after segment of the static universe. This gives the illusion that things happen.

To bring precognition into the block universe, theorists have argued that consciousness is analogous to a thin beam of light, whereas the unconscious is a much wider and more piercing spotlight. The unconscious is more expansive and infiltrates the block universe ahead of the conscious mind. Hence it perceives events before the conscious, giving the effect of seeing the future before it happens.

J.W. Dunne's book *An Experiment with Time*, published in 1927, offered other intriguing possibilities. Dunne argued that time exists in layers. When we say that time 'flows', we are measuring it against something. What if that something is another layer of time – time number two? But what is that measured against? Could it be measured against time number three?

In Dunne's theory there are numerous layers of time, the origin of which is Absolute Time, created by God. However, in order to perceive these various layers of time, we have several selves. Self number one exists in time number one, but other, non-physical selves can rise above time number one to other layers of time. And, by doing so, the future is perceived.

However, if you will excuse the pun, I have no time for any of the theories for precognition stated here. My first problem concerns that leap into the darkness of knowledge. All these theories to account for the anomalies of time are unprovable, so to attach further hypotheses to them to explain precognition is to enter the arena of belief. And to all of them the law of causality presents problems. Stated simply, this law states that cause precedes effect. A bullet must be fired before a man can be shot. It would be ridiculous to suggest otherwise. Yet most of the theories for precognition do suggest otherwise. They argue that a man can know he is going to be shot before the bullet is fired.

So where should we look in order to devise a logical theory of precognition? Perhaps the best place to begin is within the present.

Unconscious Perception

IT WAS five o'clock in the morning one day in Philadelphia in 1979. Helen Tillotson was rudely awakened by a knocking at the door. Wondering who it was, she rushed to the door and opened it. It was her mother, who lived across the street, asking why Helen had been knocking at her door a couple of minutes before. This was impossible. Helen had gone to bed at eleven o'clock and slept soundly.

'But I saw you. I spoke to you,' said the mother.

The next moment the mother's flat exploded. It was a gas explosion. Had she been in the flat she would have been killed.

The Tillotson case demonstrates most of the elements typically present in precognitions regarding disaster. They involve a psychic representation of a loved one; they suggest information regarding the immediate future; they are life-saving; they involve dream symbolism.

Vaunda Johnson is from Arkansas. She has two daughters – Karen and Yvonne. However, it is possible that she might now have only one. Vaunda was asleep when, suddenly, she got out of bed. Her destination was the girls' bedroom, where they were sound asleep in their bunk beds. Why Vaunda lifted Karen from the lower bunk she does not know. But she does know that minutes later she got out of bed again. She was answering the scream of her other daughter, Yvonne. The bunk beds had collapsed – and the two-inch-thick bar joining the upper and lower bunks was embedded in the pillow where Karen's head would have been.

Sometimes such intuitions of the future can infect a whole community.

At Aberfan, Wales, on 21 October 1966, a slag heap slithered down a hillside and buried a school, killing over a hundred children. After the event some two hundred premonitions, or feelings of impending disaster, were reported, beginning some two weeks before the tragedy. The psychiatrist Dr John Barker researched these premonitions and identified some sixty which he thought were genuine. So convinced was he by the premonitions that he became a founder member of the British Premonitions Bureau.

Most of the premonitions occurred in dreams, where impressions of choking, gasping, coal dust and black clouds were reported. One girl said she had dreamt of 'something black' falling on to the school. Another girl dreamt that when she went to school there was nothing there – ' . . . just a big black hole'.

But to explain these premonitions we don't have to accept them as glimpses into a definite future. We input far more information than we consciously perceive. The electromagnetic spectrum, for instance, is made up of numerous waves of various frequencies. The range goes from radio waves, through microwaves, infra-red, ultra-violet and X rays, to gamma rays. In between infra red and ultra violet is a tiny range of waves we call visible light. This is the only part of this huge spectrum that we can consciously perceive. Many species of animals, though, have a wider perception range. The only reason our range is not extended is the limitation placed on our perception by the known senses. Another factor is cryptomnesia. Unconsciously we register every perception we make, and only a tiny percentage of these are registered by the conscious mind.

However, in dreaming and other altered states of consciousness we have access to a far greater range of information and, knowing this, we must ask some simple questions.

A gas explosion is usually preceded by a gas leak and attendant smell. Could it be that Helen Tillotson's mother had simply smelled the gas in her sleep?

Bunk beds do not collapse without prior creaks and strains. Could Vaunda Johnson simply have heard these sounds in her sleep?

Could a slag heap have suddenly fallen on a school without any prior movement, however slight? Is it really feasible to say that no strain had developed prior to the event? Or is it more likely that tiny disturbances – even small falls of coal dust – had been occurring for days before the actual slide?

The chances are that, in these three cases, smell, sound or movement, no matter how slight, were perceived by the unconscious – and in the dream state it surfaced in the conscious and was played out as a dream.

Here I believe we have a viable and logical answer to the vast majority of cases of premonition and precognition. They do foretell future events but they do so not by supernatural means but through people's unconscious assessment of happenings in the present.

The Collective Psyche

THERE ARE, though, some cases of precognition that are not adequately explained as manifestations of a wider unconscious awareness of the present.

Take the instance psychic researcher Tom Lethbridge experienced in Devon in the late 1960s. In a dream he saw a face he didn't recognize, and hands moving about, in a kind of frame. Out driving next day, he saw the face and hands in the windscreen of a passing car, the hands moving as they turned the steering wheel.

Around the same time a similar precognitive intuition was experienced by researcher Montague Ullman when he was at the Maimonides Dream Laboratory in New York. One night he dreamt he met fellow researcher Stanley Krippner, who, he was surprised to see, had a massive bleeding wound on his face. Later that day, in a part of New York he was unfamiliar with, he saw a man resembling Stanley Krippner. When Ullman approached him, he realized that the man had a wound on his face like the one he had seen in his dream.

Tom Lethbridge and other researchers, including J.W. Dunne, used to record their dreams on a regular basis and were fascinated by the fact that many of these dreams foretold future events. This is interesting on two counts.

First of all, it suggests that if we all recorded our dreams we might all experience glimpses into the future. And, secondly, the intuitions of Lethbridge and Ullman are extraordinary in their mundaneness. As an intuition of the future they are seemingly of no value whatsoever. So why is such a fantastic ability wasted on matters of no consequence?

When we are going to a party we consider possibilities relating to that party – who's going to be there, what will there be to drink, what time should I arrive? Could it be that a higher communal mind might work in a similar way? Could the mental reflections of all those going to the party filter into a communal mind-model, causing a communal mind to offer similar assessments which can filter into the dream state?

If this is possible, then Tom Lethbridge's dream is explained as his unconscious reflections on his drive the following day intermingling with the other driver's contemplation of the future, with the higher, communal mind suggesting to Lethbridge, through a dream, that in the future he will see this man. As for Montague Ullman, a similar reflection throws up the fact that if he goes to that particular part of New York he will see a man who looks similar to his colleague, Stanley Krippner.

The communal unconscious – the memory shop – can take an average assessment of future possibilities to 'design' the future before it happens. This explains both the mundaneness of many precognitive intuitions and why most people who record their dreams seem to have these intuitions. We all do, every night of our lives. It is a common ability, shrouded in secrecy simply because most of us have never looked for evidence of it.

The theory also makes the future event remain only a possibility until it actually happens. Lethbridge could have decided, up to the last minute, not to take his car journey. Hence, man is still left with his free will and an exact future is not mapped out. The law of causality is left intact. All that is suggested is a probability of a future event happening.

Even if we do not remember dreams on a regular basis, we have all been to certain locations and felt a strong sense of *déjà vu*, as if we had been there before. Quite possibly we had – in a forgotten dream the night before.

Prophecy

URSULA SONTHEIL was an ugly, deformed woman who lived in fifteenth-century Yorkshire. She was both revered and feared in her day as a prophetess and witch. She is better known today as Mother Shipton. She is said to have foretold the steam engine, the motor car and the telegraph. Cardinal Wolsey eventually decided enough was enough and set off to York to burn her at the stake. On hearing of her fate, she is said to have advised that he would 'see York but never enter it'. Wolsey rested on his journey to York about ten miles outside the city. Here he was arrested for treason and he died on the journey back to London.

The word 'prophecy' is from the Greek; loosely, it means 'speaking before'. Prophecies, once thought of as divinely inspired visions, are common in history. One estimate suggested that there have been as many as 240,000 prophets, all offering their own versions of the future.

One element of prophecy which is often forgotten today is that the future was not the only concern of prophets. As the representatives and spokesmen of gods, they were often called upon to give advice about contemporary life. Rulers often consulted them on matters of state. In this role, the prophet was like a political adviser today, rather than the mystical crackpot he is often perceived to be.

Prophets, or seers, often reflected the social structure of the societies in which they worked. In Babylon, Greece, Egypt and Rome, they were invariably celibate women. Their virginity symbolized the pureness of the divine; their womanhood represented the goddess of ancient, pagan fertility cults.

To the Hebrews, though, the pagan goddess was anathema. God was the only deity, and he was essentially male. Hence the early monotheistic leaders were patriarchs and the prophets were men. However, just to show how important prophecy still was, eighteen of the thirty-nine books in the Old Testament are attributed to prophets.

Men continued to be the main prophets during the Dark Ages and right up to the Enlightenment. For most of this period the fate of the female who claimed prophetic powers was usually to be hanged or burnt at the stake as a witch. Society was man-centred with a male God and male establishment. These early feminists were simply not tolerated.

By early medieval times society was regulated by the written words of God, as contained in the Bible and the Koran. The political and social function of the prophet was taken over by the secular politician. Prophets lost authority and respect – they were no longer regarded as divine agents but simply crackpots. From this grew the ridicule usually poured upon prophets today.

This ridicule is not always undeserved and, arguably, many modern prophecies should be taken with a pinch of salt. Take for instance, America's great prophetess, Jeane Dixon. Mrs Dixon's fame rests upon one of the most famous prophecies of our age, her prediction of President Kennedy's assassination. One version of the story states that in 1952 Mrs Dixon had gone into St Matthew's Cathedral in Washington D.C. to pray. Standing before a statue of the Virgin Mary, she had a vision of the White House. The number 1960 appeared above it. A young, blue-eyed man stood at the door and a voice told her that he was a Democrat and would be assassinated.

This vision, recounted often *after* Kennedy's assassination, was timely, for it was one of a few predictions that came true from many of Mrs Dixon's that did not. But it differs from the story told, and the prediction made, *before* the assassination, in a Sunday newspaper supplement, *Parade*, on 13 May 1956: 'As for the 1960 election, Mrs Dixon thinks it will be dominated by labor and won by a Democrat. But he will be assassinated or die in office, though not necessarily in his first term.'

This is a different story. No blue eyes. There is a fifty-fifty chance of any president being a Democrat; there is only one other party. She does not specify assassination. But most important of all, there was a jinx which used to hang over American presidents. It went in twenty-year cyles. Every president elected in 1860, 1880, 1900, 1920 and 1940 was either assassinated or died in office. Chances were high that it would happen to the president elected in 1960 – Kennedy. (The jinx was finally broken by Reagan, who was elected in 1980.) So Mrs Dixon's prophecy seems to add up to nothing but common sense plus the tiniest bit of luck.

As for her other major predictions, Communist China did not plunge the world into war in 1958; the Soviet Union did not invade Iran in 1953; and Fidel Castro did not die in 1966.

Arch-debunker James Randi is cynical about seers. Indeed, he offers guidelines for their success. Make lots of predictions, hoping that some will come true. If they do, build them up and ignore the others. Always be vague in your predictions. Use lots of symbolism so believers can attach the interpretations they want to. No matter how often you're wrong, keep going. The believers won't notice the mistakes. And finally, predict lots of catastrophes. The people like them.

So how does the greatest prophet of all time stand up to investigation? We must look closely at the French physician and astrologer Michel de Nostradame, or Nostradamus. Up to his death in 1566 Nostradamus wrote ten volumes of verses, a total of 942 verses in all. They were published in centaines, or centuries of one hundred verses each. In them he is credited with predicting the rise of Hitler, the French Revolution, and practically every event between, right up to the end of the world. One adaptation of his verses says: 'In 1999 and seven months the Great King of Terror shall come from the skies.' This is seen as the beginning of the destruction, with the 'city of the seven hills' being destroyed.

Some see this city as Los Angeles, but then again it could be Rome. But maybe Nostradamus was confused. For he supposedly boasted that his verses would continue to predict world events right up to the year 3797. Perhaps we need not worry about the world coming to an end in 1999.

Let us look at his predictions about Hitler. First of all, the name he uses is 'Hister'. He speaks of turbulence concerning 'Venus'. Was he talking of Vienna, where Hitler spent many of his pre-Nazi days?

In his book *The Mask of Nostradamus* Randi puts forward the credible theory that Nostradamus was writing about events in his own time. He wrote in riddles to avoid upsetting the Church and the governments he attacked. This becomes apparent when we look at the seer's supposed prediction of the Great Fire of London in 1666. Erica Cheetham, in her book *Prophecies of Nostradamus*, decoded a particular verse as including the following: 'The blood of the just will be demanded of London, burnt by fire in three times twenty plus six.'

Nothing could be simpler. 'Three times twenty plus six' is clearly sixty-six. Except for one thing. The verse says nothing of the sort. Consider a more accurate translation:

> The blood of the innocent will be an error at London,
> Burned by thunderbolts (or fire), of twenty three, the six,
> The senile lady will lose her high position,
> Many more of the same sect will be slain.

Although it is not known what 'twenty three' signifies, it most certainly does not say 'three times twenty'. This has been pointed out by other translators, who claim the 'senile lady' is St Paul's Cathedral. Hence the verse, they argue, is a prediction of the London Blitz. However, if we look at the verse in terms of events at the time of Nostradamus, the 'senile lady' may be identified as Bloody Mary who, at the time, was burning Protestants. They were frequently executed in groups of six. Victims were often offered bags of gunpowder to tie between their legs to ensure a swifter, more merciful death. This way they didn't burn, but exploded like 'thunderbolts'.

Alternative possibilities exist for all of Nostradamus's riddles. A re-writing of one of Nostradamus's riddles, making it predict a great earthquake that would cause parts of California to sink into the sea, caused a mass exodus from Los Angeles in 1988. The fleeing residents went home rather sheepishly.

However, Nostradamus did seem to get it right once, with a series of predictions about the French Revolution. Although not spot on, there are some remarkable hits here. But how can this be? Were subtle powers at work?

Following World War 1 and the Peace of Versailles, the French Marshal Foch observed the demoralized state of the humiliated German people and said, 'This is not peace. It is an armistice for twenty years.' This political assessment was almost exactly right. Had Foch not been a military man but, like Nostradamus, of a mystical bent, I wonder if this would have been classed as a great, supernatural look into the future?

And this is how I would initially approach Nostradamus's predictions. He was a clever assessor. But clever assessors have a tendency to be used. This is because people want to believe in such abilities as prophecy. I call it the 'donkey factor', after the triumphal entry into Jerusalem of Jesus, riding on an ass. How relevant to his decision to use this mode of transport was the fact that a prophecy had said that the Messiah would enter Jerusalem in this way?

With the French Revolution we must consider the possibility that the instigators of the Revolution understood the donkey factor, planned their operations accordingly and unleashed a revolution that was 'fated' to be.

But consider one specific riddle concerning the Revolution:

> By night will come through the forest of Reines
> Two partners, by a tortuous valley,
>   Herne the white stone,
> The black monk in grey to Varenne:
> Elected capet, cause tempest, fire, blood and slicing.

Could 'two partners' refer to Louis XVI and Marie Antoinette? At a point in the Revolution the two of them fled to Varennes, this being the town's only real mention in French history. They fled there through the Forest of 'Reines', in which they got lost (the 'tortuous valley'). The outcome of their flight was the Terror, and they ended up under the guillotine ('blood and slicing'). 'Capet' was the name of a dynasty of French kings and Louis was the first French king who could ever be called 'elected' – allowed to stay in power not by divine right but after giving in to reforms insisted upon by an assembly.

And it doesn't stop here. Louis XVI was a sombre man who also happened to be impotent ('the black monk'), and he was dressed in 'grey' when he fled. Marie Antoinette was dressed in 'white'.

The number of hits in this riddle seem to defy rational explanation. So surely it hints strongly at an ability to see into the future?

Not necessarily. There is an alternative possibility.

There is a higher, communal mind which creates reality as it goes along, based upon the prevalent wishes of society. Hence it could be argued that, when the French Revolution began, the higher mind became a form of conductor, helping to play out contemporary affairs in a way perceived by the communal wishes and hopes of the people. In other words, when Nostradamus wrote that riddle, he pre-destined it to become a truth by the subtle manipulations of a communal mind yielding to the needs of the people. The higher, communal mind looked at their wishes and created the outcome they wanted – a time slip, writ large.

I accept that this theory is both fanciful and, in a way, ridiculous. But the question the reader must ask is, does it fit the pattern I have highlighted throughout this book? If so, it is a viable scenario to offer, a scenario in which the fundamental reality of the universe is a subliminal connection of all that exists within the universe, including us, mankind. We are one, communal – a product of our universe, and, in a way, slaves to the machinations of that universe. But it could also be correct to say that the way the universe reacts to man is based on how we, ourselves, wish our society to be. As a species we have access to the communal mind, for it is the sum total of our thoughts. Hence, when we look at the conflict and the fragmentation of our world, we may be able to see, very clearly, who is really to blame.

CONCLUSION

EARLIER (pp. 205–6) I told the story of the night before my first son's christening, when I heard footsteps coming up the stairs and saw the bedroom door opening. I gave the impression that this was an isolated event, but perhaps I should tell of the events surrounding it.

The manifestation occurred as my wife was coming out of post-natal depression, during which she had had many hallucinations, including seeing horns on my son's head, so there was already a form of altered reality in the house. Following my hallucination, my wife spoke about it to a neighbour, who told her that this presence had been haunting *her* for some time. The neighbour had had a string of unfortunate miscarriages.

After this, the rumour circulated that the presence was a monk, who had been causing supernatural happenings for some time about the small estate we lived on. By the time my wife heard this rumour she had sensed the presence many times. It seemed to centre around my son, making his bedroom very cold at times. Finally, knowing it was a monk, and being very religious herself, she lost her fear of the presence, and it vanished from our house.

Round the corner was an empty house. It had been empty since the tenants had moved after the wife kept hearing the voice of a child, as if it was in water. They later discovered that a family that used to occupy the house had lost a daughter through drowning.

Soon after our presence had gone, a woman down the road miscarried. She, too, was religious, and one day, in front of a witness, all the religious pictures on the wall turned face against the wall. Obviously, there was much discussion about all these strange events, and for a while after, every time the men from the estate went away on military exercises, an unseen prowler was heard trying the doors of the houses.

I record these events simply to show just how prevalent psychic happenings can be, or be thought to be. I like a pint or two of beer, so I can often be found in a pub. And whenever it comes out that I write about the paranormal, you can guarantee everyone I talk to can recount several paranormal incidents in their life. One day I was talking to a sceptic about the poltergeist phenomenon. He dismissed it as total rubbish. When I pointed out that there was a poltergeist at work at that very moment within five miles (eight kilometres) of where we were, he disbelieved me. A level-headed friend walked in at that moment and joined in the conversation. The sceptic was left with his mouth open wide when this friend told us that a poltergeist was causing trouble in the home of one of the girls in his office. It seems the paranormal is with us as a very close bedfellow.

The sceptic's usual answer to claims of the paranormal is that reality doesn't allow paranormal events to take place. The reality we appreciate daily is so well mapped out that if paranormal happenings occurred, then we would have understood them by now. Hence, the paranormal does not exist.

If such a comment was applied to the supernatural, I would be inclined to agree, for there is no hint of scientific acceptance of supernatural influences. But if he applies it to the paranormal, the sceptic is talking bunkum.

Enshrined in occult philosophy is the belief that the mind is all-embracing and can interact with reality. This is paranormality, as opposed to supernatural influences, which dictate the actions of gods and spirits. To the occultist, each individual is a god – or has the ability to become one – through the abilities of the mind. So rather than the paranormal being supernatural, it can best be understood through psychology, or through what has come to be known as parapsychology.

Yet, even with this explanation of the processes of the paranormal, sceptics still insist that paranormal events don't happen. And in a way they are quite right. In normal reality they don't. But if the all-embracing mind is enshrined in the occult, modern science is similarly showing that normal reality is nothing more than a simplistic model of a deeper truth.

When Newton devised his theory of universal gravitation, it was believed that the search for the truth of the universe was complete. Newton's theories explained normal reality perfectly well. And they still do. In normal happenings, we need nothing more than the theory of gravity to explain the mechanics of the universe. However, while these theories work normally, under the microscope or at high speed, Newtonian gravity fails to provide the complete answer. Rather, science has invoked two new models of reality, enshrined in quantum and relativity theory. In normal life such theories are not required, but in extraordinary, or paranormal, circumstances, they are. Hence, we have differing levels of scientific reality.

There is also a strong case to suggest that normal reality, as experienced by us all daily, is in fact a 'masking' reality to hide higher truths. To show what I mean here, all you have to do is stand still. When you stand still, in normal reality you are doing just that – standing still. But in the truth of a higher reality, due to the rotation of planet earth, you are spinning like a top. In fact, not only are you spinning, but, because the earth is orbiting the sun, you are rocketing through space at thousands of miles per hour. One might also add that you are rocketing through space in another direction too – this time at hundreds of thousands of miles per hour, because of our solar system's movement within the spinning Milky Way.

Such facts as these hint strongly that normal reality is, in fact, a delusion. And this point can also be seen by looking into a mirror.

In normal reality, when you look into a mirror, you see your face, a rather peculiar mass of skin and bone. However, under the reality of the microscope, skin and bone dissolve to an intricate system of cells and genes. This reality can be further shrunk to an electric field of atoms and even smaller particles. At this level of reality, the process of atomic structure becomes almost the same for a lump of granite as it is for your face. Indeed, these particles are not even yours – they were cooked up in stars billions of years ago. This 'stardust' is only borrowed.

Again we see the possibility that normal reality is a delusion. And if it works in this way for physics and for genetic structure, then why can't it work similarly for psychology?

Well, in actual fact academe has already proved that it does. At present, science has only begun to tap the realities that exist under the normal reality of the mind. This is done with hypnosis, where the subject is placed in an altered state of consciousness that is anything but normal. So if, as is suggested by other areas of science, the mind also has ever-deepening regions of reality, then I suppose that if you really want to see the paranormal in action, you need do nothing more than observe the closed-reality mind of the sceptic.

My hopes for this book are that it will nudge science to move on from its present intransigent stance concerning the paranormal. It is, perhaps, a forlorn hope, but a hope all the same. However, at the beginning of this book I pointed out that understanding such phenomena could be vital for understanding, and actually living, life. In this conclusion let me just show a few areas where this could be so. Consider, for instance, our historical advancement.

The hundreds of gods available to early historic man left mankind in a cauldron of barbarism as civilization grasped reality from the shadows of prehistory. The first significant attempt at order came with the realization of monotheism – the idea of the one god – by Abraham. From here, monotheism was shaped by Moses, and later Jesus. Shortly after the crucifixion, St Paul devised the early Christian Church, the movement eventually receiving political and social acceptance through Constantine the Great. As the Roman Empire came crashing down it was saved by the monastic system, which was essentially the concept of St Augustine of Hippo. In these six men we have the genesis of monotheism. Yet they all shared a similar trait.

The Bible states quite clearly that Abraham did not come to monotheism by his own volition. Rather, God said to him: 'Go from your country and your kindred and your father's house to the land that I will show you. . . . ' Moses, too, acted upon instruction, this time from a burning bush. Jesus, rather than acting upon instruction, is thought of as God Himself, made flesh.

St Paul, too, had a calling. He was struck down on the road to Damascus and asked, by Jesus, 'Why are you persecuting me?' A similar thing is said to have happened to Constantine. While he was fighting to amalgamate the Roman Empire into a cohesive whole after a period of near civil war, God showed him a vision of a cross and told him to place it on his soldiers' shields. In thanks for his subsequent victory, Constantine granted toleration to Christians. And in St Augustine we have a man who, in his early years, bore little resemblance to a man of Christian virtues – he lived in sin and had an illegitimate child. Then his whole life changed after God reprimanded him during a spiritual experience.

This shows that all the main players in the genesis of Christianity were influenced by some form of clairaudient or clairvoyant experience, which manifested itself through the vehicle of an existent archetypal entity, and led to an inspirational advancement within their culture.

But there is no historic proof of the existence of Moses or Abraham, or, indeed, Jesus. They could have been symbolic representations of wider political movements. The synthesizing of Christianity into Roman culture could be easily explained as a shrewd political move to provide stability. Saints Paul and Augustine were both very much non-Christian prior to their conversions, Paul being instrumental in the murder of the first Christian martyr. Hence, their conversions could be seen as guilt trips. However, the influence recorded in such accounts does not only exist within Christianity. Just look at scientific folklore.

Archimedes had an inspired thought about water displacement while in the bath, causing him to run naked through the streets shouting 'Eureka'. Newton is said to have discovered gravity after noticing an apple fall. Mandeleev claimed that he understood the Periodic Table of elements upon waking from a dream. Einstein arrived at the theory of relativity after dreaming of what he would see if he rode on a beam of light.

Again, such stories may be purely symbolic representations of the facts, but we again have the idea of sudden flashes of inspiration, occurring in the dream state or during deep relaxation. And it is not confined to science.

Percy Bysshe Shelley once wrote, 'Poetry is not like reasoning, a power to be exerted according to the determination of the will. A man cannot say: "I will write poetry". The greatest poet even cannot say it.' William Wordsworth often spoke of the 'sublime invasion' of material. Robert Louis Stevenson pre-shadowed the split personality in *Jekyll and Hyde*, revealed to him in a dream. Samuel Coleridge dreamed his poem 'Kubla Khan'. Robert Burns achieved his insights as if touched by a Muse (one of the goddesses who presided over the arts and sciences in Greek mythology). Goethe claimed that his songs made him, not he the songs.

Philosophy has a similar tradition. Socrates said that his philosophies came from his 'demon'. Descartes, the father of modern, rational thought, had a life-changing experience in which he had three dreams which told him of his destiny to unify the sciences. Great philosophers such as Hegel and Nietzsche were of a mystical bent. And even a hard materialist like Bertrand Russell admitted that solutions to problems were more likely to come during the hours of sleep.

Throughout religion, science, the arts and philosophy there is the notion of 'invasions' of the mind within the altered state of consciousness, leading to inspirations and cultural advancement for all. Throughout history, men have risen to further our knowledge through impressions received from a higher mind, through clairaudient and clairvoyant manifestations, indicating that we have only arrived at our present culture through paranormal happenings, arising from our communality.

This idea is, in fact, similar to the theories of maverick British biologist Rupert Sheldrake. Indeed, when Sheldrake suggested that a rabbit knows it has to be a rabbit because of the existence of 'species fields' at a fundamental level of life, one prestigious science journal classed his book as fit for burning. This is hardly surprising. It was a new and revolutionary suggestion.

Sheldrake's species – or morphogenetic – field is an advancement on Jung's collective racial unconscious in many respects. Sheldrake postulated the principle of 'formative causation'. In its simplest sense he is saying that it is easier to do something that has been done before, regardless of the lack of physical connection between attempts to do it. And, he claims, the principle works throughout life, whether involving the replication of physical form, or the ideas in a man's head. This non-causal interconnection he calls 'morphic resonance'.

Here again we have the idea of the individual being a product of the communality of the species through not-yet-understood influences. And this idea may not just give a clearer impression of the processes of history. It could also answer many problems of the present and offer indications of our future.

One of the main propositions of this book is the idea that Colin Wilson's concept of close-upness can be understood in terms of an evolved consciousness, with the conscious shrinking because of the increasing amount of information that technology has thrust upon it. From this we could extrapolate that, as the information available continues to increase we shall have further to shrink our conscious mind to allow concentration. Hence, we could possibly look forward to the time when the sheer mass of information is such that our conscious mind is so small that it is practically non-existent. However, take away consciousness from man and what are you left with? You have a zombie, unable to interact properly within society.

Now look at society today, infested with our culture of mass information. Look how small-minded we have become, imbued with greed; with specialization coming to the point that we are only able to concentrate on a tiny area of life, and unable to conceptualize a wider world view. Such is the flood of information that we become fanatics, looking only through our tunnel vision.

Now look at the members of modern society who cannot think at all. Look at the declining standards in education, at the constant trivia which are thrown our way via soap operas, tabloid newspapers *et al*. I can see the time when our conscious mind is so small that the media becomes the new collective unconscious, born of the microchip and regulating a utopia of mindless non-entities, revelling in nothing but inconsequential trivia.

Colin Wilson was far-sighted enough to realize a similar concept many years ago. To him close-upness created a state of upside-downness. This shortsighted state of mind makes man suffer the delusion that the trivia of life are important. Negative values impinge on his intellect and his values turn upside down. Hence, boredom results in further boredom, rather than giving man the impetus to rise out of his lethargic state and grasp meanings within the world.

The mystical experience tells us that there are meanings in the world, but such meanings have to be sought by contemplation and a re-introduction to our deeper mind, where the real humanity lies. To a place where man and knowledge are unified. Indeed, the experimental mystic P.D. Ouspensky tells us what the world is really like, the world he returned to after the ecstasy of his search for true knowledge in the mystical experience:

> The experiments almost always ended in sleep. During this sleep I evidently passed into the usual state and awoke in the ordinary world, in the world in which we awake every morning. But this world contained something extraordinarily oppressive, it was incredibly empty, colourless and lifeless. It was as if everything in it was wooden, as if it was an enormous wooden machine with creaking wooden wheels, wooden thoughts, wooden moods, wooden sensations; everything was terribly slow, scarcely moved, or moved with a melancholy wooden creaking. Everything was dead, soulless, feelingless.
>
> They were terrible, these moments of awakening in an unreal world after a real one, in a dead world after a living, in a limited world, cut into small pieces, after an infinite and entire world.

Is it any wonder that those within society who seek to drop out descend into the hallucinatory world of drugs – the feeble, vain attempt to connect with the wonder of hidden realities – to escape from the disintegrated meaninglessness of this trivial thing we call Western culture, infested, as it is, with information?

This is the lot of humanity if my theories are anywhere near correct. Through the paranormal, though, we could just pull ourselves back from the brink and learn to think once more. This is how important psychic understanding could be – no less than the true understanding of our psychic self.

Of course it could be argued that a descent to our deeper mind could equally lock us in a prison, not of mindless trivia, but of identical, instinctual behaviour, returning us totally to the instinctual controls of Nature. And this is quite true. But we are unique in known reality in that we have the choice to form a balance, to grasp the best of both worlds.

But also, remember this. Information is not the same thing as knowledge. Information can be of no substance, whereas knowledge is a far more substantial thing. Information is a clutter of unrelated factors, whereas knowledge is an understanding of who we are.

This book is an attempt to identify who we are, and what we are capable of as a species. If mankind wants to go forward in a frame of mind bordering on pessimism, existing in a 'wooden' world, then we shall reap what we ask. But alternatively, if we look deeper into ourselves for knowledge, if we become, through such understanding, more optimistic, then the future will cede to our wishes. We, en masse, can change our communal reality and life will become that much more pleasurable. As we create our own bad luck with the personal mind, so, too, with the communal. So our future is very much in our communal hands.

But this book also suggests something else. If such a creative, higher mind does exist as I have suggested, underlying the very universe, then it is the sum total of more than simply a species such as man. For the quantum field is the underlying reality to everything. And we have a word for such a concept. In our trivial way we may have bastardized it, devising various 'self'-induced modes of thought – of religions – to understand it. But that word is 'God'.

Select Bibliography

Bannister, Paul, *Strange Happenings*, Grosset & Dunlap, 1978

Barrett, Francis, *The Magus*, University Books, 1967 (original 1801)

Bernstein, Morey, *The Search for Bridey Murphy*, Doubleday, 1965

Blackmore, Susan, *Beyond the Body*, William Heinemann, 1982

Bohm, David, *Wholeness and the Implicate Order*, Routledge & Kegan Paul, 1980

Buchanan, Joseph Rhodes, *Manual of Psychometry: The Dawn of a New Civilisation*, Holman Brothers, 1885

Canetti, Elias, *Crowds and Power*, Victor Gollancz, 1962

Carrington, Hereward and Muldoon, Sylvan, *The Projection of the Astral Body*, Rider & Co., 1968

Cheetham, Erica, *Prophecies of Nostradamus*, Corgi, 1973

Churton, Tobias, *The Gnostics*, Weidenfeld & Nicolson, 1987

Cleckley, H.M. and Thigpen, C.H., *The Three Faces of Eve*, Secker and Warburg, 1957

Crick, Francis, *The Astonishing Hypothesis: the Scientific Search for the Soul*, Simon & Schuster, 1995

Dennett, Daniel, *Consciousness Explained*, Little, Brown, 1991

Denton, William, *The Soul of Things*, Aquarian Press, 1988 (original 1863)

Dunne, J. W., *An Experiment with Time*, Faber & Faber Ltd, 1927

Ellenberger, H.F., *The Discovery of the Unconscious*, Fontana, 1994 (original 1970)

Fairley, John and Welfare, Simon, *Arthur C. Clarke's World of Strange Powers*, Collins, 1984

Forman, Joan, *The Mask of Time*, Macdonald & Jane's, 1978

Freud, Sigmund, *The Interpretation of Dreams*, The Modern Library, 1950

Garrett, Eileen, *My Life*, Psychic Book Club, 1939

Gauld, A. and Cornell, A.D., *Poltergeists*, Routledge & Kegan Paul, 1979

Graves, Robert, *Goodbye to All That*, Berghahn Books, 1957

Gregory, R.L. (editor), *The Oxford Companion to the Mind*, Oxford University Press, 1987

Grey, Margot, *Return from Death*, Arkana, 1985

Guiley, Rosemary Ellen, *Harper's Encyclopedia of Mystical and Paranormal Experience*, HarperCollins, 1991

Gurney, E., Myers, F.W.H. and Podmore, F., *Phantasms of the Living*, Trubner & Co., 1886

Harris, Melvin, *Sorry You've Been Duped*. Weidenfeld & Nicolson, 1986

Hasted, J., *The Metal Benders*, Routledge & Kegan Paul, 1981

Hudson, Thomson Jay, *The Law of Psychic Phenomena*, G.P. Putnam & Sons, 1902

Inglis, Brian, *Science and Parascience*, Hodder & Stoughton, 1984

Iverson, Jeffrey, *More Lives than One?*, Souvenir Press, 1976

Jaynes, Julian, *The Origin of Consciousness in the Breakdown of the Bicameral Mind*, Houghton Mifflin Company, 1976

Jung, C.G., *Memories, Dreams, Reflections*, Collins and Routledge & Kegan Paul, 1963

Kardec, Allan, *The Spirit's Book*, Lake Livraria Allan Kardec Editions Ltd., 1972

LeShan, Lawrence, *Clairvoyant Reality*, Turnstone, 1974

Levi, Eliphas, *History of Magic*, Samuel Weiser, Inc., 1973

Lewinsohn, Richard, *Science, Prophecy and Prediction*, Harper & Bros, 1961

Lewis, I., *Ecstatic Religion*, Penguin, 1971

Marais, E., *The Soul of the White Ant*, Jonathan Cape, 1971

Maslow, Abraham, *Religious Values and Peak Experiences*, State University Press, Ohio, 1962

McLeish, Kenneth (editor), *Guide to Human Thought*, Bloomsbury, 1993

Meade, Marion, *Madame Blavatsky, the Woman behind the Myth*, Putnam, 1980

Monroe, Robert, *Journeys Out of the Body*, Doubleday, 1971

Moody, Raymond, *Life after Life*, Bantam, 1975

Moravec, Hans, *The Mind Children*, Harvard, 1990

Myers, F.W.H., *Human Personality and its Survival of Bodily Death*, Longman's, 1903

Penrose, Roger, *Shadows of the Mind*, Oxford University Press, 1994

—— *The Emperor's New Mind*, Oxford University Press, 1989

Picknett, Lynn (editor), *Encyclopedia of the Paranormal*, Macmillan, 1990

Playfair, Guy Lyon, *The Flying Cow*, Souvenir Press, 1975

—— and Grosse, Maurice, *This House is Haunted*, Souvenir Press, 1980

Polkinghorne, J. C., *The Quantum World*, Longman, 1984

Price, Harry, *The End of Borley Rectory*, Harrap, 1947

Prince, Walter Franklin, *The Enchanted Boundary*, Little, Brown, 1930

Puharich, Andrija, *Uri: a Journal of the Mystery of Uri Geller*, W. H. Allen, 1974

Randi, James, *The Mask of Nostradamus*, Prometheus, 1995

Randles, Jenny, *Sixth Sense*, Robert Hale, 1987

Rhine, J.B., *Extra Sensory Perception*, Society for Psychical Research, Boston, 1934

Rogo, D. Scott, *Mind Beyond the Body*, Penguin, 1978

Shallis, Michael, *On Time*, Burnett Books, 1982

Schatzman, Morton, *The Story of Ruth*, Zebra Books

Sheldrake, Rupert, *A New Science of Life*, Blond & Briggs, 1981

Sinclair, Upton, *Mental Radio*, Werner Laurie, 1930

Sizemore, C. and Pitillo, E., *Eve*, Doubleday, 1977

Stevenson, Ian, *Twenty Cases Suggestive of Reincarnation*, (2nd edition) University Press of Virginia, 1974

Targ, Russell and Puthoff, Harold, *Mind Reach*, Delacorte, 1977

Tyrrell, G.N.M., *Apparitions*, Gerald Duckworth & Co., 1953

Underwood, Peter and Tabori, Paul, *The Ghosts of Borley Rectory*, David & Charles, 1973

Unexplained, The, (part work) Orbis, 1980-83

Urmson, J.O. and Ree, Jonathan (editors), *Concise Encyclopedia of Western Philosophy and Philosophers*, Routledge, 1991

Wambach, Helen, *Recalling Past Lives*, Harper & Row Perennial Library, 1978

Watkins, Alfred, *The Old Straight Track*, Abacus, 1974 (original 1925)

Watson, Lyall, *Beyond Supernature*, Hodder & Stoughton, 1986

Wilson, Colin, *The Occult*, Hodder & Stoughton, 1971

—— *Mysteries*, Hodder & Stoughton, 1978

—— *Poltergeist*, New English Library, 1981

—— *Aleister Crowley: The Nature of the Beast*, Aquarian Press, 1987

—— *Beyond the Occult*, Bantam, 1988

—— *The Mammoth Book of the Supernatural*, Robinson, 1991

Wilson, Ian, *Mind Out of Time?*, Victor Gollancz, 1981

—— *The After Death Experience*, Weidenfeld & Nicolson, 1987

—— *The Bleeding Mind*, Weidenfeld & Nicolson, 1988

Index